Phonics and Structural Analysis for the Teacher of Reading

Phonics and Structural Analysis for the Teacher of Reading

Programmed for Self-Instruction

Tenth Edition

Barbara J. Fox

North Carolina State University

Allyn & Bacon

Boston New York San Francisco
Mexico City Montreal Toronto London Madrid Munich Paris
Hong Kong Singapore Tokyo Cape Town Sydney

Executive Editor: Aurora Martínez Ramos
Series Editorial Assistant: Jacqueline Gillen
Executive Marketing Manager: Krista Clark
Production Editor: Mary Beth Finch
Editorial Production Service: Omegatype Typography, Inc.
Composition Buyer: Linda Cox
Manufacturing Manager: Megan Cochran
Electronic Composition: Omegatype Typography, Inc.
Interior Design: Omegatype Typography, Inc.
Cover Administrator: Linda Knowles

For related titles and support materials, visit our online catalog at www.pearsonhighered.com.

Library of Congress Cataloging-in-Publication Data

Fox, Barbara J.
Phonics and structural analysis for the teacher of reading programmed for self-instruction / Barbara J. Fox. — 10th ed.
p. cm.
Rev. ed. of: Phonics for the teacher of reading, c2005.
Includes bibliographical references.
ISBN-13: 978-0-13-208094-1 (pbk.)
ISBN-10: 0-13-208094-X (pbk.)
1. Reading—Phonetic method—Programmed instruction. 2. Teaching—Aids and devices. I. Title.
LB1573.3.F69 2009
372.46'5—dc22

2008050911

Printed in the United States of America

10 9 8 7 6 5 4 3 2 1 13 12 11 10 09

Allyn & Bacon
is an imprint of

www.pearsonhighered.com

ISBN-10: 0-13-208094-X
ISBN-13: 978-0-13-208094-1

Contents

Part VII  Structural Analysis: Morphemes, Prefixes, Suffixes, Contractions, and Compound Words 185

Preface

Phonics and Structural Analysis for the Teacher of Reading presents the content of phonics and structural analysis as two skills used to identify and learn new words. *Phonics* is the relationship of letters and sounds. It encompasses a system for teaching these relationships and a word identification strategy for the recognition of unfamiliar words. Knowledge of phonics is important because the English language writing system is based on the alphabetic principle—the principle that letters represent speech sounds. *Structural analysis* is a word identification strategy that entails dividing unfamiliar words into meaningful units, such as prefixes, suffixes, and root words. Knowledge of structural analysis is important because these meaningful units are the building blocks of many English words, especially the words in books for third-, fourth-, and fifth-graders.

For classroom teachers, reading teachers, and special education teachers who will soon be entering teaching, learning the content of phonics and structural analysis will help you better understand the teaching methods and materials you will be using in your classroom. For practicing classroom, reading, and special education teachers, studying the content of this book will sharpen your knowledge of phonics, onsets and rimes, syllables, and structural analysis. In sum, the information in this book will help you learn how the alphabetic principle works in English, how syllables affect pronunciation, and how words are built from units. In addition, this book will provide a resource you can turn to in future years as you make decisions about the teaching of word identification skills.

How Is This Text Organized?

Phonics and Structural Analysis for the Teacher of Reading is a self-paced program of instruction that has proven a useful technique for presenting background on the letters and sounds of phonics, onsets–rimes, syllables, and word structure to future and practicing teachers. The text will guide you through a series of small steps to help you learn the terminology associated with word identification skills and ensure your understanding of letter and sound relationships, onsets and rimes, syllables, and structural analysis.

Seventeen Study Guides are interspersed throughout the text to help you review and to provide you with a quick source of information. To assist you in applying your knowledge while teaching, appendixes list all the letter and sound relationships of phonics, the key English sounds (phonemes) and words that represent these sounds, syllable patterns, and guidelines for spelling when adding prefixes and suffixes to words. A brief history of the events that shaped English spelling will give you insight into how the English spelling system evolved and why spelling is not always a perfect match for sound.

Scattered throughout the book are 10 boxed features that explain some of the more intriguing aspects of the history of the alphabet. These sections take a closer look at a few of the sounds of language and explain the reasons certain letters and letter combinations are used in the English language today. These brief accounts will enhance your insight into and appreciation for the American-English spelling system.

 New to This Revision

To further assist you in your study, this latest revision of *Phonics and Structural Analysis for the Teacher of Reading* includes a detailed explanation of **structural analysis.** This discussion includes morphemes, prefixes, suffixes, contractions, and compound words. **Seven guidelines** have been added to **Appendix A** to help you understand the conventions that frequently determine the spellings of words with prefixes and suffixes. **New Study Guides** offer an in-depth view of useful prefixes and suffixes, present a list of contractions, and provide a consolidated list of spelling generalizations for adding suffixes. To help you solidify your understanding, you will find a short, **comprehensive Review of Phonemes,** with page numbers telling you where information is located in the book, and four Recaps. The **Recaps** will help reinforce your understanding of consonants, vowels, syllables, and structural analysis. You will read a concise, **updated overview of the research foundation for teaching phonics** just before you begin your study of the content of phonics and structural analysis. I hope this book will help you understand phonics and structural analysis and give you the knowledge base you need to be an effective teacher.

 Acknowledgments

I would like to thank the reviewers of this text. I appreciate their insightful guidance: Linda Amspaugh-Corson, University of Cincinnati; Ward Cockrum, Northern Arizona University; and Yvonne Taylor, Shippensburg University.

Phonics and Structural Analysis for the Teacher of Reading

Self-Evaluation I

A Pretest

This is a test designed to give an indication of your present knowledge in the field of phonics. Read each item, including **all** the choices. Indicate the answer you consider best by circling the appropriate letter (a, b, c, d, or e) or marking the appropriate letter on an answer sheet. Be sure to respond to every item. Time: 30 minutes.

I. Multiple Choice. Select the best answer.

1. A requirement of a syllable is that

- **a.** it contain at least one consonant letter.
- **b.** it contain no more than one vowel letter.
- **c.** it contain no more than one vowel phoneme.
- **d.** it contain no more than one phoneme.
- **e.** All of the above

2. Which of the following most adequately completes this sentence? The consonant speech sounds in the American-English language are represented by

- **a.** the distinctive speech sounds we associate with the 21 consonant letters of the alphabet.
- **b.** 18 of the consonant letters of the alphabet plus certain digraphs.
- **c.** the single-letter consonants plus their two- and three-letter blends.
- **d.** The American-English language is too irregular to represent the consonant speech sounds with any degree of accuracy.

3. The letter *y* is most likely to be a consonant when

- **a.** it is the first letter in a word or syllable.
- **b.** it is the final letter in a word or syllable.
- **c.** it follows *o* in a syllable.
- **d.** it has the sound of *i* as in *might.*
- **e.** None of the above

4. Generally, when two like consonants appear together in a word,

- **a.** only one is sounded.
- **b.** one is sounded with the first syllable and the other with the second.
- **c.** both are sounded when the preceding vowel is *i.*

d. both are sounded when the following vowel is *e.*
e. neither is sounded.

5. The second syllable of the nonsense word *alithpic* would be expected to rhyme with

a. *aright.*
b. *brick.*
c. *kith.*
d. *pyth* (as in *python*).
e. *hit.*

6. The open syllable in the nonsense word *botem* would most likely rhyme with

a. *coat.*
b. *hot.*
c. *rah.*
d. *low.*
e. *gem.*

7. A diphthong is best illustrated by the vowels representing the sound of

a. *ow* in *snow.*
b. *ou* in *mouse.*
c. *oo* in *foot.*
d. *ai* in *said.*
e. a and b

8. The sound of the schwa is represented by

a. the *a* in *baited.*
b. the *e* in *early.*
c. the *e* in *happen.*
d. the *w* in *show.*
e. All of these

9. How many phonemes are represented in *knight?*

a. one **b.** two **c.** three **d.** four **e.** six

10. An example of a closed syllable is

a. *desk.*
b. *hot.*
c. *tight.*
d. All of these
e. None of these

11. The consonant cluster is illustrated by

a. the *sh* in *shirt.*
b. the *ng* in *thing.*
c. the *ph* in *graph.*
d. the *br* in *brought.*
e. a, c, and d

12. Which of the following has an incorrect diacritical mark?

a. căll **b.** sĕll **c.** ĭll **d.** hŏt **e.** ŭp

13. Which of the following has an incorrect diacritical mark?

a. māde **b.** sēe **c.** tīme **d.** lōve **e.** ūse

14. When the single vowel *i* in an accented syllable is followed by a single consonant and a final *e,* the *i* would most likely have the sound of

a. the *i* in *active.*
b. the *y* in *my.*
c. the *i* in *easily.*
d. the first *e* in *bee.*
e. None of the above

15. If *o* were the only and final vowel in an accented syllable, that *o* would most likely represent the same sound as

a. the *o* in *nothing.*
b. the *a* in *wanted.*
c. the *o* in *do.*
d. the *ew* in *sew.*
e. None of these

16. The letter *q* could be removed from the alphabet because it could adequately and without conflict be represented by

a. the soft sound of *c.*
b. *ch* as in *chair.*
c. *k* as in *keep.*
d. All of the above
e. The idea is foolish; *qu* represents a distinctive consonant sound.

17. If *a* were the single vowel in an accented syllable ending with one or more consonants, that *a* would most likely represent the same sound as

a. the *ai* in *plaid.*
b. the *ay* in *ray.*
c. the *a* in *all.*
d. the *a* in *any.*
e. None of these

18. When *o* and *a* appear together in a syllable, they usually represent the same sound as

a. the *o* in *bottle.*
b. the *o* in *labor.*
c. the *o* in *toil.*
d. the *o* in *come.*
e. None of these

19. The symbol *s* is used in the dictionary to show the pronunciation of the sound heard in

a. *shall.*
b. *his.*
c. *sugar.*
d. *seem.*
e. Both b and d

20. If *e* were the only vowel in an open syllable, the *e* would most likely represent the same sound as

a. the *e* in *pine*.
b. the *ea* in *meat*.
c. the *y* in *my*.
d. the *e* in *set*.
e. None of these

21. The word *if* ends with the same sound as

a. the *ph* in *graph*.
b. the *f* in *of*.
c. the *gh* in *taught*.
d. the *gh* in *ghetto*.
e. Both a and b

22. The letter *c* followed by *i* is most likely to represent the same sound as

a. the *s* in *sent*.
b. the *c* in *cello*.
c. *c* followed by *o*.
d. *c* followed by *e*.
e. Both a and d

23. The letter *g* followed by *o* is most likely to represent the same sound as

a. the *j* in *joke*.
b. the *g* in *ghost*.
c. the *g* in *swing*.
d. *g* followed by *e*.
e. Both a and d

24. The final *y* changes to *i* before a suffix is added to a word that

a. ends in a consonant followed by the letter *y*.
b. ends in two consonants.
c. ends in a vowel followed by the letter *y*.
d. has two or more syllables.
e. consists of no more than one syllable.

25. A free morpheme is illustrated by

a. *-ing*.
b. *-un*.
c. *-ous*.
d. *fame*.
e. *-ment*.

26. A word that includes both a free and a bound morpheme is illustrated by

a. *unhappy*.
b. *easily*.
c. *famous*.
d. None of these
e. All of these

27. Add *-es* to a word that ends in

a. the letter *s.*
b. the letters *sh.*
c. the letters *ch.*
d. the letter *x.*
e. All of these

28. A suffix may

a. change the meaning of a word.
b. make the meaning of a word more specific.
c. change the part of speech.
d. Both a and b
e. All of the above

29. Which word includes a derivational suffix?

a. *furious*
b. *camels*
c. *enjoyment*
d. *laughed*
e. Both a and c

30. Double the final consonant before adding a suffix to a one-syllable word to indicate that the

a. vowel represents a long sound.
b. vowel is a diphthong.
c. vowel represents a short sound.
d. vowel sound changes from short to long.
e. All of the above

31. The guideline for adding a suffix to a word that ends in an *e* is illustrated by

a. *timely.*
b. *nicer.*
c. *replacing.*
d. *largest.*
e. All of the above

32. Which word includes an inflectional suffix?

a. *serious*
b. *player*
c. *statement*
d. *childhood*
e. None of these

33. Which underlined item illustrates a free morpheme?

a. *playful*
b. *illegal.*
c. *disappear*
d. *reappoint*
e. a, b, and c

34. A contraction is illustrated by

a. *Sue's.*
b. *teachers'.*
c. *could've.*
d. *Jones's.*
e. *cannot.*

35. Which word below shows the correct syllable division?

a. en' erg y
b. gin' ger snap'
c. journ' al
d. rem' ed y
e. None of these

36. A compound word is illustrated by

a. *cheekbone.*
b. *rattled.*
c. *disability.*
d. *chickadee.*
e. *fistful.*

37. *They'd* is composed of which of the following two words?

a. *They should*
b. *They will*
c. *They would*
d. *They had*
e. Both c and d

38. A suffix that begins with a consonant is illustrated by

a. *furious.*
b. *painter.*
c. *statehood.*
d. *largest.*
e. All of these

II. Multiple Choice. Where does the accent fall in each of the words or nonsense words given at the left? Indicate your answer by selecting the last two letters of the accented syllable found in the same row as the word.

Look at the example: *showboat.* The first word in a compound word is generally accented: *show boat.* Look for the last two letters of *show, ow,* in the row to the right. You would circle b or mark b on your answer sheet.

Example:

	showboat	**a.** ho	(**b.**) ow	**c.** bo	**d.** at	
39.	contract (noun)	**a.** co	**b.** on	**c.** nt	**d.** ra	**e.** ct
40.	frottomly	**a.** ro	**b.** ot	**c.** to	**d.** om	**e.** ly
41.	plargain	**a.** la	**b.** ar	**c.** rg	**d.** ga	**e.** in
42.	desridly	**a.** de	**b.** es	**c.** ri	**d.** id	**e.** ly

43. cidaltion **a.** ci **b.** id **c.** da **d.** al **e.** on

44. phight **a.** hi **b.** ig **c.** gh **d.** ht

III. Multiple Choice. Three words are provided for each item (a, b, c). Select the word in which you hear the same sound as that represented by the underlined part of the word at the left. You may find that the sound is heard in all three words; if so, mark d. If none of the words contains the sound, mark e.

45. mention **a.** special **b.** sugar **c.** machine **d.** All **e.** None

46. then **a.** third **b.** mother **c.** think **d.** All **e.** None

47. jet **a.** gnome **b.** gentle **c.** sang **d.** All **e.** None

48. into **a.** thick **b.** watch **c.** hoped **d.** All **e.** None

49. success **a.** cheese **b.** knee **c.** queer **d.** All **e.** None

50. home **a.** honor **b.** night **c.** who **d.** All **e.** None

51. tall **a.** talk **b.** fault **c.** gnaw **d.** All **e.** None

52. food **a.** look **b.** blood **c.** bought **d.** All **e.** None

53. boil **a.** mouse **b.** employ **c.** riot **d.** All **e.** None

54. would **a.** whom **b.** once **c.** cow **d.** All **e.** None

55. sang **a.** ranger **b.** ponder **c.** thinker **d.** All **e.** None

IV. Multiple Choice. Select the letter(s) at the right that represents the onset in each one-syllable word.

56. splurge **a.** sp **b.** ge **c.** lur **d.** spl **e.** urge

57. cherry **a.** ch **b.** erry **c.** her **d.** cher **e.** erry

58. throw **a.** thr **b.** ro **c.** ow **d.** th **e.** row

59. fluid **a.** uid **b.** id **c.** lui **d.** fl **e.** flu

60. roast **a.** roa **b.** oa **c.** st **d.** oast **e.** r

V. Multiple Choice. Select the letter(s) at the right that represents the rime in each one-syllable word.

61. steam **a.** ea **b.** eam **c.** st **d.** team **e.** ste

62. rhyme **a.** rh **b.** yme **c.** rhy **d.** hyme **e.** rhy

63. catch **a.** atch **b.** tch **c.** cat **d.** ch **e.** at

64. school **a.** ch **b.** choo **c.** ool **d.** hool **e.** sch

65. dress **a.** ess **b.** dr **c.** dre **d.** ress **e.** re

VI. Multiple Choice. Select the word in each row that is **incorrectly** syllabicated.

66. **a.** ro bot **b.** ro bin **c.** ro bust **d.** ro tor **e.** rouge

67. **a.** let hal **b.** rab bit **c.** re cov er **d.** mer cy **e.** con nect

68. **a.** un der line **b.** un e qual **c.** un ite **d.** pre dic a ment **e.** re mit

69. **a.** home work **b.** book man **c.** eye ball **d.** now here **e.** egg nog

VII. Multiple Choice. Complete each sentence by selecting the word for which the correct pronunciation is indicated.

70. I went to the park for a

a. pĭc' nĭc **b.** wôk **c.** rəst **d.** păr' tē **e.** rĭde

71. When I picked my vegetables, I dropped a

a. lĕt' ĭs lēv **b.** kūk'ŭm bər **c.** kăr'ŏt **d.** kăb'ĭg **e.** bēt

72. The tree we planted was a

a. pälm **b.** wĭl'ou **c.** māp'le **d.** kŏt' ən wŭd **e.** sĭk'ə môr

73. I went to the men's store to get (a)

a. sŏgz **b.** sho͞oz **c.** trou'sərs **d.** chərt **e.** nək' tī'

74. The wall is

a. krăkt **b.** smo͞oth **c.** rôf **d.** pānt əd' **e.** tℏĭk

75. The comittee was composed of

a. klûr' gĭ mĕn **b.** book mĭn' **c.** băngk' ərz **e.** tē zhərs **e.** jŭd'jĭs

(See p. 227 for answers to Self-Evaluation I.)

Number correct ________________

Part I

General Knowledge and Terminology

What kind of background do you have in phonics and structural analysis? To help determine the depth of your present knowledge or lack of knowledge, and to aid in evaluating your growth, this text includes a pretest and a posttest. Do not examine the posttest now. You may wish to remove the posttest and file it away, awaiting the completion of your study of this programmed text.

Turn to page 1 and take the pretest now. Correct it. At your next sitting, turn back to this section and continue reading.

Now that you have completed the pretest, you are ready to continue with this program.

Events That Shaped English Spelling

The English language did not exist in the middle of the fifth century when three Germanic tribes, the Angles, the Saxons, and the Jutes, sailed across the North Sea and marched onto the shores of the British Isles. There they found the Celts, a peace-loving people who were overwhelmed by the invaders. The Saxons became the dominant tribe, and eventually, distinctions among the tribes disappeared. As the Anglo-Saxons settled down to life in their new homeland, their Germanic-based language began to change. These naturally occurring changes marked the beginning of the English language.

The early Anglo-Saxons were relatively illiterate (Bryson, 1990). Their meager use of the runic alphabet left few records, save for inscriptions on stones used in religious ceremonies. All this changed at the end of the sixth century when monks made their way into Great Britain, bringing with them the Christian religion, the Roman alphabet, and literacy (Burnley, 2000). As literacy spread across Great Britain, scribes used the Roman alphabet (with some modifications) to create a written record of regional dialects.

The imported Roman alphabet had only 26 letters to represent approximately 44 English sounds (phonemes). The problem of having too few letters could have been solved by inventing new letters or using diacritical marks to indicate pronunciation. Rather than add letters or use diacritical marks, English made up for the shortfall by combining letters (*oi* and *oo,* for instance), forming letter patterns (the final silent *e* indicating that the preceding single vowel is long), and using one letter to represent more than one sound (the *o* in *hot, doll,* and *for,* for example).

The spellings of many English words had not yet been established when the French-speaking Normans conquered Great Britain in 1066, and legions of French-speaking scribes poured into England. When asked to spell English words, a language they did not know, the scribes turned to letter combinations related to French spelling, introducing into the English spelling system combinations such as *qu, ou,* and *ch.* The Normans more or less ignored English, a second-class language spoken only by the working classes. The Norman French indifference created a fertile climate in which many different English dialects developed. Dialectical variation is significant because it affected English spelling when the speakers of one dialect adopted the spellings of another (Bryson, 1990).

Wholesale borrowing from classical languages also affected English spelling. In the 17th century, zealous scholars borrowed words from the Latin and Greek languages, perhaps in the belief that these two respected languages would raise the stature of English. Not only did the scholars borrow from Latin and Greek, but they also changed the spelling of some existing English words to suggest a Latin influence, even though the spellings were not particularly consistent with English pronunciation.

By the mid-17th century, the English language spelling system was more or less standardized. Unfortunately, this standardization was quickly followed by a shift in pronunciation (Burnley, 2000). For example, the initial *k* (*knight*), *g* (*gnat*), some instances of initial *w* (*write*), and the *l* in some positions (*chalk*) were no longer pronounced. As a consequence, some contemporary spellings represent 17th century pronunciation (Bryson, 1990).

English spelling continues to change and evolve in the 21st century (Burnley, 2000). Pronunciation is changing, and foreign words (*peso*) are finding their way into English. Yet in spite of military intervention and social change, the use of only 26 letters to represent 44 sounds, and a plethora of foreign words entering the English language, phonics still gives readers insight into pronunciation. This brings us to a discussion of research on the teaching of phonics.

What Does the Research Say about Teaching Phonics?

Phonics is the relationship among the letters of the alphabetic writing system and the sounds in spoken words, as well as an approach for teaching these relationships. Readers use phonics to associate sounds with the letters in unfamiliar written words and then blend the sounds to pronounce familiar spoken words. Beginning readers know many spoken words but relatively few written words. It is not surprising, then, that teaching phonics is most important in the early stages of reading, when children are beginning to build their reading vocabulary. Likewise, learning phonics is important for many struggling readers, who lack sufficient knowledge of letter and sound relationships to support word learning and spelling.

Phonics, reading comprehension, and listening comprehension are highly interdependent (Hagtvet, 2003). Children who learn phonics early and well are better readers and better spellers in the early grades than children who struggle with phonics (Christensen & Bowey, 2005). Phonics contributes to developing skill in word identification, having a large vocabulary of instantly recognized words (Connelly, Johnston, & Thompson, 2001), being able to spell, and being able to read independently (National Reading Panel, 2000), regardless of children's social or economic backgrounds (Schwanenflugel, Hamilton, Kuhn, Wisenbaker, & Stahl, 2004).

Although knowledge of phonics does not cause reading fluency, it contributes to fluency through its effect on reading vocabulary (Eldredge, 2005). Phonics makes it possible for beginning readers to learn new words through a process of changing the letter and sound relationships of unfamiliar written words into familiar spoken words. The more children analyze, read, and write the same words, the stronger their memory and the faster their word recognition (Ehri, 2004). Fast, automatic word recognition, in turn, makes it possible for children to pay full attention to meaning, rather than word identification. Having a large vocabulary of instantly recognized words also makes it possible for children to read fluently—expressively, accurately, and at a pace appropriate for the text and the reading situation.

Phonics instruction improves the decoding skills, vocabulary, comprehension, and fluency of English language learners (Lesaux & Siegel, 2003; Otaiba, 2005) and increases the achievement of struggling English-only readers who have an incomplete understanding of letter and sound relationships (Torgesen, 2004). Phonics instruction also helps to prevent reading problems in children at risk and to close the achievement gap between struggling and average readers (Hatcher, Hulme, & Snowling, 2004; Jeynes, 2008; Vadasy, Sanders, & Peyton, 2005). Research shows that high- and average-readiness kindergartners become good decoders in the first grade. Low-achieving kindergartners do not reach the same level of phonics knowledge until the third grade (Foster & Miller, 2007). By the time low-achieving kindergartners reach third grade, their knowledge of phonics is equivalent to their better-performing peers. However, their comprehension falls far below that of their average-achieving classmates.

An extensive body of research shows that **phonemic awareness**—the understanding that words consist of sounds and the ability to act on this understanding (explained in the next section)—is necessary for using phonics to identify and learn words and contributes to success in learning to read (National Reading Panel, 2000). Researchers agree that teaching phonics along with phonemic awareness is more effective than teaching either of these skills alone (Foorman, Chen, Carlson, Moats, Francis, & Fletcher, 2003; Hatcher, Hulme, & Snowling, 2004; Qudeans, 2003).

In fact, there is a close and reciprocal relationship among phonemic awareness, phonics, and success in learning to read (Foy & Mann, 2006). An increase in one—phonemic awareness, phonics, or reading achievement—coincides with an increase in the others (Torppa et al., 2007). The most likely reason for this three-way reciprocal relationship is that awareness of the individual sounds in words—phonemic awareness—helps beginning readers make sense of the letter–sound relationships of phonics. Learning phonics, in turn, improves awareness of sounds and the ability to learn new words. A large and growing reading vocabulary is, of course, necessary for gains in reading achievement.

In addition to teaching phonics and phonemic awareness together, effective phonics instruction includes the teacher's modeling of how and when to use phonics (Schunk, 2003) and ample opportunities for children to apply phonics as they read and write. Phonics instruction is most effective when it is (1) done early, intensely, directly, and systematically (National Reading Panel, 2000; Schwanenflugel et al., 2004); (2) combined with instruction in reading comprehension (Berninger et al., 2003; Blachman et al., 2004); (3) taught throughout the day; and (4) integrated with ongoing classroom instruction in spelling (Ehri, 2004; Roberts & Meiring, 2006).

While phonics instruction is important, the same amount and intensity of instruction is not equally beneficial for all children. It is important for the teacher of phonics to remember that children who begin school with good letter knowledge will likely require less intense instruction than their classmates who have relatively limited knowledge (Juel & Minden-Cupp, 2004). In order for you, the teacher, to be effective in teaching phonics, you need to understand how written English uses the 26 letters of the alphabet to represent as many as 44 different speech sounds.

Basic Elements of Phonics

spoken	**1.** The language of any people is the **sound** system by which the individuals communicate with one another. The written language is merely a system of **symbols,** a code, used to represent the ____________ language. (written, spoken)
code (or symbols)	**2.** Therefore, one of the basic steps in the reading process is **decoding:** translating the ____________ into the sounds of the spoken language.
symbols (or code)	**3.** We study phonics to learn the code so that we can translate the written ____________ into the spoken sounds. But to our regret, the code is not perfect; part of our study involves its inconsistencies. We shall begin our study by examining the basic elements of the code, the **phoneme** and the **grapheme.**
phoneme	**phoneme** **grapheme** **4.** The suffix *-eme* denotes a basic structural element of a language. *Phon* (telephone, phonograph, etc.) refers to voice or sound. One speech sound is called a ____________ (*phon* + *eme*).
sound	**5.** These word pairs illustrate the definition of a phoneme. As you pronounce each pair, notice the sound that makes the top word different from the one beneath it. *pin* / *tin* *pin* / *pen* *pin* / *pit* *pin* / *chin* **A phoneme is the smallest unit of ____________ that distinguishes one word from another.**
t	**6.** To attain a better understanding of a phoneme, let us examine these words more closely. For example, how does *pin* differ from *tin?* The sounds **represented** by the *p* and the ____________ are the smallest units of sound that distinguish *pin* from *tin.*

sound e	**7.** Compare the phonemes represented by the underlined letters in the set of words below. *pin pen* Remember that the phoneme is a _____________, so say the words aloud. The sounds that are represented by the _____________ and the _____________ are the smallest units that distinguish *pin* from *pen.*
n, t	**8.** Pronounce the words below. *pin pit* The sounds that are represented by the _____________ and the _____________ are the smallest units that distinguish *pin* from *pit.*
/r/ /p/	**9.** We can hear sounds, but we cannot write sounds. For example, we cannot write the sound of *l*. We can say, "the sound represented by *l*" or "the phoneme recorded by *l*." There is also a symbol, / /, which indicates that we are referring to the phoneme of the specific letter or letters enclosed with slashes: /*l*/. How will we write symbolically the phoneme we associate with the letter *r?* _____________ The phoneme represented by the key symbol *p?* _____________ **The symbol /*b*/ refers to the phoneme represented by the key symbol *b*.**
allophone	**allophone** **10.** *Allo*(*o*) denotes a variant form (*allegory, parallel*). We have learned that *phon* refers to the voice or sound (*phoneme, telephone*). A variant form of the same phoneme is called an _____________ (*allo* + *phone*).
no allophones /b/	**11.** Pronounce each of the words below. Listen carefully to the sound represented by the underlined letter. bee brown lab blue tub Do you hear precisely the same sound in each word? _____________ The slight variations in pronunciation are called _____________. How would you symbolically represent the phoneme? _____________
phoneme	**12.** The first sound in *pin,* the second sound in *spin,* and the last sound in *stop* are allophones. Even though we pronounce the allophones differently, we we treat them as the same _____________.

BOX 1.1

Green Glass or Green Grass?

Two English Phonemes

Use your knowledge of the phonemes in the English language to answer the three questions below. Read each question aloud, and write the answer on the line.

1. The second phoneme in *glass* and the second phoneme in *grass* are ________________.
   (the same, different)

2. The first phoneme in *late* is ________________ the first phoneme in *rate.*
   (the same as, different from)

3. *Fire* and *file* are ________________ English words.
   (the same, different)

The /r/ and /l/ phonemes (here presented between two slashes) are distinctly different in the English language. Therefore, you hear two separate phonemes and, by extension, two different words when you pronounce *glass* and *grass.* These phonemes, which are entirely distinct to you, a fluent speaker of the English language, are not so distinct and so simple to differentiate for native speakers of the Japanese language.

The Japanese language does not have an equivalent phoneme for the English /r/. Because the Japanese *r* is a combination of the English /r/ and /l/, speakers of Japanese may perceive the /l/ and the /r/ as variations (**allophones**) of the same phoneme. Not only do speakers of the Japanese language have difficulty in distinguishing the English language /r/ from the /l/, but they may well confuse these two phonemes when pronouncing English words, perhaps saying "grass" when the intended word is "glass."

We listen for and perceive those phonemic differences and similarities that are particular to the language that we speak. Not all languages share exactly the same phonemes, however. Children bring to your classroom—and to the speaking, reading, and writing of the English language—an awareness of the phonemes in their home, or native, languages. You can, therefore, anticipate that some children who speak Japanese as their first language may occasionally confuse the /r/ and /l/ when pronouncing, reading, and spelling English words. When children who are English language learners have opportunities to hear, speak, read, and write English in your classroom, they develop greater sensitivity to the English language sound structure and, in so doing, create mental categories for those English phonemes that differ from the phonemes in their native languages.

allophones phonemes	**13.** Let us review what we have learned about allophones and phonemes. Allophones are variant forms of a single phoneme. The sounds represented by the underlined letters in bag and brag are ___________. The underlined letters in bat and pat represent two different ___________. It is the phonemes that are important for learning phonics.
grapheme	**14.** Sounds cannot be written! Letters do not speak! We use a letter or letters to **represent** a phoneme. *Graph* means "drawn, written, recorded." The ___________ (*graph* + *eme*) is the written representation of the phoneme. It is the unit in the written code.
p i n *p i n*	**15.** When you say the word *pin,* you hear three phonemes. We represent these three phonemes with the letters _____ _____ _____. Put another way, the three graphemes in *pin* are _____ _____ _____. **The grapheme is the written representation of the phoneme. As the phoneme is the unit in the sound system, the grapheme is the unit in the written code.**
phonemes one	**16.** Reread frame 5. We used word pairs to illustrate the definition of a phoneme. When you said the word *chin,* you heard three ___________. *Ch* represents **one** unit of sound; you cannot divide it. Since the grapheme is the written representation of the phoneme, *ch* is ___________ grapheme(s). (How many?)
ch i n *ch*	**17.** We represent the three phonemes in *chin* with the graphemes __________ __________ __________. The sounds represented by the *p* and the ___________ are the smallest units of sound that distinguish *pin* from *chin.*
ch	**18.** We represent the first phoneme in the word *chart* with the grapheme _______.
phoneme	**19.** A **grapheme** is the written symbol of the ___________. It may be composed of one or more letters.
grapheme phoneme graphemes *k, c, q*	**20.** A **phoneme** is a speech sound. A ___________ is composed of the symbols we use to picture the sound on paper. Say the words *keep*, *come*, and *quit.* In each one you will hear the ___________ that we commonly associate with the underlined grapheme. Three different ___________ are used to represent this phoneme. They are ___________, ___________, and ___________.

BOX 1.2

An Allophone Experiment

You have learned that **allophones** are naturally occurring variations in the phonemes of the English language. You know that, if you listen carefully, you can hear these slight variations. For example, you can identify variations in /*b*/ as it is pronounced in the words *brick, crab,* and *blank.* But can you also feel the difference when you pronounce some allophones? Try this to find out.

1. Put your hand in front of your mouth, palm toward your face and fingers near your lips.
2. Say "pin." Notice that you feel a puff of air when pronouncing the /*p*/ in *pin.* Phonemes that produce a puff of air are called **aspirated.**
3. Say "spin." Notice that you do not feel a puff of air when pronouncing the /*p*/ in *spin.* Phonemes that do not produce a puff of air are called **unaspirated.** When /p/ follows /s/ in English words, /p/ is unaspirated (*spoon, speed*).

Although the /*p*/ in *pin* is aspirated and the /*p*/ in *spin* is unaspirated, we treat them as the same sound because each is an allophone of the same English phoneme, the /*p*/.

You have now demonstrated, through this experiment, that the aspirated and unaspirated allophones of /*p*/ can, indeed, be both heard and felt.

	21. The words **grapheme** and **letter** are not synonymous. A grapheme never consists of less than a letter, but it may consist of more than one letter. The grapheme represents the phoneme.
three *three* *w, a* *sh* *sh*	Examine the word *wash. w a sh* Say it aloud. *Wash* consists of ____________ phonemes. Therefore, it consists of ____________ graphemes—one grapheme to represent each phoneme. The graphemes are ___________, ___________, and ___________. What letters comprise the final grapheme of the word *wash?* ____________
phonemes (or speech sounds)	**22.** Although there are hundreds of different speech sounds (consider the variations due to dialect, individual speech patterns, change in stress, etc.), for all practical purposes, in the task of teaching reading, **we can consider the American-English language to contain 44 separate ____________.**
phoneme, grapheme	**23.** If the code were consistent (that is, if we had one grapheme for each ____________ and one phoneme for each ____________), the task of teaching children to read would be much simpler than it is now.
26 phonemes	**24.** The truth is that we have only ____________ letters in our alphabet, only 26 symbols to represent 44 ____________.

phonemes	**25.** We add symbols to our system by using combinations of letters (such as as *ch, th*) to represent the ____________ not represented by the 26 letters of the alphabet.
phoneme, *a*	**26.** We also add symbols by using one letter to represent more than one ____________. The letter ____________, for example, represents three different phonemes in the three words *ate, pan, all.*
k, g, h	**27.** Another of the many complications is the use of symbols that do not represent any sound: *Knight* has three letters that do not represent sounds: the ____________, ____________, and ____________.
gh, ph phoneme	**28.** Besides lacking a one-to-one correspondence between the letters of the alphabet and the phonemes needed, the spelling of the English language is further complicated by its many inconsistencies. One of the greatest of these is the use of different symbols to represent the same phoneme. For example, the sound we associate with *f* is represented by *f* in *fine,* by ____________ in *cough,* and by ____________ in *elephant.* This is an example of three graphemes representing one ____________.
letter (or symbol or grapheme)	**29.** Sometimes when a grapheme represents more than one phoneme, there are clues within the word to indicate which sound the ____________ represents. A teacher of reading should be able to recognize these clues.
phoneme phonemes, graphemes	**30.** Our alphabet represents speech at the level of the ____________. Therefore, learning the code requires that readers separate (segment) spoken words into ____________ and associate ____________ with these phonemes.
rhyme	**31. Phonological awareness** is the understanding that spoken language consists of words, syllables, rhymes, and phonemes. Readers who are phonologically aware know that the words *man, pan,* and *van* ____________.
phonemes	**32. Phonemic awareness** refers only to the understanding that spoken words are composed of ____________ and the understanding that individual phonemes, when blended together, form meaningful words.

	33. Reread the definition in the previous frame. You will see that phonemic awareness consists of two understandings:
phonemes	(1) The understanding that spoken words are composed of ____________, and
	(2) The understanding that phonemes, when blended together, form
words	recognizable ____________.
	34. Let us consider the first understanding. Readers who are aware of the individual phonemes in spoken words can segment, or separate, words into sounds.
three	Pronounce the word *tip* aloud. *Tip* is composed of ____________ phonemes. (How many?)
four	Say the word *trip. Trip* is composed of ____________ phonemes. (How many?)
segement (or separate)	When you count the phonemes in a word, you ____________ the word into individual sounds.
	35. Now try *meadow, cough,* and *admit.* (Do not be misled by the number of letters in a word's spelling!)
four	The word *meadow* consists of ____________ phonemes, *cough* of (How many?)
three, five	____________ phonemes, and *admit* of ____________ phonemes. (How many?) (How many?)
/p/	**36.** Say the word *pin* aloud. *Pin* begins with the phoneme ____________.
/i/	The phoneme in the middle of *pin* is ____________.
/n/	*Pin* ends with the phoneme ____________.
segment	You have demonstrated the ability to ____________ the word *pin* into phonemes. (segment, blend)
	37. Segment each of the following words by saying it aloud and then writing each phoneme enclosed with a slash.
/p/, /a/, /n/	The word *pan* consists of the phonemes ______, ______, and ______.
/m/, /i/, /l/, /k/	*Milk* consists of the phonemes ______, ______, ______, and ______.
/s/, /e/, /n/, /s/	*Sense* consists of the phonemes ______, ______, ______, and ______.
phoneme	**38.** Our alphabet represents speech at the level of the ____________. Therefore, readers of the English language must be able to segment
phonemes (sounds)	or separate spoken words into ____________.

	39. Review frames 34 through 37. In frames 34 and 35, you were asked to
count	______________ the phonemes in a word. (count, note the position of)
note the position of	Frame 36 required that you ______________ the phonemes by (count, note the position of)
	identifying the beginning, middle, and last phonemes in a word. Frame 37 asked you to pronounce the phonemes one-by-one.
	40. We will now consider three other activities that the teacher of reading may use to develop and demonstrate phonemic awareness in the beginning reader.
	In **phoneme addition,** the reader attaches one or more phonemes to a word or word part. Use your awareness of the phonemes of the English language to complete the phoneme addition activities below. Combine the phonemes to pronounce a word. Write the new word on the line beside each activity.
man	**A.** Add /*m*/ to /*an*/. The new word is ________.
	B. Start with the word *bike.* Add /*s*/ to the end. What is the new word?
bikes	________.
sit	**C.** What word do we make when we add /*s*/ to /*it*/? ________
	41. Phoneme deletion, the next activity we will examine, is defined as removing one or more phonemes from a word. Complete the phoneme deletion activities below. Write the new word on the line beside each activity.
at	**A.** Say *flat.* Now say it again without the /*f*/. The new word is ________.
top	**B.** What is left when we take the /*s*/ from /*stop*/? ________
eat	**C.** Say *seat.* Now say it again without the /*s*/. What is the new word? ________
	42. Phoneme substitution, the last activity we will consider, requires that the reader delete one or more phonemes from a word (or word part) and replace them with one or more different phonemes. Complete the phoneme substitution activities below. Write the new word on the line beside each activity.
	A. Say *can.* Say it again, but this time say /*m*/ instead of /*c*/. The new word
man	is ________.
pin	**B.** Say *pan.* Change /*a*/ to /*i*/. What is the new word? ________
fat	**C.** Begin with *fan.* Change /*n*/ to /*t*/. What is the new word? ________

deletion noting the positions of phonemes in words substitution counting phonemes addition segementing (or separating)	**43.** We have studied activities that the teacher of reading may use to develop or demonstrate phonemic awareness in the beginning reader. These activities ask the reader to consciously and intentionally count phonemes, note the positions of phonemes in words, fully segment a word by pronouncing its phonemes one-by-one, and add, delete, and substitute phonemes. Write the name of the activity on the line beside the description. Read all the descriptions before answering! **A.** Removing the /*s*/ from /*sat*/ to form the new word *at* is an example of phoneme ____________. **B.** Pronouncing the middle phoneme in a three-phoneme word is an example of ____________. **C.** Exchanging /*h*/ for /*f*/ in /*fat*/ to pronounce the new word *hat* is an example of phoneme ____________. **D.** Telling how many phonemes are in a spoken word is an example of ____________. **E.** Adding /*b*/ to /*at*/ to pronounce the new word *bat* is an example of phoneme ____________. **F.** Saying each phoneme in *mat* one by one (/*m*/ /*a*/ /*t*/) is an example of fully ____________ a spoken word into phonemes.
blend	**44.** We will now turn our attention to the second aspect of phonemic awareness: the ability to ____________ individual phonemes into meaningful spoken words.
/*l*/ /*a*/ /*f*/ no	**45.** Use your knowledge of phonics to say the phoneme represented by each grapheme in the word *laf.* The grapheme *l* represents the phoneme ____________. The grapheme *a* represents the phoneme ____________. The grapheme *f* represents the phoneme ____________. You have now pronounced each phoneme in isolation. Have you pronounced a word? ____________
blend	**46.** To identify the spoken word that the graphemes in the word *laf* represent, you must associate a phoneme with each grapheme, and then you must ____________ the phonemes together.

laugh	**47.** Now blend the phonemes together. Say the phonemes aloud as you blend. The phonemes /l/ + /a/ + /f/ form a word you recognize in speech. Write the word the way that you would normally spell it. ____________
decoding cat lame tent gem	**48.** Sometimes blending is described as "folding sounds together." The reader blends, or folds, the phonemes together so that the phonemes form a whole spoken word. Blending is an essential aspect of ____________. Try blending the phonemes below. Write each word the way that it is normally spelled. /k/ + /a/ + /t/ = ____________ /l/ + /a/ + /m/ + /p/ = ____________ /t/ + /e/ + /n/ + /t/ = ____________ /j/ + /e/ + /m/ = ____________
phonemic awareness phonemes, blend	**49.** We have learned that readers who are successful at using phonics to decode words have developed ____________. These readers can segment words into their individual ____________ and can ____________ individual phonemes to pronounce the words we use in everyday conversation.

Graphophonic, Syntactic, and Semantic Cues

graphophonic	**1.** For the purposes of learning phonics, **graphophonic cues** consist of the 26 letters and combinations of these letters (graphemes), the 44 sounds (phonemes), and the system of relationships among the letters and the sounds (phonics). Readers use ____________ (*grapho* + *phonic*) cues to translate the written code into the sounds that form the words of spoken language. In this book we will focus our attention on the letter–sound associations of our alphabetic writing system. Therefore, we will consider **letter–sound** to be a synonym of **graphophonic**. You may use either term as you complete the frames in this section.
cot coat	**2.** Pronounce the words below. *hot boat rod road top coal* Graphophonic or letter–sound cues indicate that the *o* in *rod* represents the same sound as the *o* in ____________ (*cot, coat*) and that the *oa* in *road* represents the same sound as the *oa* in ____________. (*cot, coat*)

BOX 1.3

Spanish Phonemes

Different languages use different phonemes and different graphemes. Let us consider four Spanish phonemes that do not have exact English language equivalents and the graphemes that represent them.

1. The Spanish *ñ* is pronounced like the *ny* in the English word *canyon,* and is represented by the grapheme *ñ.* We hear this phoneme in the Spanish loan words *El Niño* and *La Niña.*
2. The Spanish trilled *r* is pronounced by rolling the *r* on the upper palate. A single *r* is the grapheme that indicates a slightly trilled pronunciation; a double *rr* represents a strongly trilled pronunciation. The Spanish word for *dog, perro,* is pronounced with a strongly trilled *rr.*
3. In Latin America, the *ll* is the grapheme that represents the sound of the *y* in *yellow.* In Spain, the *ll* is pronounced like the *lli* in *million. Tortilla,* a cornmeal flat bread used in tacos and other dishes, is an example of a Spanish loan word in which the *ll* is pronounced like the *y* in *yellow* or the *lli* in *million.*
4. The Spanish *j* is pronounced like the English /*h*/ in *happy,* only farther back in the throat and with more emphasis. *Javelina,* the wild pig of the southwestern United States, is an example of a Spanish loan word in which the letter *j* represents /*h*/.

The native speaker of English who wishes to speak the Spanish language must learn to pronounce the four Spanish phonemes that are not among the 44 American-English phonemes. The best ways to do this are to speak Spanish and to listen to Spanish as it is being spoken. Similarly, Spanish-speaking children who learn English as a second language benefit from many and varied opportunities to speak and listen to English, to participate in English conversations, and to hear English books read aloud.

syntactic	**3.** Besides graphophonic or letter–sound cues, readers use **syntactic cues** and **semantic cues** to determine the identity of words. **Syntax** is the manner in which words are ordered to form phrases, clauses, and sentences. Therefore, readers who use ____________ clues recognize the manner in which word order and grammatical function are clues to the identity of a word.
hit syntactic	**4.** Consider the word order and grammatical function to determine the missing word in this sentence: The batter ____________ the ball to the right fielder. You know to choose a word that is a verb because English syntax requires the use of an action word in the structure of this sentence. When you decide that the missing word is a verb, you use ____________ cues. (graphophonic, syntactic)

semantic	**5. Semantic** refers to the meaning of language. Therefore, the meaning of a passage provides readers with ____________ cues.
semantic (meaning)	**6.** Consider once again the word omitted from the sentence in frame 4. To determine that the missing word is *hit,* you must combine a background knowledge of baseball with an understanding of the meaning of this sentence. This is an example of the use of ____________ cues.
truck Semantic *truck*	**7.** Now read the following sentence: The dog barked at the red and blue ____________. (*truck, tree*) ____________ cues within the sentence indicate that the missing word (Syntactic, Semantic) is ____________.
graphophonic cues syntactic cues semantic cues	**8.** The three types of cues used to identify unfamiliar words are ____________, which consist of letter and sound relationships, ____________, which consist of grammatical relationships, and ____________, which consist of meaningful relationships.
graphophonic or letter–sound syntactic semantic, sense	**9.** Readers frequently combine the information from graphophonic, syntactic, and semantic cues to determine the identities of words. Readers use ____________ cues to translate the written code into speech sounds. Readers use ____________ cues to identify words that are consistent with grammatical order and function. Readers use ____________ cues to identify words that make ____________ in a sentence.
graphophonic or letter–sound syntactic, semantic	**10.** You have learned that readers use ____________ cues to determine the pronunciations of words they do not recognize. However, the process of word identification is strengthened when graphophonic cues are used in combination with ____________ cues and ____________ cues.
phonemes sound (or phoneme)	**11.** We have noted that the alphabet is a symbolic representation of our speech sounds (or ____________), that there is not a one-to-one correspondence between the symbol and the ____________, and that there are many inconsistencies in the symbolic system. The code is far from perfect.

	12. However, there are certain symbols that are reliable and there are patterns of reliability within the inconsistencies. The teacher of reading must be aware of these. It is the purpose of this program to aid you in your understanding of one set of word recognition skills, that of phonics.
letters (graphemes)	We shall begin our study with the most reliable of the 26 ____________ of the alphabet, the **consonants.** (letters, phonemes)

The Reviews should give you some indication of the effectiveness of your study and provide means for additional reviewing. Write the answers to the Reviews on another sheet of paper. Correct them and analyze the results. Then recheck yourself after a few days by answering the Review questions again. Keep track of your scores so that you will know where additional study and review are needed.

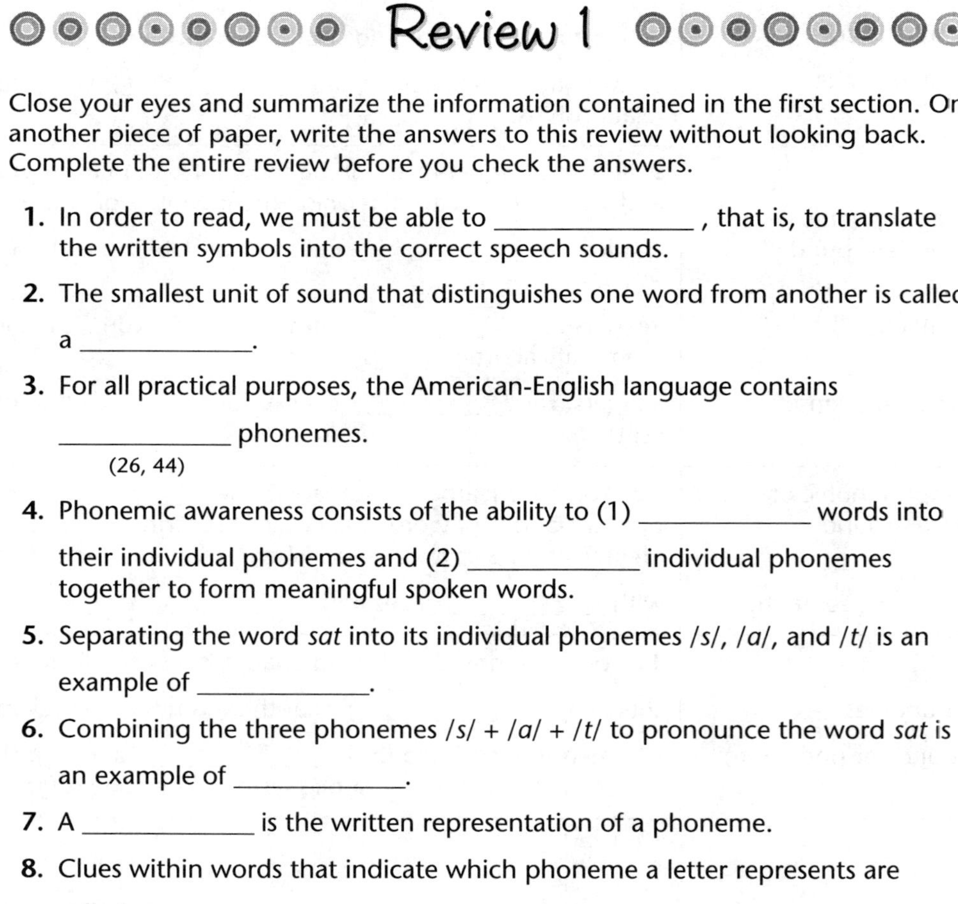

Review 1

Close your eyes and summarize the information contained in the first section. On another piece of paper, write the answers to this review without looking back. Complete the entire review before you check the answers.

1. In order to read, we must be able to ______________ , that is, to translate the written symbols into the correct speech sounds.
2. The smallest unit of sound that distinguishes one word from another is called a ____________.
3. For all practical purposes, the American-English language contains ____________ phonemes. (26, 44)
4. Phonemic awareness consists of the ability to (1) ____________ words into their individual phonemes and (2) ____________ individual phonemes together to form meaningful spoken words.
5. Separating the word *sat* into its individual phonemes /*s*/, /*a*/, and /*t*/ is an example of ____________.
6. Combining the three phonemes /*s*/ + /*a*/ + /*t*/ to pronounce the word *sat* is an example of ____________.
7. A ____________ is the written representation of a phoneme.
8. Clues within words that indicate which phoneme a letter represents are called ____________ cues.

9. The way that words are ordered and function in sentences provides ____________ cues to word identification.

10. The meaning of a passage provides readers with ____________ cues to the identities of words.

Turn to the Answers to the Reviews section, page 229, and check your answers. You should have answered all the questions correctly. If you did not succeed, analyze your study procedure. Is your mind active? Are you writing all the answers? Do you complete a frame before you move the mask down? Did you summarize your learnings before you started the review? Study the appropriate parts of the Introduction again. Congratulations to those who had a perfect score! Your learning should be very profitable.

References

Berninger, V. W., Vermeulen, K., Abbott, R. D., McCutchen, D., Cotton, S., Cude, J., Dorn, S., & Sharon, T. (2003). Comparison of three approaches to supplementary reading instruction for low-achieving second-grade readers. *Language, Speech, and Hearing Services in Schools, 34,* 101–116.

Blachman, B. A., Schatschneider, C., Fletcher, J. M., Francis, D. J., Clonan, S. M., Shaywitz, B. A., & Shaywitz, S. E. (2004). Effects of intensive reading remediation for second and third graders and a 1-year follow-up study. *Journal of Educational Psychology, 96,* 444–461.

Bryson, B. (1990). *Mother tongue: English and how it got that way.* New York: William Morrow.

Burnley, D. (2000). *The history of the English language: A source book* (2nd ed.) Edinburg Gate, England: Pearson.

Christensen, C. A., & Bowey, J. A. (2005). The efficacy of orthographic rime, grapheme–phoneme correspondences, and implicit phonics approaches to teaching decoding skills. *Scientific Studies of Reading, 9,* 327–340.

Connelly, V., Johnston, R., & Thompson, G. B. (2001). The effect of phonics instruction on the reading comprehension of beginning readers. *Reading and Writing: An Interdisciplinary Journal, 14,* 423–457.

Ehri, L. C. (2004). Teaching phonemic awareness and phonics: An explanation of the national reading panel meta-analysis. In P. McCardle & V. Chhabra (Eds.), *The voice of evidence in reading research* (pp. 153–186). Baltimore: Paul H. Brookes.

Eldredge, J. L. (2005). Foundations of fluency: An exploration. *Reading Psychology, 26*(2), 161–181.

Foorman, B. R., Chen, D. T., Carlson, C., Moats, L., Francis, D. J., & Fletcher, J. M. (2003). The necessity of the alphabetic principle to phonemic awareness instruction. *Reading and Writing: An Interdisciplinary Journal, 16,* 289–324.

Foster, W. A., & Miller, M. (2007). Development of the literacy achievement gap: A longitudinal study of kindergarten through third grade. *Language, Speech, and Hearing Services in Schools, 38,* 173–181.

Foy, J. G., & Mann, V. (2006). Changes in letter sound knowledge are associated with development of phonological awareness in pre-schoolchildren. *Journal of Research in Reading, 29*(2), 143–161.

Hagtvet, B. E. (2003). Listening comprehension and reading comprehension in poor decoders: Evidence for the importance of syntactic and semantic skills as well as phonological skills. *Reading and Writing: An Interdisciplinary Journal, 16,* 505–539.

Hatcher, P. J., Hulme, C., & Snowling, M. J. (2004). Explicit phoneme training combined with phonic reading instruction helps children at risk of reading failure. *Journal of Child Psychology and Psychiatry and Allied Disciplines, 45,* 338–350.

Jeynes, W. H. (2008). A meta-analysis of the relationship between phonics instruction and minority elementary school student academic achievement. *Education and Urban Society. 40*(2), 151–166.

Juel, C., & Minden-Cupp, C. (2004). Learning to read words: Linguistic units and instructional strategies. In R. B. Ruddell & N. J. Unrau (Eds.), *Theoretical models and processes of reading* (5th ed., pp. 313–364). Newark, DE: International Reading Association.

Lesaux, N. K., & Siegel, L. S. (2003). The development of reading in children who speak English as a second language. *Developmental Psychology, 39,* 1005–1019.

National Reading Panel. (2000). *Report of the National Reading Panel. Teaching children to read: An evidence-based assessment of the scientific research literature on reading and its implications for reading instruction: Reports of the subgroups* (NIH Publication no. 00-4754). Washington, DC: U.S. Government Printing Office.

Otaiba, S. A. (2005). How effective is code-based reading tutoring in English for English language learners and preservice teacher–tutors? *Remedial and Special Education, 26,* 245–254.

Qudeans, M. K. (2003). Implication of letter–sound concepts and phonological awareness skills of blending and segmenting: A pilot study examining the effects of instructional sequence in word reading for kindergarten children with low phonological awareness. *Learning Disabilities Quarterly, 26,* 258–280.

Roberts, T. A., & Meiring, A. (2006). Teaching phonics in the context of children's literature or spelling: Influences on first-grade reading, spelling, and writing and fifth-grade comprehension. *Journal of Educational Psychology, 98*(4), 690–713.

Schwanenflugel, P. J., Hamilton, A. M., Kuhn, M. R., Wisenbaker, J. M., & Stahl, S. A. (2004). Becoming a fluent reader: Reading skill and prosodic features in the oral reading of young readers. *Journal of Educational Psychology, 96,* 119–129.

Schunk, D. H. (2003). Self-efficacy for reading and writing: Influence of modeling, goal setting, and self-evaluation. *Reading and Writing Quarterly, 19,* 159–172.

Torgesen, J. K. (2004). Lessons learned from research on interventions for students who have difficulty learning to read. In P. McCardle & V. Chhabra (Eds.), *The voice of evidence in reading research* (pp. 355–382). Baltimore: Paul H. Brookes.

Torppa, M., Poikkeus, A.-M., Laakso, M.-L., Tolvanen, A., Leskinen, E., Leppanen Paavo, H. T., Puolakanaho, A., & Luytinen, H. (2007). Modeling the early paths of phonological awareness and factors supporting its development in children with and without familiar risk of dyslexia. *Scientific Studies of Reading, 11*(2), 73–103.

Vadasy, P. E., Sanders, E. A., & Peyton, J. A. (2005). Relative effectiveness of reading practices or word-level instruction in supplemental tutoring: How text matters. *Journal of Learning Disabilities, 38*(4), 364–380.

Part II

Consonants

Place the mask over the left-hand column. As you work through these sections, it will be necessary for you to make sounds out loud. Be sure that you are seated where this is possible. Now work out the first frame, move the mask down to check, and proceed as you did in the first section. Keep an active mind! You may need to study the entire frame before you make your response.

Introduction

consonants	**1.** The 26 letters of the alphabet can be divided into two major categories: vowels and ______________.
consonants	**2.** There is, however, a degree of overlapping between these categories. Certain letters, notably the *w* and *y,* sometimes function as vowels and at other times as ______________.
consonants, 21	**3.** Recognizing the fact that we are oversimplifying the situation, we shall, in this part of the program, consider all letters except *a, e, i, o, u* to be ______________. There are then ______________ (How many?) consonant letters.
is not	**4.** We have noted previously that in the American-English language, there ______________ (is, is not) a consistent one-to-one correspondence between letter and phoneme. Let us now see how this applies to consonants.

21, 25 is not	**5.** There are (for our purposes in the teaching of reading) 44 phonemes, 25 of these being consonant phonemes. There are ______________ (How many?) consonant letters and ______________ (How many?) consonant phonemes. There ______________ (is, is not) one letter for each phoneme.
grapheme	**6.** There are more phonemes than letters. We gain seven additional phonemes through the use of the two-letter ______________ (grapheme, phoneme).
digraph	**7.** We call these two-letter combinations **digraphs.** Note the spelling—*di* for two; *graph* referring to writing. The two-letter combination *ch,* as in *chair,* is called a ______________.
not	**8.** Pronounce the word *chair* as though each consonant were sounded. You said either "s-hair" or "k-hair." Now pronounce *chair* as it should be pronounced. Note that you hear neither the sound represented by the *c* nor by the *h.* The combination *ch* represents a phoneme ______________ (already, not) represented by a single consonant letter. It functions like another letter of the alphabet.
c *h*	**9.** **A digraph is a two-letter combination that represents a single speech sound.** The **digraph** *ch* does not represent the sound of the ______________ and the ______________ with which it is spelled.
is not	**10.** The phonemes of our language are very familiar to us, but to prepare ourselves to teach others to read, it is necessary to identify *each* of the 44 phonemes. Since there ______________ (is, is not) a one-to-one correspondence between sound and letter, it will be helpful to designate a key symbol for *each* phoneme. In this way we will know the sound to which we are referring no matter how it is represented in the word (that is, no matter how it is spelled).
yes	**11.** When possible, the key symbol will be the same as the letter we ordinarily associate with the sound. For example, *b* will serve as the key symbol for the sound we hear at the beginning of the word *box.* Would you expect *d* to serve as the key symbol for the sound heard at the beginning of the word *dog?* ______________

44 25 phonemes	**12.** There are 44 phonemes; 25 of these are consonant phonemes. We will, therefore, identify ____________ key symbols altogether, of which (How many?) ____________ will be consonants. (How many?) **There will be one key symbol for each phoneme.** **Each phoneme will have one key symbol.** There will be a one-to-one correspondence between key symbols and ____________.
symbol letter boat	**13.** Most of the consonants are reliable with respect to sound. Therefore, in most cases, the key ____________ that designates a certain phoneme heard in a word will be the same as the consonant ____________ seen in that word. For example, *b* will serve as the key symbol for the initial sound we hear in the word ____________. (*boat, comb*).
no (The final *b* represents no phoneme: It is a silent letter.)	**14.** Will *b* serve as the key symbol for the final sound we hear in the word *bomb?* ____________
4, 4 g, r, a, ph f	**15.** The word *graph* has __________ phonemes and therefore __________ (How many?) (How many?) graphemes. They are ________, ________, ________, and ________. So that we have a clue to its pronunciation, the logical key symbol to assign to the final phoneme in *graph* is the letter ________.
ph f	**16.** Pronounce *photo.* The initial grapheme is ____________. The key symbol to represent this sound is ____________.
  key symbols digraphs	**17.** We can divide the 25 consonant phonemes into two major groups: (1) Eighteen consonant phonemes identified by key symbols composed of **single letters;** and (2) Seven consonant phonemes identified by ____________ composed of **two-letter combinations** called ____________.

Review 2

Summarize your learnings. What new words have you learned thus far? Define them.

1. Is there a one-to-one correspondence between the consonant letters and the consonant phonemes? ______________
2. We shall learn to identify a key symbol for each of the consonant ______________ of the American-English language.
   (letters, phonemes)
3. The *m* is a very dependable letter; it is the key symbol for the initial sound heard in *man.* We would expect the key symbol representing the sound heard at the end of the word *jam* to be ______________.
4. Dictionaries also use ______________ as the key symbol to represent the sound heard at the beginning of the word *man.*
5. Most of the key symbols will be single letters; however, seven of the consonant symbols will be composed of ______________ letters called ______________.
6. We can divide the consonant phonemes into two groups according to whether the key symbol representing the phoneme is composed of one or two ______________.
7. *Ch,* a ______________, represents how many phonemes?

See the Answers to the Reviews section for the answers to Review 2, page 230.

Single-Letter Consonants

18

18

phonemes

~~a~~ b ~~c~~ d ~~e~~ f g h ~~i~~ j k l m n ~~o~~ p ~~q~~ r s t ~~u~~ v w ~~x~~ y z

1. Place the mask firmly over the responses at the left. Do not move it until the entire frame is completed.

A. Write the 26 letters of the alphabet, in order, in the column at the right.

B. Draw a diagonal line through each of the five vowel letters.

C. Three of the 21 consonant letters do not represent distinctive sounds. Draw a horizontal line through each of the three unnecessary letters.

A puzzle? Clue: Say the words below, listening for the sounds that are represented by the underlined consonant letters.

city and *cold*

antique and *quiet*

exam and *reflex*

As single letters, *c*, *q*, and *x* do not represent distinctive phonemes.

When these words are spelled so that each consonant letter represents a distinctive phoneme, the words look like this:

sity and *kold*

antikue and *kuiet*

egzam and *refleks*

Eliminating the three unnecessary letters leaves us with

_______________ single consonant letters that have distinctive sounds. In other words, our alphabet supplies us with

_______________ single-letter graphemes to represent 18 of

the 25 consonant _______________ of our language.

phonemes
3

b	*boat*
d	*dog*
f	*fish*
g	*goat*
h	*hat*
j	*jeep*
k	*kite*
l	*lion*
m	*moon*
n	*nut*
p	*pig*
r	*ring*
s	*sun*
t	*table*
v	*van*
w	*wagon*
y	*yo-yo*
z	*zipper*

2. As you repeat the letters of the alphabet, write the 18 consonant letters (the **key symbols**) that represent 18 distinctive ____________.

You will omit the ______ consonant letters that do not represent distinctive phonemes.

How can we know exactly which phoneme has been assigned to each of the key symbols? We use a key word that has that phoneme as its initial sound. The selected key words follow, but they are out of order. Write each key word next to its key symbol.

Key Words

kite	*pig*	*van*	*boat*	*goat*	*dog*
ring	*moon*	*wagon*	*zipper*	*jeep*	*yo-yo*
sun	*lion*	*table*	*fish*	*nut*	*hat*

Key Symbols	Key Words
________	________
________	________
________	________
________	________
________	________
________	________
________	________
________	________
________	________
________	________
________	________
________	________
________	________
________	________
________	________
________	________
________	________
________	________

---

m	*moon*	*g*	*goat*
y	*yo-yo*	*h*	*hat*
s	*sun*	*r*	*ring*

3. Which key symbol and key word should be used to identify the initial sound heard in each of these words? Refer to frame 2 for the key words.

mats ______ __________ *got* ______ __________

yellow ______ __________ *have* ______ __________

city ______ __________ *ride* ______ __________

---

j	*jeep*	*f*	*fish*
j	*jeep*	*k*	*kite*
k	*kite*	*b*	*boat*
g	*goat*	*g*	*goat*

4. Which key symbol and key word should be used to identify the initial sound heard in each of the following words? Use frame 2 for the key words.

jelly ______ __________ *fat* ______ __________

gerbil ______ __________ *candy* ______ __________

cat ______ __________ *book* ______ __________

ghost ______ __________ *gone* ______ __________

Now check your answers. If you missed any, say aloud the key word you selected while you listen carefully to the first phoneme. Substitute that sound in the specific study word above. Correct it so the initial sound in the study word is the same as that in the key word.

Answers	Frame
girl gym goat	**5.** Now, when we use a key symbol such as *g,* we will know that we are referring to the sound heard in ______________ *(girl, gym)* and not to that heard in ______________ *(girl, gym)*. Check yourself. Is the phoneme you have selected the same as that heard in the key word ______________?
key	**6.** As we study each consonant letter, we need to ask certain questions: **A.** How reliable is it? Does it always represent the sound we associate with its ______________ symbol? Are there patterns of reliability? Patterns of inconsistencies? **B.** Does it have distinctive characteristics? The consonant letters have been grouped to facilitate our study in answering the above questions.

m, q, r, v

Answers	Frame
symbol *m m moon* *r r ring* *v v van*	**1.** Four of the 21 consonant letters are extremely dependable: *m, q, r,* and *v.* When we see *m, r,* or *v* in a word, we can be sure it represents the phoneme we associate with its key ______________ and is the initial sound heard in its key word. Fill in the columns at the right with the key symbols (2), and the key words (3). Select the words from the following: *van queen fish ring kite moon*
q k kite	**2.** Since *q* is an unnecessary letter, how can we call it dependable? When we see *q,* we know it represents the sound we associate with the key symbol *k.* In other words, /*q*/ = /*k*/. We can depend on it! Now write the key symbol and key word for *q* above.
k *kite*	**3.** We did not use *q* for a key symbol because the sound it represents had already been assigned to the letter ______________. We have selected one symbol to represent each of the 25 consonant sounds of our language. The key word we have selected to help identify /*k*/ is ______________.

1	2	3
m	________	________
r	________	________
v	________	________
q	________	________

k *k, u, e* *opak, unik* *plak, antik*	**4.** Study the words below. The *que* combination at the end of a word represents the phoneme we associate with the key symbol ______________. Or we might say that the *q* represents the sound we associate with __________, while the __________ and __________ are silent. Rewrite these words using the proper key symbol to stand for each of the consonants. Omit the silent *ue* combination and the silent consonants. Copy the vowels as they are, pronouncing them as they would sound in the real word. *opaque* _________ *unique* _________ *plaque* _________ *antique* _________
u *k*	**5.** The letter *q* is almost always followed by the letter ________. In *unique* the *u* that follows the *q* is silent. There are a few words that begin with *q* in which the *u* is also silent, as in *quay,* or the *u* is pronounced as *u,* as in *queue.* We may miss this point because we may be mispronouncing these words. *Quay* is pronounced as though it were spelled *key; queue* is pronounced as though it were spelled *cue.* The first phoneme in both *key* and *cue* (therefore in *quay* and *queue*) is represented by the key symbol ________. Pronounce *quay* and *queue* correctly several times (*quay* as key; queue as *cue*). Practice reading this: *The people boarding the ship formed a queue on the quay. Three of them wore queues.*
  k *w*	**6.** More commonly, the *u* following the letter *q* becomes a consonant and represents the sound we associate with the key symbol *w.* Say these words: *quilt, equal, quiet, quill.* In these words, the *q* represents the sound we associate with ______________, and the *u* represents the sound we associate with ______________.
 kwick, kwit *kwiz, kween* *k* consonant, *w*	**7.** Pronounce the words below aloud. Rewrite each word below using the proper key symbols to show the pronunciation of the *qu* combination. *quick* _________ *quit* _________ *quiz* _________ *queen* _________ In these words, the letter *q* represents the sound we associate with the key symbol ____________, and the letter *u* represents the sound of the ______________ letter ________. (consonant, vowel)

	8. Let us summarize:
	The letters *m, q, v,* and *r* are very dependable. The *m, v,* and *r* represent distinctive sounds of their own.
k	**The q always represents the same sound as the _______.**
	The letter *q* has a distinctive characteristic: It is almost always followed by the
u	letter ________________. This *u* may be silent or represent the sound of the
consonant, *w*	__________________ __________. (consonant, vowel)

BOX 2.1

How Would a Duck Quack without Q?

Without a sound of its own, the letter *Q* is tantamount to an alphabetical orphan in the modern English alphabet. Let us take a look at how we got this extra letter in our alphabet. The letter *Q,* known as *koppa* in the archaic Greek alphabet, fell out of use and did not survive long enough to become part of the classical Greek alphabet. We would not have the letter *Q* in our own alphabet today had not the Etruscans revived the *Q.* They passed it along to the Romans who used *Q* to spell /kw/ words (*quake, question*). Western languages inherited the Latin alphabet, although the Anglo-Saxons did not borrow this letter from Latin. The French language did borrow the Latin *Q,* however, and it was the French who added the *Q* to the English alphabet. After the Norman Conquest in 1066, French scribes began to use *Q* when spelling English words—perhaps because adding the *Q* made English words look more like French words. By sometime around 1500, the letter *Q* had become part of the English alphabet, where it remains today. If the letter *Q* were to disappear from our alphabet as it did from the classical Greek alphabet, we would use the letters *kw* and *k* in its place, depending on the sounds in the words to be spelled, such as *kwest, technik, kwiz, kwilt, opak, kwip,* and *kwit.* Consider this *kwestion:* If you could choose, would you discard the letter *Q* or keep it as the 22nd letter of the English alphabet?

Ouaknin, M. C. (1999). *Mysteries of the alphabet: The origins of writing* (J. Bacon, Trans.). New York: Abbeville Press.

Review 3

1. How many phonemes are there in *panda*? How many graphemes?
2. How many phonemes are there in *chat*? How many graphemes?
3. We do not have a sufficient number of consonant letters in our alphabet to represent all the consonant sounds. Rather, we supplement the single letters with seven ______________.
4. Which letters have not been assigned key symbols of their own? Why?
5. To establish our code, we select key ______________ and key ______________ to represent each phoneme.
6. What key symbol represents /*m*/? ______________ /*q*/? ______________ /*r*/? ______________ /*v*/? ______________
7. *Q* is followed by ______________ in English words. The *u* may be ______________, as in *antique,* or have the sound of the consonant ______________, as in *quilt.*
8. Using our code, how would we write the consonants in these words?
   mover ______________ *quiver* ______________
9. What do we mean when we say "The *v* is a very dependable letter"?

See the Answers to the Reviews section for answers to Review 3, page 230.

b, h, k, l, p

b	*b*	*boat*
h	*h*	*hat*
k	*k*	*kite*
l	*l*	*lion*
p	*p*	*pig*

1. The five consonants *b, h, k, l,* and *p* are very dependable except for the fact that on occasion, they represent no phonemes. When you see one of these letters in an unknown word, you expect it to represent the sound you hear in its key word. Complete the table at the right with the letter (1), key symbol (2), and key word (3) for each.

1	2	3
______	______	______
______	______	______
______	______	______
______	______	______
______	______	______

Select the key words from the following:

lion *cat* *hat* *pig* *queen* *boat* *kite*

boat consonant	**2.** You will associate *b* with the sound heard at the beginning of the key word ______________. Can you say that sound aloud? It is very difficult. Many consonant phonemes cannot be pronounced easily without adding a bit of the vowel sound. Some teachers, trying to pronounce the initial phoneme in *boat,* say "buh." This will not help the child to identify the word *boat: buh-oat* is not *boat!* Some experts advise teachers to say "the first sound we hear in *boat*" or "the last sound we hear in *tub*" rather than to attempt to sound the phoneme in isolation. Keep in mind that it is very difficult to sound some ______________ phonemes in isolation. (consonant, vowel)
vowel	**3.** Try pronouncing /*m*/, /*v*/, /*l*/, and /*r*/. Listen to the sounds you give them in *hum, dove, call,* and *car.* Say them aloud again. These are fairly easy to sound in isolation. Now say /*b*/, /*k*/, and /*p*/ aloud. Listen to them in the words *tub, back,* and *help.* Do not hang on to the sound (as you can in *hummmmmmm*); just softly expel your breath. Try to sound them with as little of the ______________ phoneme as possible.
silent silent	**4.** Sometimes these consonant letters have no phonemes. It is common practice to call them "______________ letters." Certain patterns help determine whether these letters represent a phoneme or are ______________ in an unknown word.
one *muff̸in, mufin, lett̸er, leter, purr̸, pur, ribb̸on, ribon, happ̸en, hapen, less̸, les*	**5.** One pattern is very common to almost all consonants: **Two like consonants appearing together in a word generally represent one phoneme.** Say these words aloud. How many phonemes do the two like consonants represent? ______________ Make a slash through the second like consonant to depict the silent letter. Then rewrite the words omitting the silent consonant. *muffin* ____________ *letter* ____________ *purr* ____________ *ribbon* ____________ *happen* ____________ *less* ____________
clim, lam *bom, number* *b, m*	**6.** Pronounce the words below. Rewrite these words, omitting the silent letters. (Do not be concerned with the vowel sounds at this point. We will indicate the vowel sounds later.) *climb* ____________ *lamb* ____________ *bomb* ____________ *number* ____________ The ______________ is silent when it follows an ______________ in the *same* syllable.

syllable, *m*	**7.** In frame 6 the *b* is not silent in *number,* because it is not in the same ____________ as the ____________.
is is not syllables	**8.** Pronounce the words *bomb* and *bombard.* The *b* when followed by the *m* in *bomb* ____________ silent. (is, is not) The *b* in *bombard* ____________ silent. (is, is not) The second *b* and the *m* in *bombard* are in different ____________.
dout, det *obtain, sutle* *t* *subtle* *t*	**9.** Pronounce the words below. Rewrite the words, omitting the silent consonants. *doubt* ____________ *debt* ____________ *obtain* ____________ *subtle* ____________ The *b* is silent when it is followed by a ____________ in the same syllable. Which word does not belong in the set? ____________ Notice that *b* is silent even though the *b* and the ____________ are in different syllables.
b	**10.** Let us summarize: **When *b* follows *m* or precedes *t* in the same syllable, the ____________ is usually silent.**
/h/ hat final	**11.** *H,* as a single letter (phoneme / /, key word ____________), has a distinctive characteristic: It is never heard as the ____________ sound in a word or syllable. (initial, final)
oh̸, hurrah̸, shah̸ no	**12.** *H* is silent when it follows the vowel in a word or syllable. Put a slash through the silent *h* in each of the following words: *oh* *hurrah* *shah* Check carefully. Do you hear the /*h*/ at the end of each word? ____________
heir, hour, honest	**13.** The *h* may even be silent when it appears as the initial consonant of a word. There are no clues to tell us whether the initial *h* represents a phoneme. In fact, some people consider the *h* to be silent in *homage, humble,* and *herb.* Circle the words below in which the initial *h* is silent. *here* *heir* *hour* *happy* *honest*
g, k, r	**14.** Study the words below. *ghost* *khaki* *rhyme* *ghastly* *khan* *rhino* The letter *h* is silent when it follows the consonants _____, _____, and _____.

gost, kaki, ryme, gastly, *kan, rino*	**15.** Rewrite the words in the preceding frame, omitting the silent consonants: __________, __________, __________, __________, __________, __________.
khaki, ghost, rhino ***hurrah*** ***hour***	**16.** Review by filling in these blanks. Use the words below to assist you. *hurrah* *khaki* *hour* *ghost* *rhino* **The letter *h* is silent when it follows the consonants *k* (as in __________), *g* (as in __________), or *r* (as in __________). *H* is silent when it follows a vowel (as in __________). Sometimes *h* is silent at the beginning of a word (as in __________).**
6 (or 5. You would not be incorrect if you omitted *wh* /hw/.) *laugh, wish, phone change, white, thorn*	**17.** Aside from the fact that *h* is often silent, as a single letter grapheme, it is reliable. However, we cannot say that whenever we see an *h* in a word, we know it will either be silent or represent the initial sound heard in *hat. H* is a component of several digraphs (a two-letter combination that represents a single speech sound). Study the words below. How many digraphs contain the letter *h* but not /*h*/? __________ Underline them. *laugh* *wish* *phone* *change* *white* *thorn*
phoneme *kite*	**18.** Except when silent, the *k* is a very dependable letter. Let us be sure we understand: There are other graphemes that represent the sound we associate with the key symbol *k* (*queen, choir, coat*), but when we see the letter *k* in a word, we can be quite sure that when we hear the word, we will hear the same __________ as that heard at the beginning of its key word, __________.
nob, nown *nit, nee* ***n***	**19.** Study the words below to discover the "silent *k*" pattern. *knob* ________ *known* ________ *knit* ________ *knee* ________ **The *k* is silent at the beginning of a word or syllable when followed by ________.** Rewrite these words, omitting the silent *k* in each. Pronounce aloud the words you have written.
nife, buble, hero *clim, onor, nee*	**20.** Rewrite the following words, omitting the silent consonants. *knife* ________ *bubble* ________ *hero* ________ *climb* ________ *honor* ________ *knee* ________

lion /l/	**21.** The consonant *l* is another very reliable letter. To help distinguish its phoneme, we have chosen the key word _____________. We can represent its phoneme thus: / /.
    baloon, dolar *jely, bel*	**22.** However, the *l* may be silent. Study the words below to see if this generalization applies. **Two like consonants appearing together in a word generally represent one phoneme.** Rewrite these words, omitting the silent consonants. *balloon* ___________ *dollar* ___________ *jelly* ___________ *bell* ___________
    cam (kam), pam, yok *chak, woud, shoud*	**23.** To discover another pattern, study the words below. **The letter *l* is sometimes silent when followed in the same syllable by *m, k,* or *d.*** Rewrite these words, omitting the silent consonants. *calm* ___________ *palm* ___________ *yolk* ___________ *chalk* ___________ *would* ___________ *should* ___________ (Do you hear the /l/ when you say *calm* and *palm?* If so, this is a regional difference in pronunciation and a natural variation in the way we pronounce words.)
no *gold, tak, film* *milk, caf, wak*	**24.** Is this a completely dependable pattern? _____________ Rewrite the words below, omitting the silent consonants. *gold* ___________ *talk* ___________ *film* ___________ *milk* ___________ *calf* ___________ *walk* ___________ (Pronouncing the /l/ in *gold, film,* and *milk* is not a consequence of regional differences. These are true exceptions to the pattern.)
  p *help*	**25.** Next we turn our attention to the consonant *p.* In this study, we are establishing a key symbol for each phoneme in our language. The logical key symbol to use to identify the first phoneme heard in *pig* is _____________. It is the last phoneme heard in _____________. (*help, graph*)
  p	**26.** We establish a key symbol and a key word to help distinguish this phoneme from any other. *Pig* is the key word we have selected to identify the sound represented by _____________.
  p	**27.** Next we examine its dependability. *P,* as a single consonant, is very reliable. When we see *p,* we can expect to hear the sound we are associating with the key symbol _____________.

Study Guide

Consonants b, h, k, l, m, p, q, r, v

Consonant	Key Symbol	Key Word
b	*b*	*boat*
h	*h*	*hat*
k	*k*	*kite*
l	*l*	*lion*
m	*m*	*moon*
p	*p*	*pig*
q	no key symbol	no key word
r	*r*	*ring*
v	*v*	*van*

Bb is usually silent when it follows *m* or precedes *t* in the same syllable (*climb, doubt*).

Hh is silent when it follows the consonants *g* (*ghost*), *k* (*khaki*), or *r* (*rhino*). H is also silent when it follows a vowel in a word or syllable (*hurrah*). Sometimes *h* is silent at the beginning of a word (*hour*).

Kk is silent at the beginning of a word or syllable when followed by *n* (*knee*).

Ll is sometimes silent when followed, in the same syllable, by *m* (*calm*), *k* (*chalk*), or *d* (*should*). If you hear an /l/ in *calm,* this is a regional difference in pronunciation.

Mm is a very dependable letter. When we see *m* in a word, we can be sure that it represents the phoneme we associate with the key word *moon.*

Pp is usually silent when followed by *s* (*psychology*), *t* (*pterodactyl*), or *n* (*pneumonia*) at the beginning of a word.

Qq has no key symbol. The *q* may represent the /*k*/ (*antique*). *Q* is almost always followed by the letter *u.* The *u* may be silent or represent the sound of the *w.* When the *u* represents the sound of *w,* the *qu* stands for *kw* (kween).

Rr is a dependable letter. When we see *r* in a word, we can be sure that it represents the sound we associate with the key word *ring.*

Vv is a dependable letter. When we see *v* in a word, we can be sure that it represents the sound we associate with the key word *van.*

Silent Consonants

Two like consonants appearing together in a word generally represent one phoneme (*bubble, puddle, waffle, jelly, summer, dinner, puppet, carrot, buzz*).

no *f*	**28.** Do we expect to hear the sound we associate with the key symbol *p* in *phone?* ______________. The two-letter grapheme *ph* represents the sound we associate with the key symbol ______________.
silent *aple, hapy* *pupet, pupy*	**29.** Sometimes, however, the *p* has no phoneme; it is ______________. Rewrite the following words, omitting the consonant letters that represent no phonemes. *apple* ____________ *happy* ____________ *puppet* ____________ *puppy* ____________
no *p*	**30.** Is *p* sounded in the following words? ______________ *pseudo* *psychology* *psalm* *pterodactyl* *pneumonic* *pneumonia* We can generalize: **When *p* is followed by *s, t,* or *n* at the beginning of a word, the ______________ is usually silent.**
silent	**31.** **The consonants *b, h, k, l,* and *p* as single letters are very reliable.** However, they are not always sounded; each has "__________ letter" patterns.

Review 4

1. Phonics is used to decode unknown words. The pronunciation of each of these nonsense words is unknown to you. Using the generalizations you have studied, decide which key symbol should represent each of the underlined consonants. Rewrite the "words," omitting the silent consonants.

   a. *knoh* **b.** *psaph* **c.** *mell* **d.** *plarrah* **e.** *ghaeve* **f.** *lalm* **g.** *psimb*
   h. *ptovom* **i.** *rolk* **j.** *rhimb* **k.** *quimmel* **l.** *kloppem* **m.** *voubt*

2. *Ph* and *ch* are examples of ______________: Each represents ____________ phoneme(s). (How many?)
3. Why is it difficult to pronounce /*b*/, /*k*/, and /*p*/ aloud?
4. Why did we omit *q* in our list of key symbols?

See the Answers to the Reviews section for the answers to Review 4, page 230.

d, f, j, n, z

Answers	Frame
d d *dog* f f *fish* j j *jeep* n n *nut* z z *zipper*	**1.** Each of the five consonants *d, f, j, n,* and *z* has minor irregularities. Complete the table at the right with the letter (1), key symbol (2), and key word (3) for each of these consonants. Select the key words from the following: 1 ______ 2 ______ 3 ______ (five rows) *jeep* *nut* *fish* *gerbil* *dog* *zipper* *moon*
f f, f, f f, v, f	**2.** Say the word *fish.* Now start to say the word again but hold the first sound. This is the sound we represent by the key symbol ________. The *f* is, in general, a reliable letter. Write the key symbol for the sound represented by *f* in each of the words below. Listen carefully! *fiesta* ________ *fan* ________ *effect* ________ *off* ________ *of* ________ *if* ________
v	**3.** The *f* represents the sound we associate with the key symbol ________ in the word *of.* (Try to pronounce *of* using /f/.)
silent off	**4.** One *f* in the word *effect* is not sounded. It is clear then that *f* can be a ________ letter. Another example of an unsounded *f* in the list in frame 2 is in the word ________.
f /v/ gh ph	**5.** We have noted that *f* is, in general, a reliable letter: When we see *f* in a word, we expect, when the word is spoken, to hear the sound represented by the key symbol ________. Exception: in *of,* the *f* is pronounced / /. However, there are other letters that are used to stand for the sound represented by the key symbol *f.* We will digress to study them here. What letters represent the /f/ in the word *enough?* ________ In the word *phonics?* ________
fone, nit, dou *enouf, gost, lam* *graf, taut, hi*	**6.** The *gh* digraph can be silent. Rewrite the words below using key symbols for all consonants and omitting silent letters. Copy the vowels as they are, pronouncing them as they would sound in the original word. *phone* ________ *knight* ________ *dough* ________ *enough* ________ *ghost* ________ *lamb* ________ *graph* ________ *taught* ________ *high* ________

b r t, s t, t *t*	**7.** Study the words below. *bright* ___________ *sight* ___________ *ought* ___________ The *gh* digraph is usually silent when followed by ___________. What consonants are sounded in these words?
gh */f/* beginning, *h*	**8.** Study these words: *ghost, high, rough.* The digraph ___________ is silent or represents / / when it appears after the vowel in a syllable. When it appears at the ___________ of the syllable, the ___________ in the two-letter combination is silent.
ph	**9.** Study these words: *phone, graph, phrase.* The digraph ___________ can be found at the beginning or end of a syllable (that is, both before and after the vowel).
foto, fork, foneme *alfabet, foot* *f*	**10.** Rewrite the words below to indicate their pronunciations. Use the key symbols for the consonants. Copy the vowels as they appear. *photo* ___________ *fork* ___________ *phoneme* ___________ *alphabet* ___________ *foot* ___________ **The digraph *ph* represents the sound we associate with the key symbol ___________.**
first, laugh, phone *after, cough, nephew* *lift, enough, graph* *f, f, f* **silent**	**11.** We have identified three graphemes that represent /f/. Pronounce each of the words below. Underline the grapheme in each word that represents /f/, and write the key symbol on the line below. *first* *laugh* *phone* *after* *cough* *nephew* *lift* *enough* *graph* _______ _______ _______ **The *gh* may represent /f/ or it may be ___________ (*high, through*).**
j *jeep*	**12.** Say *jeep* out loud. Now pronounce the first phoneme in that word. We will represent the initial sound heard in *jeep* with the key symbol ___________. *J* is a very reliable letter. When we see a *j* in a word, we will use the same sound as that in its key word ________.
y	**13.** There is one exception! Pronounce *Hallelujah.* You see a *j,* but you do not say /j/. Can you determine what key symbol you would use to represent the *j?* ___________

---

14. It might be well at this time to look at a combination of letters that represents /j/, the *dg.* Rewrite these words to indicate their pronunciations. Omit each silent *e* and copy the other vowels as they are.

juj, nowlej, ej — *judge* __________ *knowledge* __________ *edge* __________

Perhaps you hear the /d/, but try pronouncing the words as though /dg/ = /j/. It comes out the same, does it not?

---

15. Study the one-syllable words below. Does the *dg* digraph occur at the

no — beginning of English words? __________

fudge *budget*
dodge *pidgin*
judge *gadget*

The *dg* is a very reliable digraph. What key symbol do we

j — **use to represent the phoneme?** __________

---

16. We shall represent the initial phoneme heard in *dog* with the key symbol

d — __________. Say *dog* aloud. Listen carefully as you say the initial phoneme in *dog.*

---

17. The *d* is fairly dependable. It, however, may be silent, as in *ladder* and *sudden.* Rewrite these words, omitting silent consonants.

lader, suden — *ladder* __________ *sudden* __________

---

18. But let us examine more closely the sounds the *d* represents. The key symbol represents the sounds heard in *doll, did, day, led.* Now read these words out loud to discover another sound that the *d* represents: *jumped, clipped, hoped, missed.*

t — Here *d* represents the sound we associate with the key symbol __________.

---

19. Study each word below.

missed *mist*
hopt — *hoped* __________
jumpt — *jumped* __________
slipt — *slipped* __________

Missed, for example, has four phonemes. Rewrite each word showing the pronunciation of the consonants by using key symbols.

one — In spite of their appearance, these are all __________ -syllable words.
(one, two)

t one *d*	**20.** We have noted that the *d* sometimes is pronounced as though it were ______________ (as in *kissed*). Now examine the words below. *played* *smiled* *called* They are also ______________-syllable words. The final consonant represents the sound we associate with the key symbol ____________.
two, -*ed* *d* *t, d*	**21.** Notice the sound the *d* represents when the suffix -*ed* forms a separate syllable. Say each of these words below out loud. *seated* *wanted* *waited* *needed* *sanded* *folded* These are __________-syllable words. In each, the suffix __________ forms a separate syllable. The final *d* represents the sound assigned to the key symbol __________. Look at the the letters preceding the suffixes (*seated*). They are either __________ or __________.
syllable ***d*** *d*	**22.** **In general, the suffix -*ed* forms a separate ________ when it is preceded by *t* or _______.** When the -*ed* forms a separate syllable, the final *d* represents the sound we associate with the key symbol ______________.
d ***t***	**23.** To summarize: **When the suffix -*ed* forms a separate syllable, the *d* represents the sound associated with the key symbol _______. When the suffix does not form a separate syllable, the *d* may represent the sound associated with the key symbol *d* or with the key symbol ______________.**
/*j*/ *soljer, fuj*	**24.** We have noted that *dg* forms a special combination representing / /. Occasionally, a *d* or *di* represents the /*j*/. Perhaps you hear /*j*/ when you pronounce *graduation.* Rewrite these words using key symbols to represent the consonant sounds and omitting any silent consonant letters. Copy the vowels as they are. *soldier* ______________ *fudge* ______________
sudden *jumped, soldier* *fudge*	**25.** We have seen that *d* can be silent, as in ______________. *D* can represent (*sudden, debt*) /t/, as in ______________, and /*j*/, as in ______________, and /*j*/ as a part (*jumped, pulled*) (*gem, soldier*) of the combination *dg* as in ______________. (*fudge, handgrip*)

nut colum, maner	**26.** The /*n*/, identified by the first phoneme in the key word ____________, can be silent, as in *running,* and when preceded by *m,* as in *hymn.* Rewrite these words, omitting the silent letters. *column* ____________ *manner* ____________
1 yes, 2 no	**27.** *N* is very reliable with one common but confusing exception. First, let us note that *n* is a part of the digraph *ng* as heard in *sing.* The *n* and the *g* represent ____________ phoneme(s) in *sing.* Is *ng* a digraph in *bring?* (How many?) ____________ The *n* and *g* represent ____________ phoneme(s) in *ungrateful.* Is the *ng* a digraph in *ungrateful?* ____________ (How many?)
yes think	**28.** Say *thing.* Is the *ng* a digraph? ____________ Add the phoneme represented by *k* to *thing* (*thing* + *k*). We do not spell this word *thingk:* We spell it ____________. The letter *n* represents /*ng*/ in *think!*
thang + k	**29.** There are many words in which you hear /*ng*/ but see only *n.* These words follow a pattern: Generally the letter following the *n* is either *k* or *g.* Pronounce *thank.* Which of these "keys to pronunciation" is correct? ____________ *than* + *k* *thang* + *k*
fing ger	**30.** Pronounce the "words" below. This is hard! *fin ger* *fing ger* *fing er* Which set of key symbols (consonant sounds only) indicates the correct pronunciation of *finger?* ____________
ng g	**31.** In *finger,* the *n* represents the sound we associate with the key symbol ____________. The *g* represents the sound we associate with the key symbol ____________. To show pronunciation, we need both the *ng* and the *g.*
kang ga roo sing gle	**32.** Which set of symbols below indicates the pronunciation of *kangaroo?* Of *single?* *kan ga roo* *kang ga roo* ____________ *sin gle* *sing le* *sing gle* ____________
ran bank (bangk)	**33.** It is clear that the grapheme *n* sometimes represents the phoneme associated with the key symbol *n,* as in ____________ (*ran, rang*), and sometimes with the digraph *ng,* as in ____________ (*bank, band*).

BOX 2.2

Why Z Comes Last

The letter *Z* has not always been the last letter of the alphabet. Thousands of years ago, *Z* was the seventh letter in the Phoenician (tenth-century B.C.) and the Greek (eighth-century B.C.) alphabets. When the Greeks passed their alphabet to the ancient Romans, the letter *Z* became part of the Latin alphabet as well. Although the *Z* represented a speech sound in the Greek language, it served no real purpose in Latin because the Latin language did not use the sound represented by the letter. The *Z* may have stayed in the Latin alphabet had it not been for the fact that the letter *C* represented two Latin phonemes, the /k/ in *kite* and the voiced /g/ in *goat.* The Romans wanted to give the voiced /g/ its own letter, so they introduced a new letter, the letter *G*. The letters *G* and *C* are visually quite similar, which is not surprising since the Romans created the letter *G* by modifying the letter C. To keep the order of the letters in the Latin alphabet intact, the Romans decided to delete the useless letter *Z*, and to replace it with the newly created letter *G*. The letter *G* then became the seventh letter in the Latin alphabet, as it is in our own English alphabet. When later contact with the Greeks made it necessary for the Romans to translate Greek words into Latin, the Romans found that they needed to add the letter *Z* to the Latin alphabet. Putting the letter *Z* into its old slot as the seventh letter would have changed the letter sequence, something the Romans did not want to do. The Romans solved their problem by adding the letter *Z* to the end of the alphabet, where it remains today in our own English alphabet.

Ouaknin, M. C. (1999). *Mysteries of the alphabet: The origins of writing* (J. Bacon, Trans.). New York: Abbeville Press.

engage	**34.** We have also noted that when we see *n* and *g* together in a word, the *ng* may represent the two separate phonemes that we associate with the separate symbols *n* and *g,* as in ______________. *(engage, clang)*
solemn *banker*	**35.** We have seen that the letter *n* may be silent, as in ______________. *(solemn, rang)* The single letter *n* may also represent the */ng/*, as in ______________. *(ingredient, banker)*
zipper *buzz*	**36.** The key symbol *z* represents the phoneme heard at the beginning of its key word ______________. In general, it is fairly reliable. It may be silent as, for example, one *z* is silent in ______________. *(zigzag, buzz)*
s, azure *size*	**37.** The *z* occasionally stands for the sound represented by the key symbol __________, as in *quartz,* and the *zh,* as in ______________. *(size, azure)* Pronounce *size* and *azure* aloud. Which has the phoneme you hear in *zoo?* ____________

Study Guide

Consonants d, f, j, n, z
Digraphs dg, gh, ph
Suffix -ed

Consonant	Key Symbol	Key Word
d	*d*	*dog*
f	*f*	*fish*
j	*j*	*jeep*
n	*n*	*nut*
z	*z*	*zipper*
Consonant	**Key Symbol**	**Key Word**
dg	*j*	*jeep*
gh	*f, g,* or silent	*fish, goat* (or no key word when silent)
ph	*f*	*fish*
Suffix	**Key Symbol**	**Key Word**
-ed	*d*	*dog* (*folded*)
-ed	*t*	*table* (*hoped*)

Dd may be silent (*ladder*), or may represent /*t*/ (*jumped*) when part of the *-ed* suffix.

Ff is, in general, a reliable letter, with a notable exception in the word *of,* in which the letter *f* represents /*v*/.

Jj is a very reliable letter (*jelly*).

Nn may be silent when preceded by *m* (*autumn*). The single *n* may represent /*ng*/ (*thank*).

Zz represents the /*z*/ in the key word *zipper* and occasionally stands for /*s*/ (*waltz*) and the /zh/ in *azure.*

dg The *dg* digraph represents /*j*/ (*fudge, budget*).

gh The *gh* digraph is usually silent when followed by *t* in a syllable (*night*). The *gh* is silent (*through*) or represents /*f*/ (*cough*) when it follows the vowel in a syllable. When *gh* occurs at the beginning of a word, the *h* is silent (*ghost*). There are only a handful of English words that begin with *gh.* They include: *ghost, ghetto, ghastly,* and *ghoul.*

ph The *ph* digraph represents /*f*/ and may occur at the beginning (*phone*) or end (*graph*) of a syllable (that is, before or after the vowel).

***-ed* Suffix** The *-ed* suffix forms a separate syllable when it is preceded by *t* or *d* (*salted, folded*). When the *-ed* forms a separate syllable, the final *d* represents /*d*/ (*folded*). When the suffix does not form a separate syllable, the *d* may represent the sound associated with /*d*/ (*played*), or with /*t*/ (*hoped*).

zero, prize	**38.** Check the words below in which the *z* stands for the phoneme heard at the beginning of the word *zipper.* *zero* *waltz* *prize* *azure*
of *missed* *bank* *waltz* *azure*	**39.** We have noted that the consonants *d, f, j, n,* and *z* have irregularities. In the next two frames, select the word at the right that illustrates the irregularity described. **The consonant may represent a phoneme other than that of its key symbol:** *f* = /v/ *fish, of* *d* = /t/ *missed, list* *n* = /ng/ *bank, bone* *z* = /s/ *zoo, waltz* *z* = /zh/ *his, azure*
phone *rough* *fudge*	**40.** **The key symbol may be represented by a different letter or digraph:** *ph* = /f/ *phone, puff* *gh* = /f/ *bough, rough* *dg* = /j/ *jug, fudge*

Review 5

1. Write the key symbols that represent the sounds of the consonant letters in each of these words:

a. *bough* **b.** *tough* **c.** *hedge* **d.** *of* **e.** *phone* **f.** *tight*
g. *ghastly* **h.** *soldier* **i.** *gender* **j.** *huffed* **k.** *planted*
l. *quilt* **m.** *zero* **n.** *sleigh* **o.** *column*

2. In which words do you hear the same phoneme as that represented by the underlined part of the first word?

a. *dog*	*clapped*	*don't*	*ride*	*soldier*	*moved*
b. *fish*	*fine*	*graph*	*of*	*photo*	*off*
c. *jeep*	*wedge*	*soldier*	*gold*	*hallelujah*	*Roger*
d. *nut*	*sling*	*hymn*	*knot*	*stranger*	*lank*
e. *zipper*	*his*	*puzzle*	*does*	*seizure*	*waltz*

See the Answers to the Reviews section for the answers to Review 5, page 231.

c, g, w, y

c g goat w w wagon y y yo-yo	**1.** Each of the four consonants *c, g, w,* and *y* is very irregular. However, each has a pattern of consistency within its inconsistencies. The *c* and *g* have some patterns in common as do the *w* and *y*. *C* has been omitted in the table at the right because it has no phoneme of its own. Complete the table for each of the other three with the key symbol (2) and key word (3). Select the words from the following: **1** / **2** / **3** g ______ ______ w ______ ______ y ______ ______ *yo-yo jeep wagon why goat kite van city*
goat no guess, glass, go, begin	**2.** *G* is the key symbol for the phoneme we hear at the beginning of its key word ______________. Check its reliability: Does it always represent the sound we associate with the *g* in *goat?* ______________ Pronounce these words using /*g*/ whenever you see a *g*. Then pronounce them correctly. Check those in which you hear /*g*/. *guess huge page ginger glass* *go enough gnat begin sing*
guess glass, go, begin huge page, ginger gnat enough, sing	**3.** It is clear that *g* is a very unreliable letter. In the list of words in frame 2, *g* represents its hard sound (/*g*/, as in *goat*) in the words ______________, ______________, ______________, and ______________. *G* represents the soft phoneme, /*j*/, in the words ______________, ______________, and ______________. *G* is silent when followed by *n*, as in ______________. *G* is part of a digraph, representing a different sound from either of its components in ______________ and ______________.
j j g	**4.** *G* is the key symbol for the hard sound we hear at the beginning of *goat.* We have noted that the letter *g* often represents the *soft* sound we associate with the key symbol __________. Are these used interchangeably, or is there a pattern to the words that might give a clue as to whether the *g* represents the soft sound we associate with the key symbol __________ or the hard sound we identify with the key symbol __________? Let us examine some known words to see.

1. *gate* 2. *gem* 3. *giant* 4. *gone* 5. *gum* 6. *gym*	**5.** Study the numbered sets of words below. Add a word from the list at the bottom of the frame to each set. Choose a word in which the *g* represents the same phoneme as the other underlined letters in the set and has the same vowel following the underlined *g*. **1** / **2** / **3** / **4** / **5** / **6** *gain* / *gentle* / *giraffe* / *go* / *gulp* / *gypsy* *against* / *age* / *engine* / *wagon* / *regular* / *energy* _____ / _____ / _____ / _____ / _____ / _____ *gone* *gem* *gum* *get* *gym* *gate* *giant*
e, i, y	**6.** **The letter *g* usually represents the sound we associate with the key symbol *j* (the soft sound) when it is followed by the vowel ______, ______, or ______.** Carefully study the sets of words above before you answer.
get *j* *get*	**7.** The word *usually* in the generalization indicates that this is not always true. The word __________ (*gem, get*) is an exception. When *g* is followed by the letter *e*, the *g* usually represents the sound we associate with the key symbol ______. The word __________ (*get, gentle*) does not follow this generalization.
a, o, u	**8.** Make a generalization about the phoneme that we associate with the key symbol *g:* **The letter *g* usually represents the sound we associate with the key symbol *g* when it is followed by the vowels ______, ______, or ______.**

e, i, y hard (or the one associated with *g*)	**9.** What happens when other letters follow *g?* Study the words below. *great* *ghost* *pilgrim* *gleam* *egg* The generalization will read: **The *g* usually represents the soft sound when followed by _____, _____, or _____. When followed by any other letter or when it appears at the end of a word, the *g* represents the _____ sound.** Memorize these sets: /*j*/—*e i y* /*g*/—*a o u* You may wish to compose a phrase to help you remember, such as "*an ornery ugly goat.*"
e, i, y g	**10.** Do not forget that there are exceptions. The generalization above, however, is a useful one. When you see a word you do not recognize, a word that contains a *g,* try the generalization. Try the phoneme represented by the key symbol *j* when the *g* is followed by _____, _____, or _____; otherwise, try the hard sound, represented by the key symbol _____.
j yes	**11.** Many words end in the letters *ge.* Pronounce the words below. *huge* *sponge* *cage* *orange* The key symbol that represents the final sound in each of these words is _____. Does the generalization apply to words that end in the letters *ge?* _____
guard, guilt, ej gastly, naw, paj guilt	**12.** Rewrite each of these words to show the pronunciation of the consonant letters. Omit each silent consonant and silent *e.* Copy the other vowels as they are. *guard* _____ *guild* _____ *edge* _____ *ghastly* _____ *gnaw* _____ *page* _____ (It is interesting to note that an unnecessary *u* has been added to many words that makes the *g* hard and so eliminates many exceptions, for example, _____ above.)
symbol, word	**13.** The letter *c* is also very irregular, but on top of that, it has no phoneme of its own and therefore no key _____ or key _____. (See Frame 1, page 31.)

BOX 2.3

Why Not K for Cat?

Alphabetically speaking, the letter C has a rather checkered past. The Greeks called the letter C, *gamma,* and used it to represent the voiced /g/ heard in *goat* (the hard *g*). The Etruscans, who inherited the alphabet from the Greeks, did not use the voiced /g/ in their spoken language. Rather than eliminate the letter C altogether, the Etruscans decided to use it to represent the /k/ heard in *kite.* In changing the sound represented by the gamma from a /g/ to a /k/, the Etruscan alphabet came to represent /k/ with four different letter sequences. In the Etruscan alphabet, the /k/ could be represented with *ka, ce* or *ci,* and *qu!* The Etruscan alphabet subsequently passed to the Latin alphabet, and eventually to our own English alphabet. Today we continue the practice that was passed down from the Etruscans, using the same three letters to represent the /k/ in English words: *k, c,* and *q* (as in *antique*).

Ouaknin, M. C. (1999). *Mysteries of the alphabet: The origins of writing* (J. Bacon, Trans.). New York: Abbeville Press.

c *k* *s*	**14.** Study these words: *cute, city.* Both start with the letter ________. The first phoneme in *cute* represents the sound we associate with the key symbol ________. The first phoneme in *city* represents the sound we associate with the key symbol ________.
k *s*	**15.** As a single-letter grapheme, the *c* not only represents no phoneme of its own but commonly serves to represent two other phonemes, the ___________ and the ___________. There are some clues to guide us to the sounds the *c* represents in words we do not know.
1. *cat* 2. *cent* 3. *city* 4. *coat* 5. *cup* 6. *bicycle*	**16.** Study the numbered sets of words below. For each set, choose a word from the words at the bottom of the frame in which the *c* represents the same phoneme as the other underlined letters in the set and has the same vowel following it.

1	2	3	4	5	6
cane	*center*	*cider*	*cook*	*current*	*cymbal*
became	*mice*	*decide*	*bacon*	*cut*	*encylopedia*
_______	_______	_______	_______	_______	_______

coat *bicycle* *city* *cup* *cent* *cat*

Answers	Frames
1, 4, 5 a, o, u	**17.** Which sets of words in frame 16 have a *c* that represents the hard sound, that of the /*k*/? ________ What vowels follow the *c* in each of these groups? ________
a, o, u	**18.** Complete the generalization: **The letter *c* usually represents the sound we associate with the *k* when it is followed by ____ , ____ , or ____.**
s, e, i, y	**19.** What about the soft sound? **The letter *c* usually represents the sound we associate with the ____ when it is followed by ____ , ____ , or ____.**
The letter *g* usually represents the soft sound (*j*) when it is followed by *e, i,* or *y.*	**20.** What is the generalization about the phoneme we associate with the soft sound of *g?*
yes a, o, u e, i, y a, o, u	**21.** Are there similarities between the generalizations concerning the sounds represented by *c* and *g?* ________ The combined generalization might read: **The consonants *c* and *g* represent their hard sounds when followed by ____ , ____ , and ____. They usually represent their soft sounds when followed by ____ , ____ , and ____.** If you remembered the phrase "*an ornery ugly goat,*" you might relate it to "*an ornery ugly kid.*" *C* generally represents the sound heard in *kid* when followed by ____ , ____ , or ____.
k *g*, hard hard	**22.** Study the words below. *regret* *glad* *crow* *magic* *climb* *big* What happens when other letters follow *c* and *g?* The *c* then represents the sound we associate with ________ and the *g* with the sound we associate with ________. These are the ________ sounds. What happens when *c* or *g* is the last letter in the word? In that position, they also represent their ________ sounds.
hard	**23.** Let us summarize the generalizations: **The *c* and *g* usually represent their soft sounds when followed by *e, i,* or *y.* When followed by any other letter or when they appear at the end of the word, the *c* and the *g* represent their ________ sounds.**

cello, girl, gift, give	**24.** Now apply the generalizations to the words below. Check the words that **do not** follow the generalization. *cube* *cello* *cotton* *cash* *receive* *giant* *girl* *guide* *gift* *give*
siense, skool, sene *skalp, skale, skold* *skreen, skum* silent	**25.** There are many words in which *s* is followed by *c*. Examine the words below. Rewrite each word, using key symbols for the consonants. *science* ________ *school* ________ *scene* ________ *scalp* ________ *scale* ________ *scold* ________ *screen* ________ *scum* ________ Note that *c* can be a ________ letter.
ch *k*	**26.** You have learned that *c*, as a single letter, is unnecessary. Examine these words: *chair, child, check.* We have no substitute for the *c* in the digraph ________. We cannot get along without the *c*. We could get along without the *q*, because ________ substitutes perfectly.
only one is sounded	**27.** Complete the generalization: **When two like consonants appear together in a word, usually** ________.
k *s*	**28.** Does this hold for the *c?* This generalization does not hold when the consonants represent different sounds. In the word *success,* the first *c* represents the sound we associate with the key symbol ________ , and the second *c* represents the sound we associate with the key symbol ________.
akses, stoping *skil, aksident* *aksept, aksent*	**29.** Examine the following words. Rewrite them, using key symbols for the consonants. Omit the silent letters. *access* ________ *stopping* ________ *skill* ________ *accident* ________ *accept* ________ *accent* ________
c *n, k* *blok, duk* *blak, bak*	**30.** In words containing *ck,* the ________ is usually silent. What consonants are sounded in *knock?* ________. Rewrite the words below to show pronunciation of the consonants. *block* ________ *duck* ________ *black* ________ *back* ________

Answers	Frames
sak, poket gimik, truk	**31.** The *c* may be part of the digraph *ck*. To discover a pattern for the placement of *ck* within a word, rewrite each word below, omitting the silent consonants. *sack* ____________ *pocket* ____________ *gimmick* ____________ *truck* ____________
end ck	**32.** The *ck* is always found at the ____________ (beginning, end) of a word or syllable. The vowels in the words above represent short sounds (such as in *apple* and *igloo*). When a word with a short vowel ends in /k/, the _____ often represents the /k/.
a, o, u, end letter (consonant) digraph, *ch* silent	**33.** *C* and *g* generally represent their hard sounds when followed by ________ , ________ , or ________ ; come at the ________ of a word; or are followed by another ____________. Both *c* and *g* are part of a ________ (*c* in ____________ , *g* in *gh*). Both *c* and *g* can be ____________, as in *back* and *gnome.*
y	**34.** Say *yo-yo* aloud. Listen to the first phoneme as you pronounce this key word again. The initial sound heard in *yo-yo* will be identified by the key symbol ____________.
yo-yo *yellow, young, canyon* consonant	**35.** The *y* is very unreliable. You cannot assume that when you see *y* in a word, it will represent the sound you hear in its key word ____________. Pronounce these words aloud, using /y/ for each *y* you see: *yellow* *sky* *rhyme* *young* *sadly* *play* *canyon* Check those in which the *y* represents the phoneme you hear in *yo-yo.* When *y* represents the phoneme heard in *yo-yo,* it is a ____________.
beginning	**36.** Now pronounce the above words correctly. Listen to the sound represented by the *y* in each word. You will notice that when the *y* is at the ____________ (beginning, end) of a word or a syllable, it has the /y/ phoneme.
vowel	**37.** You will notice also that each *y* within or at the end of a syllable has a ____________ (consonant, vowel) sound (see frame 35).
consonant, /y/	**38.** The *y* is unreliable, but there is a distinct pattern to help us select those that are consonants. When the *y* appears at the beginning of a syllable, it is a ____________ and has the sound we associate with ____________ (another vowel, /y/). (Exception: some words in chemistry with a foreign origin, as in *Ytterbia.*)

consonant *yo-yo*	**39.** As a consonant, *y* is very reliable. When we see a *y* at the beginning of a syllable, we can be sure it is a ______________ and represents the sound heard in its key word ______________.
w consonant	**40.** Say *wagon* aloud. Listen to the first phoneme as you pronounce this key word again. The initial sound heard will be identified by the key symbol ______________. The *w* is very unreliable. Like the *y,* it serves as a vowel as well as a ______________.
went, always	**41.** Use the words below for this and the following five frames (42–46) to illustrate the characteristics of the consonant *w.* *once* *quilt* *went* *write* *antique* *who* *snow* *dwell* *one* *queen* *always* *W,* as a consonant, always appears before the vowel in a syllable. (Note: *w* as a vowel always follows another vowel.) *W* is generally an initial consonant in a word or syllable, as in ________________ (select a one-syllable word) and in ________________ (select a two-syllable word).
dwell (*quilt* and *queen* are okay, too!)	**42.** The phoneme represented by *w* may, however, be part of a blend of two consonants, as in ______________.
quilt, queen	**43.** The *u,* when following *q,* often represents the consonant phoneme we associate with the key symbol *w.* We hear this when we say the words ______________ and ______________.
write	**44.** The *w* is silent before *r,* as in ______________.
who (*hoo*)	**45.** Occasionally the letter *w* fools us. It appears to be a part of the digraph *wh* but is actually silent, as in ______________. (This is a puzzle. Can you solve it?) Remember to refer to frame 41.
one *once*	**46.** We are familiar with the word *won.* But note the grapheme we use in the word that is pronounced the same but spelled ______________. We use the same grapheme to represent the *w* in ______________.
vowel before *way, wring*	**47.** The *w* may be a consonant or a ______________. As a consonant, it appears ______________ (before, after) the vowel in the syllable and represents the phoneme heard in __________ (*way, blow*). It is sometimes silent as in __________ (*wish, wring*).

unreliable /g/, /j/ /ng/ /j/, silent	**48.** We have been studying four ________________ consonants: *c, g, w, y.* (reliable, unreliable) We have found that *g* may have the sound of / /, as in *goat,* or / /, as in *genius.* It may be part of a digraph that has the sound of / /, as in *sing,* or the sound of / /, as in *fudge. G* may be ________, as in *gnome.*
It has no key symbol of its own.	**49.** What is the distinctive key symbol for *c?*
/k/, /s/ digraph /k/, silent	**50.** *C* may represent the sound of / /, as in *corn,* or of / /, as in *nice.* It may, with the letter *h,* form a __________, as in *much. C,* with the letter *k,* may represent the sound of / /, as bri<u>ck</u>. It is ________ in *scissors.*
e, i *y,* /k/, *a* *o, u,* consonant end of a word, /j/ *e, i, y* /g/, *a, o, u,* consonant end of a word	**51.** *C* usually has its soft sound when followed by ________, ________, or ________. It usually has its hard sound, / /, when followed by ________, ________, ________, or any other __________ or when it comes at the __________. *G* usually represents its soft sound / / when followed by ________, ________, or ________, and its hard sound / / when followed by ________, ________, ________, or any other __________ or when it comes at the __________.
    wrote, two, who digraph	**52.** **The consonants *w* and *y* are positioned before the vowel in a syllable. The consonant *y* is never silent. The consonant *w* may be silent.** In the list below, check the words that have a silent *w.* *quit* *wrote* *wing* *two* *who* *W* may be a part of a ____________, as in *white.*

Review 6

1. What generalization helps you to determine the sound of /g/ in an unknown word?
2. Write the key symbols for the consonants in each of these words:

   a. *giant* **b.** *bank* **c.** *girl* **d.** *big* **e.** *circus* **f.** *cook* **g.** *who*
   h. *match* **i.** *yellow* **j.** *way* **k.** *quick* **l.** *write* **m.** *yet* **n.** *knack*
3. Which of the above contains an exception to the hard/soft *g* generalization?
4. What generalization helps you to determine the sound of a *c* in an unknown word?

5. The suffix *-ed* may have the sound of / / as in *folded,* of / / as in *called, or* of / / as in *jumped.*
6. What generalization helps you to determine whether *w* represents /w/ and *y* represents /y/?
7. What key symbol indicates the pronunciation of the last phoneme in each of the following words?

   a. *beg* **b.** *church* **c.** *judge* **d.** *quack* **e.** *knowledge*
   f. *back* **g.** *ache* **h.** *unique* **i.** *critic* **j.** *rough*
8. The two-letter key symbols *ch* and *ng* are called ______________.
9. Rewrite the following words using key symbols to indicate the pronunciations of the underlined parts. Omit silent consonant letters. Underline the digraphs.

   range ____________ *wrinkle* ____________ *ransom* ____________
   manger ____________ *triangle* ____________ *links* ____________
10. As a single letter, *g* can represent the hard sound we associate with the key symbol *g,* **except** when followed by ______________, ______________, or ______________.
11. When *g* is part of a ______________, as in *enough,* it is not considered a single-letter consonant: The *g* in *enough* does not represent the sound we associate with the key symbol *g* as in ______________.
    (*go, ginger*)

    The *g* in *enough* does not represent the sound we associate with the key symbol ______________, as in *gem.*

    Nor is the *g* in *enough* a ______________ letter, as it is in *knight.*

See the Answers to the Reviews section for the answers to Review 6, page 231.

s, t, x

	1. The three consonants *s, t,* and *x* are unreliable. You cannot assume that when you see one of them in a word, you will hear the same phoneme as that in its key word. Complete the table, adding key symbols (2) and key words (3). Select key words from this set:
s *s* *sun* *t* *t* *table*	*city* *sun* *chin* *she* *table* *zipper* *ax* *thin*

1	2	3
s	______	______
t	______	______

boks	**2.** Why is there no *x* in the table above? The letter *x* has no key symbol because it has no distinctive sound of its own. It represents sounds we associate with other key symbols. Pronounce *box* aloud. Try to write *box* using other letters: _______________
egzact (or *egzakt*) *box* *gz* Either is correct.	**3.** Pronounce *exact.* Rewrite it using other key symbols: _______________ The letter *x* represents the sounds we associate with *ks* as in _______________ (*box, exam*) and ___________ as in *exact.* And we often interchange them! How do you pronounce *exit?* _______________ (*egzit, eksit*) We are more apt to use /*gz*/ when *x* appears between two vowel phonemes.
/*ks*/, /*gz*/	**4.** We have seen that *x* may represent the phonemes / / or / /. This may sound confusing, but it presents no problem to an English-speaking person, who will automatically use the acceptable phoneme.
z *eks*	**5.** Then consider the word *xylophone.* At the beginning of a word, *x* consistently represents the sound we associate with the key symbol _________. Of course, at times we use *x* as a letter, such as *X-ray.* In this instance, _______________ could be used as the grapheme to represent the *x.*
siks, zylofone, egzample *boks, zeroks, egzist*	**6.** **The *x* could be omitted from our alphabet by using the letters *gz, ks,* and *z.*** Spell the words below, substituting the proper graphemes for the letter *x* in each one. *six* _____________ *xylophone* _____________ *example* _____________ *box* _____________ *Xerox* _____________ *exist* _____________
k *gz, ks, z* *ch* *s, k*	**7.** The phonemes represented by *c, q,* and *x* need no key symbols. In our one-to-one correspondence, they are already represented. We could omit the letter *q* entirely by substituting the ______. We could omit the letter *x* by substituting ______ , ______ , or ______. We do use the *c* as part of the digraph _______________ , but as a single letter, the _______________ (*city*) and _______________ (*coat*) could adequately take its place.

s *sun,* yes no, no, no, no is not cannot	**8.** The phoneme represented by *s* (key symbol ________) is heard in its key word ________. Does it represent the sound heard in *list?* ________ *has?* ________ *she?* ________ *was?* ________ *surely?* ________ The letter *s* ________ (is, is not) very reliable. When you see the letter *s* in a word you ________ (can, cannot) be sure you will hear /s/ when it is pronounced.
s, s, z	**9.** Say each of the words below aloud. Listen very carefully to the underlined part. Which key symbol represents each part? Write it in the space following the word. *this* ________ *history* ________ *his* ________
see, ask *rose, his* *sure, sugar* *television, treasure*	**10.** The grapheme *s* is used to represent different phonemes. Study the words below. *see* *ask* *rose* *his* *sure* *sugar* *television* *treasure* The single consonant *s* represents the sound we usually associate with: (1) *s* in the words ________ and ________ (2) *z* in the words ________ and ________ (3) with *sh* in the words ________ and ________ (4) with *zh* in the words ________ and ________
z *z* *z, z, z, s, s*	**11.** Pronounce *his* and *has* aloud. The key symbol that represents the final sound in these words is ________. There are many words in which the grapheme *s* represents the / /. Write the key symbol for each of the plural endings of the words below. If you have trouble, try both the /*s*/ and the /*z*/. You must say them aloud. *toys* ____ *dogs* ____ *beds* ____ *cats* ____ *hops* ____
sizorz, zylofon, fuzy *us, uz, fuz* *miks*	**12.** Rewrite the words below using the key symbol that represents the sound of each consonant. Copy the vowels as they are but omit each silent *e.* *scissors* ________ *xylophone* ________ *fuzzy* ________ *use* ________ *use* ________ *fuse* ________ *mix* ________

    rugz, iz, doez peaz, some, pleazhure roze, so, shurely	**13. The consonant *s* is unreliable: It often represents the phonemes we associate with *z, sh,* and *zh,* as well as its key symbol *s.*** Rewrite each of the following words using *s, z, sh,* or *zh* to indicate the sound the *s* represents. Copy the vowels as they are, pronouncing them as they sound in the real words. *rugs* ________ *is* ________ *does* ________ *peas* ________ *some* ________ *pleasure* ________ *rose* ________ *so* ________ *surely* ________
   s, sun *miss*	**14.** When we see an *s* in an unknown word, we have few clues to tell us which phoneme it represents. We might note the following: (1) The letter *s* usually represents the sound we associate with the key symbol __________. It is the sound heard in __________. *(sun, sure)* (2) Except for certain foreign names (as *Saar*), the *s* at the beginning of a word stands for the sound heard in __________. *(miss, rose)* (3) Except when acting as a plural, the *s* at the end of a word represents /*s*/ or /*z*/ with about equal frequency. (4) We tend to use the phoneme represented by the *z,* the voiced counterpart of /*s*/, when the preceding phoneme is voiced. (English-speaking people use the correct ending automatically; thus we have not studied voice–voiceless phonemes in this edition.)
table *th*	**15.** The letter *t* as a single consonant (as heard in its key word __________) is fairly reliable. However, we must distinguish between *t* as a single letter and *t* as part of a digraph. Pronounce these words: *this, think, with.* We do not hear /*t*/ in the two-letter grapheme ________. We will study this grapheme later.
 /*t*/ *h*	**16.** But then pronounce these words: *Thomas, thyme.* (Exceptions! Exceptions!) The *th* in each of these words does represent the phoneme / /. Or we could say that the ________ is silent.
 no *shun*	**17.** One of the common "endings" in our language is found in these words: *motion, convention, station.* Pronounce them. Do you hear /*t*/? __________ This ending could be spelled __________. *(shun, ton)*

Answers	Frames
/ch/, /ch/, /t/ /ch/, /sh/	**18.** Examine the words below. Pronounce them, paying special attention to the underlined parts. What phoneme does each part represent? Work carefully. *righteous* / / *question* / / *mountain* / / *natural* / / *action* / /
beginning	**19.** It is clear there are many word "parts" (never at the ______________ (beginning, ending) of the word) in which the *t,* in combination with a vowel, represents a phoneme other than /*t*/.
silent	**20.** Pronounce these words: *bouquet, beret, debut.* There are several common words derived from the French language in which the *t* is ______________.
t *often, soften* *listen, fasten, moisten*	**21.** When *t* follows *f* or *s,* the ______________ is sometimes silent. These words are written without the silent consonants; write them correctly. *ofen* _________ *sofen* _________ *lisen* _________ *fasen* _________ *moisen* _________
match, watch, hatch	**22.** The *t* is also silent in the *tch* combination. Pronounce the words below saying the /*ch*/ as in *chair.* Spell them correctly. *mach* ___________ *wach* ___________ *hach* ___________
soften *s, listen* *ch, catch* *letter* *ballet* *future, lotion* *father*	**23.** **The *t* is fairly reliable. However, it may be silent and often loses the /*t*/ phoneme when combined with other letters.** The words below will aid you in filling in the blanks in the following paragraph. We have noted that *t,* as a single letter, is fairly reliable. *catch* *father* *soften* *letter* *listen* *future* *lotion* *ballet* It may be silent as when it follows *f* (as in ______________) or ______________ (as in ______________) and when it precedes ______________ (as in ______________). Only one *t* is sounded in such words as ______________. It may also be silent in words adopted from the French as in ______________. In connection with a vowel, the *t* may represent /*ch*/ as in ______________ or /*sh*/ as in ______________. It is often a part of a consonant digraph as in ______________, in which case the /*t*/ is not heard.

Study Guide

Consonants c, g, s, t, w, x, y

Consonant	Key Symbol	Key Word
c	no key symbol	no key word
g	*g*	*goat*
s	*s*	*sun*
t	*t*	*table*
w	*w*	*wagon*
x	no key symbol	no key word
y	*y*	*yo-yo*

Cc does not have a key symbol. *C* usually represents /s/ (the soft sound) when it is followed by *e* (*cent*), *i* (*city*), or *y* (*cycle*). *C* usually represents /k/ (the hard sound) when followed by *a* (*cat*), *o* (*coat*), or *u* (*cut*), when it appears at the end of a word (*comic*), and when followed by any other letter (*cloud*). *C* can be silent when it follows *s* (*scene*).

Gg may represent /j/ (the soft sound) when it is followed by the vowel *e* (*gerbil*), *i* (*giant*), or *y* (*gypsy*), although with exceptions. *G* usually represents /g/ (the hard sound) when it is followed by *a* (*gate*), *o* (*go*), or *u* (*gum*), when it appears at the end of a word (*leg*), and when followed by any other letter (*glass*).

Ss, except when acting as a plural at the end of words, represents /s/ (*miss*) or /z/ (*whose*) with about equal frequency. *S* also represents /zh/ (*television*) and occasionally stands for /sh/ (*sugar*).

Tt may be silent when it follows the letter *s* (*listen*) or *f* (*soften*) and when it precedes *ch* (*catch*). In connection with a vowel, *t* may represent /ch/ (*future*) or /sh/ (*station*). When part of a digraph (th), the *t* is not heard (*father*). *T* may also be silent in words adopted from the French language (*ballet*).

Ww serves as a consonant and a vowel. As a consonant, *w* precedes the vowel (*wagon*). As a vowel, *w* follows the vowel (*snow*). The *w* is silent before *r* (*write*). *W* may also be part of a blend (*dwell*) or a diagraph (*what*). Occasionally, the letter *w* fools us. It appears to be part of the digraph *wh* but is actually silent (*who*).

Xx does not have a key symbol. It may represent /ks/ (*six*), /gz/ (*exam*), or /z/ (*xylophone*). We are more apt to use /gz/ when *x* appears between two vowel phonemes (*exempt*).

Yy serves as a consonant and as a vowel. The *y* at the beginning of a syllable acts as a consonant and represents /y/ (*yellow*). *Y* within a syllable or at the end of a syllable acts as a vowel and may be silent (*play*), or may represent a vowel sound (*rhyme*).

	24. We have noted that several different graphemes may represent the initial sound heard in *sun* as well as the initial sound heard in *zipper.* To illustrate, write the key symbol that indicates the pronunciation of each of the consonants in the words below. (If you get these, you are really thinking!)
ng z t, z, t s	*anxiety* ______ *is* ______ *its* ______
s n t, z n z	*scent* ______ *zones* ______
s r k l, z l f n	*circle* ______ *xylophone* ______
	25. We have also noted that the grapheme *s* may represent sounds other than that heard in *sun* and that the grapheme *z* occasionally represents sounds other than that heard in *zipper.* Check the words below in which the *s* stands for a phoneme letter other than that heard at the beginning of *sun.*
sugar, pleasure, hose	*sugar* *this* *pleasure* *whisp* *hose*
ks	**26.** We called *x* an unnecessary letter because it can be replaced by ______
gz, z	in *ax,* by ______ in *example,* and by ______ in *xylophone.*

Review 7

1. There are three consonants that, as single letters, represent no distinctive phonemes:

   a. The *c* usually represents the sound we associate with s when followed by

   __________, __________, or __________.

   The *c* usually represents the sound we associate with __________

   when followed by the vowel __________, __________, or

   __________, most other consonants, or when appearing at the end of a word.

   b. The *q* represents the sound we associate with __________.

   c. The *x* can adequately be represented by the consonants __________,

   __________, and __________.

2. There are other letters that represent two or more sounds, one of which is the sound we commonly associate with that particular letter (key symbol).

   a. The *g* represents "its own sound," /*g*/, (the __________ sound),
   (hard, soft)

   when followed by the vowel __________, __________,

   __________, or by another consonant, or when it appears at the end of a word.

b. The *g* usually represents its ______________ sound, that which we
(hard, soft)

ordinarily associate with the letter ______________, when followed by

______________, ______________, or ______________.

3. The two most common sounds represented by the single letter *s* are:

a. The sound we ordinarily associate with the letter *s*, as in ______________.
(some, sugar)

b. The sound we ordinarily associate with the letter ______________, as in *his.*

4. The letter *d* may represent the sound we associate with ______________ or with ______________ when it appears in the suffix *-ed.*

5. *F* occasionally represents the sound we associate with ______________, as in *of.*

6. *T* in combination with a vowel may represent different sounds, as ___________ in *question* and ______________ in *patient.*

7. Generalizations:

a. Consonant letters may represent more than one sound.

The *s* represents the sound of ____________ (as the key symbol indicates), of __________ (*sure*), of __________ (*has*), and of __________ (*treasure*).

The z represents the sound of ______________ (as the key symbol indicates), of ______________ (*quartz*), and of ______________ (*azure*).

b. Consonant sounds may be represented by more than one letter. The sound we hear at the beginning of *say* is often represented by *s*, by ______________ (*cent*), or by ______________ (*chintz*).

The sound we hear at the beginning of the word *zipper* is sometimes represented by the letters ______________ and ______________.

c. Consonant letters may represent no sound. The three consonant letters that represent no sound in *knight* are ______________, ______________, and ______________. We call them ______________ letters. The letter ______________ is ______________ in *soften, ballet,* and *latch.*

8. Reread the generalizations in question 7. Be sure you determine the differences among them. These generalizations would carry more precise meanings if the words *phoneme* and *grapheme* were used. Then they would read:

a. Consonant ____________ may represent more than one ____________.

b. Consonant ______________ may be represented by more than one ______________.

c. Consonant letters may represent no ______________.

See the Answers to the Reviews section for the answers to Review 7, page 232.

Consonant Digraphs

Answers	Frame
 26 vowels, 21 Three 18	**1.** We have been relating each of the consonant phonemes to its respective consonant letter. There are ______________ letters in the alphabet. Five are ______________ , so there are ______________ consonant letters. ______________ of these have no distinctive phonemes of their own. This leaves ______________ single-letter consonant graphemes, each of which has been assigned a key symbol so as to build up a one-to-one correspondence between symbol and phoneme.
 seven	**2.** Eighteen symbols but 25 consonant sounds! Where do we find the ______________ remaining symbols? **We use two-letter combinations called *consonant digraphs* to stand for the seven phonemes not represented by single-letter graphemes.**
 no no	**3.** The *ch* is one of the two-letter digraphs we will study. Pronounce *chair.* Does the *ch* in *chair* represent the sound we usually associate with the *c* in *cat?* ______________ Does the *h* represent the sound we usually associate with the *h* in *hat?* ______________ The digraph represents unique phonemes. The phonemes do not represent the sound usually associated with either letter when it occurs alone.
ch *ch* *chair* *sh* *sh* *ship* *th* *th* *thumb* *th* *th̸* *that* *wh* *wh* *whale* *zh* *treasure* *ng* *ng* *king*	**4.** The key symbols that represent the seven missing phonemes are listed at the right. Fill in the missing items in the table: digraphs (1), key words (3). Select the key words from these: *ship, whale, king, thumb, chair, treasure.* Pronounce aloud the word and phoneme each represents. Notice that each is a distinctive consonant sound not represented by any single letter in our alphabet.

1	2	3
______	*ch*	______
______	*sh*	______
______	*th*	______
______	*th̸*	*that*
______	*wh*	______
	zh	______
______	*ng*	______

BOX 2.4

Too Many English Sounds, Too Few English Letters: The French Solution

History books tell us that the French-speaking Normans ruled England from 1066 to roughly 1500. French became the language of the government, and hordes of French-speaking scribes were moved to England to keep the official records. The Norman French scribes were relatively unfamiliar with the English language. When the scribes realized that there were not enough English letters to represent the sounds in English words, they turned to the French writing system for a solution, introducing the *ch, sh, wh,* and *th* digraphs to represent the */ch/, /sh/, /wh/,* voiced */t̸h̸/,* and unvoiced */th/.* Let us consider why the Norman French scribes chose these particular two-letter combinations.

In Old French, the letter *h* was occasionally used to signal when the preceding consonant had an atypical pronunciation. When the French-speaking scribes wanted to represent the English */ch/,* they used the *h* in English just as it had been used in Old French—to mark the unexpected pronunciation of the consonant letter. This is the reason the *ch* digraph is spelled with a *c+h.* Following the same line of reasoning, the scribes used the letter *h* to alert the reader to the unexpected pronunciation of *s* when the */sh/* phoneme occurs in English words. The *sh* digraph reliably represents */sh/,* except in French loan words, in which the Norman scribes used the *ch* digraph to represent */sh/* (*machine, chivalry, chef, sachet*).

In Old English spelling, the *wh* in *when* was written as *hw.* The French-speaking scribes reversed the letters, thereby introducing the *wh* digraph. Say *when.* Do you hear */hw/*? The Old English *hw* letter sequence is a more accurate description of English pronunciation. Modern dictionaries use the Old English letter sequence—*hw*—to record the pronunciation of the *wh* digraph in words such as *hwen, hwite,* and *hwisper.*

Old English used two letters, the *thorn* and the *edh,* to record the voiced *t̸h̸* (*this*) and the unvoiced *th* (*thumb*). These two Old English letters were used interchangeably, so the reader did not know whether to use the voiced or unvoiced pronunciation. The Norman French scribes preferred the *th* digraph and used it to represent both the voiced and unvoiced phonemes. Eventually, both the *thorn* and the *edh* disappeared from the English alphabet. In the Middle English period, after the Old English *thorn* had dropped from the alphabet, the letter *y* was occasionally used to represent */th/* in the initial position. How would you pronounce "Ye Olde Malt Shoppe" in modern English? (If you said "The Old Malt Shop," you are right! In the word *ye,* the letter *y* represents the */th/*!)

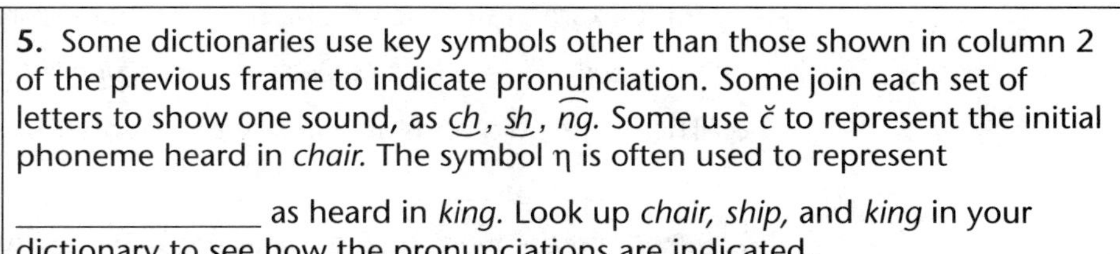

	5. Some dictionaries use key symbols other than those shown in column 2 of the previous frame to indicate pronunciation. Some join each set of letters to show one sound, as *c͜h*, *s͜h*, *n͡g.* Some use *č* to represent the initial phoneme heard in *chair.* The symbol η is often used to represent
ng	______________ as heard in *king.* Look up *chair, ship,* and *king* in your dictionary to see how the pronunciations are indicated.

f	**6.** There are other consonant digraphs as *ph* and *gh.* However, they are not listed in frame 3 because they are already represented. The key symbol ______________ indicates the sounds of the *ph* and the *gh.*

Review 8

Check yourself: Are you writing every answer and finishing each frame before moving the mask down? Are you getting almost every answer correct? Do you study more carefully when you miss one? Do you analyze your errors? Can you give yourself 100 on each review?

1. A grapheme composed of two letters that represent a single sound is called a _______________.

2. Indicate the pronunciation of the underlined part or parts of each of the following words by using key symbols:

quick   *who*   *measure*   *why*   *which*   *both*

this   *notion*   *sugar*   *wish*   *vision*   *strong*

3. In each of the following words, underline all the consonant digraphs that serve as key symbols and cannot be replaced by a single letter from our alphabet:

weather   *enough*   *whom*   *which*   *bring*

wrist   *wish*   *both*   *through*   *condemn*

4. There are 25 consonant sounds in the American-English language. We identify 18 of them with single ______________ symbols. We should have ______________ more consonant letters in the alphabet. Since we do not, we use two-letter combinations called ______________ to serve as key symbols for these phonemes. Write the seven two-letter symbols.

____

5. Our sound–symbol system is complicated by the use of other consonant digraphs standing for phonemes already represented in the system. Select three examples of such digraphs from these words:

tough   *chalk*   *sheath*   *short-sighted*   *luck*   *phoneme*

6. These three digraphs are already represented by (use key symbols)

__________, __________, __________.

7. Rewrite these words using the appropriate key symbols for the consonants. Copy the vowels as they are.

sunk   *photograph*   *know*   *alphabet*   *pheasant*   *cough*

See the Answers to the Reviews section for the answers to Review 8, page 232.

ch, sh, zh

ch no no	**1.** We have no single letter in the alphabet to represent the first phoneme we hear in the key word *chair.* We will use the logical two-letter combination, the ____________ , to identify this phoneme. Study the digraphs in these sets of words: **1**: *chair*, *chalk*, *churn* **2**: *character*, *chord*, *chaos* **3**: *chiffon*, *machine*, *chute* Each word contains the grapheme *ch.* Does each grapheme represent the phoneme we associate with the key symbol *ch?* ____________ Try pronouncing each one using the first phoneme in *chair* for each digraph. Is the digraph *ch* reliable? ____________
ch *k* If you guessed *sh,* you are right!	**2.** The digraph in each of the words in set 1 represents the phoneme we associate with the key symbol __________. The digraphs in set 2 represent the phoneme we associate with the key symbol ________. Can you guess what key symbol represents the digraphs in set 3? ____________
no *ch, k, sh*	**3.** Is the digraph *ch* reliable as to the phoneme it represents? __________ If we do not know the word, we cannot tell which key symbol to identify with it. It might be __________ , or __________ , or ________. (However, if you are an expert on language derivation, you will have clues.)
ship	**4.** The sound heard at the beginning of *ship* is very common, but there is no letter in the alphabet to represent it. We shall use the key symbol *sh* to represent the phoneme, as heard in the key word ____________. (*ship, clip*)
one no	**5.** When *s* and *h* appear together in this order in a syllable, we expect them to represent ____________ phoneme(s). Can you hear the separate (How many?) phonemes represented by *s* and *h* in *shut?* ____________ If you could, you would hear the word *hut* in *shut.*

/sh/	**6.** *Sh* is very reliable in that when we see *sh,* we can be sure we will hear / /. However, the phoneme we represent by *sh* has a variety of graphemes; that is, it is spelled in a variety of ways. Examine the words below. Look at the underlined parts. Rewrite the words, using *sh* to represent the underlined graphemes.
shure, shoe, moshon	*sure* ________ *shoe* ________ *motion* ________
shugar, mashine, speshal	*sugar* ________ *machine* ________ *special* ________
	7. The graphemes that we associate with the key symbol *sh* are:
s, sh, ti	________ in *sure* ________ in *shoe* ________ in *motion*
s, ch, ci	________ in *sugar* ________ in *machine* ________ in *special*
no	**8.** Now listen for the middle consonant sound as you say *treasure.* Is there a letter in the alphabet to represent this sound? ________
zh	**9.** We shall use the digraph *zh* as the key symbol to represent the phoneme heard in the key word *treasure,* although it is never represented in a word with the grapheme ________.
	10. Rewrite the words below to indicate, by using the key symbols, the sounds of the underlined letters.
pleazhure, vizhon	*pleasure* ______ *vision* ______ *sabotage* ______
sabotazhe, azhure, pich	*azure* ______ *pitch* ______
seizure	**11.** The *z* occasionally stands for the */zh/* as in ________. (*seizure, dozen*)
dozen	Pronounce *seizure* and *dozen* aloud. Which has the phoneme you hear in *zipper?* ________
leisure, regime	**12.** The *s* and *g* are two other graphemes that occasionally represent the */zh/* as in ________ (*leisure, base*) and ________ (*regime, age*). The *s* in the key word
treasure, do not	________ (*treasure, sun*) represents the */zh/* phoneme. We ________ (do, do not) have a grapheme to represent the */zh/* phoneme.
decision, seizure, beige	**13.** Check the words below in which the underlined graphemes represents the /zh/. If you identify all of the words in which the /zh/ phoneme occurs, you are really thinking!
collage, measure	*decision* *seizure* *beige* *collage* *person* *measure*
	14. What letter represents the sound we associate with *zh* in *measure?*
s, g	________ In *rouge?* ________

never	**15.** *Zh* ______________ appears in a word, so it is not appropriate to make (never, seldom) a statement regarding reliability.

Review 9

1. Use the key symbol to indicate the sound of each consonant in each of the following words. Underline the digraphs that represent distinctive phonemes.

   a. *shiver* **b.** *eggs* **c.** *sure* **d.** *share* **e.** *treasure* **f.** *character*

   g. *leisure* **h.** *thought* **i.** *schools* **j.** *ghosts* **k.** *charge* **l.** *chute*

   m. *quack* **n.** *lotion* **o.** *division* **p.** *Chicago* **q.** *string*

2. How does the *zh* differ from the other digraphs?

See the Answers to the Reviews section for the answers to Review 9, page 233.

th, t̶h̶, wh

no no	**1.** Listen to the first phoneme while you pronounce *that* aloud. Compare it with the first phoneme in *thumb.* Do you hear the /*t*/ in either phoneme? ______________ the /*h*/? ______________
voiced	**2.** The /*th*/ heard in *thumb* is a whispered sound, a voiceless sound. However, we use our vocal cords when we say the first phoneme in *that.* We call it a ______________ phoneme. (voiced, voiceless)
there *think* *these* *thick* *those* *thing* *this* *thank*	**3.** You have learned that the *th* digraph represents two phonemes. One phoneme is voiced (*that*); the other phoneme is voiceless (*thumb*). A **voiced phoneme** is produced when the vocal cords vibrate. A **voiceless phoneme** is produced when the vocal cords do not vibrate. Pronounce the words below. Write the words in which the *th* is voiced in Column 1 below. Write the words in which the *th* is voiceless in Column 2. *think* *there* *thick* *these* *those* *thing* *this* *thank* **Column 1: Voiced** **Column 2: Voiceless** ______________ ______________ ______________ ______________ ______________ ______________ ______________ ______________

thorn	**4.** You must say the words in frame 3 aloud or you will not hear the voiced quality. Note that the voiceless phoneme has a whispered sound even when you say it aloud. The *th* in _______________ has a whispered or voiceless sound. Our vocal cords (*this, thorn*) do not vibrate.
think, thought, thank, *through, length, both*	**5.** Many people do not realize that *th* is a grapheme that represents two sounds just as different as the sounds represented by *p* and *b* or *s* and *z*. They automatically use the correct sound for the words they have heard before. Check the words below in which the *th* represents the voiceless phoneme. You will not be able to tell the difference if you do not say them out loud! *think* *the* *though* *thought* *them* *they* *thank* *through* *length* *both*
together, think, throw	**6.** Repeat all the words in the previous frame in which the *th* represents the voiceless phoneme. Then say all the words in which the *th* represents the voiced phoneme. We shall use *th* as the key symbol to represent the voiced sound. We shall use *th* as the key symbol to represent the voiceless sound. Rewrite the following words; underline the digraphs that represent the voiceless phonemes and put a slash through the digraphs that represent the voiced phoneme. *together* ____________ *think* ____________ *throw* ____________
phoneme voiced, *their*	**7.** When we see an unknown word in our reading that contains the digraph *th,* we have no way of knowing which _______________ it represents. We can use the dictionary. Many dictionaries use the slash to indicate that the *th* represents the _______________ phoneme as in _______________. (*their, worth*)
the, bath /t/	**8.** The *th* is not a reliable digraph. It may represent the voiced sound heard in _____________, the voiceless sound heard in _____________, or, in rare (*the, third*) (*bath, bathe*) instances, the / / as in *Thomas.*
wh *what*	**9.** Another phoneme composed of two letters is _______________ as heard in *whale.* It is also heard in _______________. (*who, what*)

BOX 2.5

An Easy Way to Recognize Voiced and Voiceless Phonemes and Some Insight into Invented Spelling

You have learned that your vocal cords vibrate when pronouncing voiced phonemes and do not vibrate when pronouncing voiceless phonemes. However, sometimes it is difficult to determine from listening alone whether a particular phoneme is voiced or voiceless. To identify a voiced phoneme, you must find your voice. Here is a quick and easy way to do this:

1. Lightly place your hand over the lower part of your throat.

2. Pronounce each pair of words below:

   zap sap ban pan den ten gin kin van fan

3. Now pronounce each pair again, only this time draw out the phoneme that is represented by the underlined grapheme. When exaggerating the pronunciation of the phoneme, pay special attention to the vibration of your vocal cords. When you feel your vocal cords vibrate, you have found your voice, and you have also identified a voiced phoneme! Which phoneme in each word pair is voiced? Which is voiceless? (See answers below.)

4. To put this into a useful context for the teaching of reading, pronounce each pair once again, this time paying special attention to the way in which you form (articulate) each voiced and voiceless phoneme. Concentrate on your tongue, teeth, and lips. What do you notice about the way in which you articulate each voiced and voiceless phoneme pair? If you noticed that the phonemes in each pair represent the same articulation, and differ only in the presence or the absence of breath, you are very observant!

Understanding the voiced and voiceless phoneme pairs will help you to interpret children's misspellings. Sometimes, as children spell, they confuse phonemes that have the same articulation but differ in voicing. Suppose a child writes *bumkin* for *pumpkin.* This misspelling might be due to insufficient phonics knowledge or to misperceiving the letters *b* and *p.*

There is, however, another explanation: Perhaps the child, when thinking about the sounds of the English language, confused the */b/* and */p/* phonemes. After all, these phonemes are articulated in the same manner and only differ in their voiced and voiceless qualities. Understanding the voiced and voiceless phonemes helps you, the teacher, recognize the many ways in which children combine their knowledge of the phonemes of the English language with their knowledge of phonics in order to spell words when writing.

Answer to step 3: If you said that the voiced phonemes are */z/, /b/, /d/, /g/,* and */v/,* you are right!

w You are correct, whatever your response.	**10.** The phoneme *wh* may give you some trouble because it is rapidly disappearing from our language. If you pronounce *weather* and *whether* exactly the same, you are following the trend in the United States. Many people make the phoneme represented by the key symbol *wh* sound like that represented by the single letter ______________. What do you do? Pronounce *whistle, white.* Do they sound like *wistle, wite?* ______________
wh while	**11.** Most dictionaries note this trend but continue to indicate the pronunciations of words beginning with *wh* as *hw.* We will use the key symbol ______________ to represent the sound of the digraph, although it actually is better represented by *hw.* *Wh* represents the phoneme heard in ______________ (*whom, while*). (Pronounce *whom* and *while* carefully so that you will hear the distinction.)
beginning	**12.** The *wh,* like the consonant *w,* appears at the ______________ of the word or syllable and is followed by a vowel.

Review 10

1. We have identified each of the seven graphemes that serve as additions to our alphabet. Six of them are contained in the words below. Write the key symbol following the word in which each is found.

   swing __________ *white* __________ *measure* __________

   mother __________ *flash* __________ *porch* __________

2. One grapheme is missing from the group of digraphs above. It is found in

   ______________.
   (*breath, breathe*)

3. We have identified all 18 single-letter phonemes. They are heard in the initial position in each of the following words: *boat, dog, fish, goat, hat, jeep, kite, lion, moon, nut, pig, ring, sun, table, van, wagon, yo-yo, zipper.* Select key words from those above to illustrate phonemes represented by the underlined graphemes in the following words. Those that have no key word may be left blank.

   Examples: *work* *wagon* *psychology* ______________

   (1) *could* ______________ (9) *of* ______________

   (2) *yonder* ______________ (10) *get* ______________

   (3) *circle* ______________ (11) *honor* ______________

(4) *jumped* __________ (12) *tail* __________
(5) *gist* __________ (13) *my* __________
(6) *bomb* __________ (14) *wrong* __________
(7) *phone* __________ (15) *little* __________
(8) *ghetto* __________ (16) *rag* __________

4. The word *gem* __________ (is, is not) a key word because the *g* __________ (does, does not) represent the phoneme we associate with the key symbol *g*.

5. The word *try* is not a key word for the *y* phoneme because the *y* is not at the beginning of the syllable; it is, therefore, not a __________ (consonant, vowel) letter.

6. From the following words, select those that contain the /*t̸h̸*/ phoneme:

path	*thorn*	*write*	*wheel*
white	*theme*	*this*	*author*
father	*whip*	*mouth*	*cloth*
wrong	*feather*	*them*	*whistle*

7. Which of the words in question 6 contain the /*wh*/ phoneme?

8. What do the consonants *w* and *wh* have in common?

See the Answers to the Reviews section for the answers to Review 10, page 233.

ng

beginning follows	**1.** The phoneme /*ng*/ is different from the others represented by digraphs in that it is never heard at the __________ (beginning, ending) of a syllable, or, to put it another way, it always __________ (precedes, follows) the vowel.
bang, ranjer, stung *hinj, hunggry* yes no	**2.** Say the words below aloud. Rewrite the words to show pronunciation of the consonants. (Copy the vowels, omitting silent *e*). *bang* ______ *ranger* ______ *stung* ______ *hinge* ______ *hungry* ______ Does each contain the letters *ng?* ______ Does each contain the digraph *ng?* ______

Study Guide

Consonant Digraphs ch, sh, th, wh, ng

Digraph	Key Symbol	Key Word
ch	*ch*	*chair*
sh	*sh*	*ship*
th	*th*	*thumb*
th	*t̸h*	*that*
wh	*wh*	*whale*
	zh	*treasure*
ng	*ng*	*king*

The consonant digraphs are two-letter combinations that represent unique phonemes. The phonemes that the digraphs represent are different from the sounds associated with either of the two consonant letters when they occur alone in words.

ch The digraph *ch* is not reliable. *Ch* may represent the */ch/* (*chair*), the */k/* (*character*), or the */sh/* (*machine*).

sh The */sh/* is a common sound in the English language. The *sh* (*ship*) is very reliable.

Voiceless th The digraph *th* represents two distinct phonemes, one voiceless and one voiced. The */th/* in the key word *thumb* is a whispered sound, which we call the voiceless *th* (*thorn, thick*).

Voiced t̸h We use our vocal cords to pronounce the */th/* phoneme in the key word *that,* which we refer to as the voiced *t̸h* (*there, father*). Dictionaries may use a slash, a line, or italics to indicate the voiced digraph *t̸h* (*t̸h*, th̲, *th*). We will use the slash (*t̸h*) as the key symbol.

wh The digraph *wh* represents */hw/* (*why, white*). *Wh* occurs in the beginning of syllables, and is followed by a vowel.

zh While */zh/* occurs in English words (*measure, vision*), it is never represented in a word with the grapheme *zh.* The */zh/* may be represented by the *s* (*pleas̲ure, vis̲ion*), the *g* (*collag̲e*), or the *z* (*seiz̲ure*).

ng The digraph *ng* is never heard at the beginning of a syllable and always follows a vowel. The letters *ng* may represent */ng/* (*sing, among*). The letter *n* may also represent */ng/* when it is followed by the letter *g* (*finger—fing-ger*) or the letter *k* (*pink—pingk*). Your dictionary may use the symbol η to represent */ng/.*

/r g/ *sing, pingk, blangk, fingger* *jir jer, singk, trianggle*	**3.** Recall that *n* generally represents / / when followed by *g* or *k*. Rewrite the following words, indicating pronunciation of the consonants. Use *ng* (but underline it) to represent the digraph. Work carefully. This takes a keen ear. *sing* ________ *pink* ________ *blank* ________ *finger* ________ *ginger* ________ *sink* ________ *triangle* ________
fir ger, triangle	**4.** In which words from the preceding frame do you hear hard *g*, /*g*/, as well as /*ng*/?
 digraph *gingham* *orange*	**5.** The letters *n* and *g* together in a word are most commonly a ______________, that is, a two-letter combination representing a single phoneme, as in ______________. However, they may represent two separate (*gingham, ungrateful*) phonemes, as in ______________. (*orange, among*)
digraphs *chair* *sh* *zh* *th* *thct* *whale* *ng*	**6.** We have identified the seven ______________ that represent distinct phonemes not represented by the single letters in the alphabet. They are as follows: (1) *ch* as in ______________ (*chair, choir*) (2) ______________ as in *ship* (3) ______________ sounded like the *s* in *treasure* (4) ______________ as in *thumb* (5) *th* as in ______________ (*that, thrill*) (6) *wh* as in ______________ (*whole, whale*) (7) ______________ as in *king*

Review 11

1. Rewrite these words, showing consonant pronunciation. (This calls for acute hearing.) Underline the digraphs. Pronounce as you would in the actual word.

   a. *mango, manger, mangy*
   b. *pin, ping, pink, ping-pong*
   c. *ban, bang, bank, banking*
   d. *ran, rang, rank, ranking*
   e. *rancher, range, fancy*

2. There are 25 consonant sounds in the American-English language.
   a. We identify 18 of them with single-letter symbols. Write the 18 consonant letters.
   b. We use __________ to identify the seven additional phonemes.

      Write the seven digraphs.
3. *C* was not included in question 2a because __________.
4. What other consonant letters were not included?
5. The digraph *ph* was not included in question 2b because __________.
6. Rewrite the following words using appropriate key symbols for the consonants. Omit silent consonants. Copy vowels as they are.

whole	__________	*high*	__________
quick	__________	*gopher*	__________
wholly	__________	*phone*	__________
thatch	__________	*that*	__________
taught	__________	*comb*	__________
glistening	__________	*daughter*	__________
rustle	__________	*doubt*	__________
knot	__________	*budget*	__________
wrap	__________	*thinking*	__________

See the Answers to the Reviews section for the answers to Review 11, page 234.

Consonant Clusters and Blends

letters digraphs *bl*	1. We have identified each of the 25 consonant phonemes of the American-English language: 18 of these are represented by single __________; 7 are represented by __________. Now let us turn our attention to consonants that form a cluster in a word. What **cluster** of consonant letters do you see in the word *blue?* __________
2, *b*, *l*	2. Pronounce the word *blue.* How many consonant phonemes does *blue* contain? __________ What are they? __________ __________
one **clusters**	3. A **digraph** is a two-letter grapheme that represents __________ speech sound. The word *blue* does **not** contain a consonant digraph. Neither the *b* nor the *l* loses its identity. Both are sounded, but they are blended together. We call such combinations of consonant letters __________ and the sounds they represent **blends.** We need to study the consonant blends because in many ways, they act as one phoneme.

Answers	Frames
    bl, cl, fl, dr ft sk, fr, spr, spl Sh is a digraph. k	**4. A consonant cluster is composed of two or more consonants that blend together when sounded to form a consonant blend.** The letters do not form a digraph. The phonemes in the blend retain their individual identities. Pronounce the words below. For each, fill in the blank with the letters that form the consonant cluster. *black* _______ *clown* _______ *flying* _______ *draft* _______ *desk* _______ *fry* _______ *spray* _______ *splash* _______ Why did you omit the *sh* in *splash?* ___________________________ The *ck* in *black* represents the single consonant _________, not a blend.
  s p l, blends	**5.** Some reading series do not use the term **cluster.** In that case, **blend** refers to both letters and sounds. In the word *splash,* for example, the letters ________ ________ ________, as well as /*spl*/, are called ________.
      r, l, s	**6.** Pronounce the words in each set below. Each set has one of the common "blenders." Write the letter common to each consonant cluster in the set. **1** / **2** / **3** *brown* / *flame* / *skate* *street* / *claim* / *snow* *great* / *split* / *street* _______ / _______ / _______
r l, s	**7.** The common blenders are represented by the letters ___________, ___________, and ___________. However, there are clusters that do not contain these letters.
cluster digraph sh, ch, th	**8.** We distinguish a _____________ from a digraph by the fact that it represents two or more phonemes blended together. The _____________ represents a single sound. Check those combinations in the following list which do **not** represent consonant blends. *bl* *cr* *qu* *tr* *scr* *cl* *dr* *tw* *sh* *spr* *gl* *sk* *ch* *sm* *spl* *sl* *pr* *th* *mp* *str*

w *equal, quart, queen, quick*	**9.** It may seem strange to clssify *qu* as a consonant cluster when *u* is a vowel. The *u* in this case, however, takes the sound of the consonant ____________. So this combination is actually a /*kw*/ **blend**. Select the words with the /*kw*/ blend from the following: *equal* *quart* *unique* *queen* *opaque* *quick*
tr, tw, gr, spl, qu *pl, str, sl, pr, gr-sp* (**Not** *ch* or *sh!*)	**10.** Underline the consonant clusters in these words: *tree* *twin* *great* *splash* *chair* *quit* *please* *she* *street* *slow* *pretty* *grasp*
s, h	**11.** The *sh* in *splash* and the *sh* in *she* cannot be blends because the sounds represented by the ____________ and the ____________ are not heard.
field, lamp, bent, task *fast, hand, belt, draft*	**12.** Many consonant clusters occur in the final position in English words or syllables. Read the words below. Underline the consonant clusters that occur at the end of the words. *field* *dish* *lamp* *bent* *task* *fast* *hand* *church* *belt* *draft*
train *task*	**13.** As you have seen, clusters may appear at the beginning of a word or syllable, as in *train,* or at the end of a word or syllable, as in *task*. Underline the appropriate blend in each of these examples.
speech *speech* *rest* *church* *digraph* *digraph* *trash* *trash* *shield* *shield*	**14.** Arrange the words below in two columns: those with clusters representing blends and those with digraphs. Some words may be used in both columns. Underline to indicate the part in each word that qualifies it to be in the particular column. *speech* *church* *rest* *digraph* *trash* *shield* **Clusters** **Digraphs** ________ ________ ________ ________ ________ ________ ________ ________ ________ ________
t, h *r* *th*	**15.** There are many words in which a consonant digraph is a part of a cluster. Examine the word *throw.* The first three letters, __________ , __________ , and __________, compose a cluster. Within the cluster is the digraph __________. All blend together: /*thr*/.
thr, shr, chr, phr *ch, ph*	**16.** Draw a single line under the digraph and another line under the entire cluster in each of these words: *through* *shrimp* *chrome* *phrase* Which of the digraphs in the above words are not among the seven key symbols needed to complete the phonemes of our language? _____ _____

Study Guide

Consonant Clusters and Blends

Consonant Clusters

A consonant cluster consists of two or more consonants that blend together when pronounced to form a consonant blend (*clown, spray*). Some teachers' manuals do not use the term **cluster.** In that case, **blend** refers to both letters and sounds. We will use the more common term, **blend,** in this study guide.

Beginning Consonant Blends

The most common blends that occur at the beginning of a word or syllable include one of the letters *r, l,* or *s.*

r Blends		*l* Blends		*s* Blends			
br	*bright*	*bl*	*black*	*sc*	*scout*	*scr*	*scrap*
cr	*crayon*	*cl*	*class*	*sk*	*sky*	*spl*	*splash*
dr	*dress*	*fl*	*flower*	*sl*	*slip*	*spr*	*spring*
fr	*free*	*gl*	*glad*	*sm*	*small*	*squ*	*square*
gr	*green*	*pl*	*plan*	*sn*	*snow*	*str*	*string*
pr	*pretty*			*sp*	*spot*		
tr	*train*			*st*	*stop*		
				sw	*swim*		

tw* and *dw The *tw* (*twin*) and *dw* (*dwell*) blends are less common in English than the blends that include one of the letters *r, l,* or *s.*

qu *Qu* is a consonant blend when it represents /kw/ as in *quick* and *quiet.*

Consonant blends are taught as units, rather than as single graphemes (e.g., *st* as representing two blended phonemes, rather than an isolated /s/ and an isolated /t/).

Consonant Digraphs and Consonant Blends

Blends that occur at the beginning of a syllable may include a consonant digraph and a consonant blend, such as in *shr* (*shrimp*) and *thr* (*throw*).

Final Position Blends

Many consonant blends occur in the final position of an English syllable. Some of the more common final blends include these:

l	*old*	*nd*	*end*	*st*	*most*	*mp*	*lamp*	*lt*	*salt*
lk	*milk*	*nt*	*went*	*sk*	*desk*	*ft*	*lift*		

In teaching, vowels may be combined with consonant blends to create letter patterns that we call **rimes.** You will learn about rimes in Part V of this book. Examples of vowel and consonant blend rimes include *old* (*told*); *ild* (*wild*); *ilk* (*milk*); *alt* (*salt*); *end* (*mend*); *ent* (*went*); *ost* (*most*); *esk* (*desk*); *amp* (*lamp*); *ift* (*lift*).

Answers	Frames
str, str, scr *bl nd, sm, thr ft*	**17.** All consonant clusters (written) represent blends (spoken). Underline the consonants that represent blends in these words: *string* *strap* *scrap* *blond* *small* *thrift*
strength, /ng/, /th/	**18.** Which word in frame 17 has a cluster composed of two digraphs? _____________ The two digraphs that blend together are / / and / /.
Blends / **Digraphs** *toast* / *shelter* *grapheme* / *grapheme* *three* / *three* *clanging* / *clanging* *strike* / *altogether* / *father*	**19.** Arrange the words below in two columns: those containing clusters that represent blends and those containing digraphs. Some of these words, too, may be used in both columns, so underline to indicate the part of each word that places it in a column. **Blends** **Digraphs** *toast* *shelter* *grapheme* *three* *clanging* *strike* *altogether* *father*
phoneme	**20.** We have studied the single-consonant phonemes, the consonant digraphs, and the consonant blends. We include the blends because in many ways, one blend acts as though it were one _____________.

Review 12

1. A cluster differs from a digraph in that _____________.
2. Why were no key symbols given to represent the blends?
3. Seven specific digraphs, together with 18 single letters, supply us with the consonant sounds of our language. Which of the seven digraphs appear in the following paragraph? List them in the order in which they make their first appearance.

   It started as a pleasure trip. The driver, nearing the exit leading through the city, changed lanes. He jerked the wheel too quickly and landed on the slick shoulder.

4. There are three unnecessary single letters in our alphabet. Illustrations are in the above paragraph. Rewrite these words to show how other letters could be substituted.
5. What consonant blends are heard at the beginning of the words in the above paragraph?

See the Answers to the Reviews section for the answers to Review 12, page 234.

For a helpful summary and review of the phonemes, turn to page 135. Work through the consonant section, using a separate sheet of paper. Then you will be able to have a complete review after you have studied the vowels.

Recap I

25 phonemes word	**1.** In our study of consonants, we identified ____________ consonant ______________ (the smallest units of sound that distinguish one ______________ from another).
symbol *b, d, f, g, h, j, k, l, m, n, p* *r, s, t, v, w, y, z* digraphs *ch, sh, th, th̸, wh, zh, ng*	**2.** To know exactly to which sound we are referring, we assigned each phoneme a key ______________ and a key word. As you go through the alphabet, write the 18 consonant letters that symbolize specific phonemes: _____ _____ _____ _____ _____ _____ _____ _____ _____ _____ _____ _____ _____ _____ _____ _____ _____ _____. But we need 25 symbols. We use ______________ to complete our representation of the consonant phonemes: _____ _____ _____ _____ _____ _____ _____.
phoneme phoneme /k/, /s/ /d/, /t/ /j/, /g/ /n/, /ng/ /s/, /sh/, /z/, /zh/ /s/, /z/, /zh/	**3.** Although consonants are fairly reliable (there is a high relationship between grapheme and ______________), there are irregularities. A letter (or grapheme) may represent more than one ______________. For example: the *c* in *camp* represents / /, and in *ace* / / the *d* in *date* / /, and in *jumped* / / the *g* in *age* / /, and in *go* / / the *n* in *ran* / /, and in *rank* / / the *s* in *soap* / /, in *surely* / /, in *runs* / /, and in *measure* / / the *z* in *waltz* / /, in *quiz* / /, and in *azure* / /
/f/, *fase, lauf, fone*	**4.** A phoneme may be represented by more than one grapheme. Write the phoneme that is represented in each set of words. Then rewrite the words, using the key symbols (see frames 4 and 5). / / as in *face* ___________ , *laugh* ___________ , *phone* ___________
/j/, *paje, joke* *fuje, grajual* /k/, *ankor, antikue* *kue* /z/, *uzed, frozen* *zylofone*	**5.** / / *page* ______________ , *joke* ______________ , *fudge* ______________ , *gradual* ______________ / / *anchor* ______________ , *antique* ______________ , *cue* ______________ / / *used* ______________ , *frozen* ______________ , *xylophone* ______________

silent	**6.** A letter may represent no phoneme: it may be ______________.
	Some common silent letter patterns include the following:
t	(1) The second of two like consonants, as the ______________ in *letters* and
s	the ______________ in *dress*
b	(2) ______________ following *m,* as in *bomb,* or followed by *t* as in *doubt*
k	(3) ______________ followed by *n,* as in *know*
h	(4) ______________ following *g,* as in *ghost*
Use your dictionary to verify.	**7.** Did you feel there were any words that did not belong in the last 4 frames, words you would pronounce differently? List them here.
	8. Repeat the generalization regarding the hard–soft sounds of *c* and *g.* Check each of the following words that does not follow the generalization.
girl, give	*epic* *gem* *ghost* *girl* *cake* *gate* *cycle* *give*
before	**9.** The consonants *w* and *y* are found ______________ (before, after) the vowel in a word.
no	Is the consonant *y* is often a silent letter? ______________
k	**10.** The key symbol for *q* is ______________.

Did you get all the exercises in this recap correct? What a sense of satisfaction you must have. Congratulations! We have been studying the consonants, the most regular of all the phonemes. But the consonants cannot get along without the vowels. We will now proceed with a study of the vowels and their relationships with the consonants.

Part III

Vowels

A reminder: Do not pull the mask down until you have written your response to the entire frame.

Introduction

vowels	**1.** The 26 letters of the alphabet are divided into two major categories categories: consonants and __________.
phonemes phonemes, 19 phonemes	**2.** Although there are many variations due to dialect, individual speech patterns, and so forth, for all practical purposes in the task of teaching reading, we can consider the American-English language to contain 44 separate and distinctive __________. We have noted that 25 of these are consonant __________. Therefore, there are __________ vowel __________.
vowels	**3. The letters *a, e, i, o, u,* and sometimes *w* and *y* are classified as __________.**
yo-yo	**4.** How can you tell when *y* is a consonant and when it is a vowel? You have learned that the key symbol *y* (consonant) represents the phoneme heard in __________ *(yo-yo, say)*. *Y* functions as a consonant **only** when it represents the phoneme heard in *yo-yo.*
initial	**5.** The consonant *y* is always the __________ (initial, final) letter in a word or syllable. It is always found before the vowel.

yellow, yet, beyond consonant vowel	**6.** Study the words below. Underline each *y* that is a consonant. *they yellow yet may very beyond* The ________________ *y* is never a silent letter. (consonant, vowel) The ________________ *y* is often a silent letter. (consonant, vowel)
vowel	**7.** *Y* does not serve as a key symbol for a vowel phoneme. ***Y* represents no vowel sound of its own. When *y* is a ________________, its pronunciation is shown by the key symbols we associate with the *i* or the *e*.**
year, gym, my (c, v, v) *ready, canyon* (v, c) *canyon*	**8.** Study the function of the *y* in the words below. Place a c̲ or a v̲ above each *y* to identify *y* as a consonant or as a vowel. Check each *y* consonant to see that it represents the same sound as the initial phoneme in *yo-yo.* *year gym my ready canyon* In which word is the *y* the first letter in the second syllable? ________________
wagon	**9.** Now let us examine the *w*. You have learned that *w* as a consonant represents the phoneme heard in ________________ . (*wagon, snow*)
symbol	**10.** **As a vowel, the *w* represents no distinct phoneme of its own.** Therefore, it cannot be represented by a key ________________. **W is always used in combination with another vowel, (as in *few, cow,* and *grow*).**
thaw, threw	**11.** Underline each *w* that functions as a vowel in the following words: *water which thaw threw dwarf* (Be sure that they do not represent the phoneme you hear at the beginning of *wagon.*) The vowel *w* always ________________ another vowel. (precedes, follows)
w, y	**12.** Two of the seven vowels are not identified by distinctive key symbols because they do not represent sounds of their own. These are the vowels ________________ and ________________.

a, e, i, o, u	**13.** Now let us turn our attention to the vowels that do represent phonemes and can be assigned key symbols to distinguish them from each other. The vowel phonemes are represented by five letters. They are __________, __________, __________, __________, __________.
cannot	**14.** These five vowels, alone and in combination with another vowel, represent the 19 vowel phonemes of our language. Therefore, there ______________ a one-to-one correspondence between phoneme (is, cannot be) and letter.
a five	**15.** Study the words below. Pronounce the sound represented by the underlined vowel in each word. *same* *dare* *can* *arm* *about* We can see that one vowel, the __________, represents at least __________ different phonemes.
phoneme vowels	**16.** Each vowel letter represents more than one ______________. If we meet an unfamiliar word, how will we know which sounds its vowels represent? There are some patterns (with exceptions, of course) that will give us some help in determining the sounds represented by the ______________ in unknown words.
phonemes vowel	**17.** Our task, then, is twofold: (1) to identify the vowel ______________ of the American-English language and assign each a key symbol (2) to become acquainted with the generalizations that will aid us in associating the correct phonemes with the ______________ letters in unknown words
letters	**18.** For our study, we shall divide the vowel phonemes into two major groups: (1) those represented by single vowel letters (2) those represented by combinations of vowel letters Each of the single letters (as in group 1) and each of the combinations of ______________ represent **one** phoneme.
letter	**19.** We shall begin our study of the vowel phonemes with group 1: those represented by a single vowel ______________. (letter, phoneme)

Review 13

1. The vowel letters are ________, ________, ________, ________, ________, and sometimes ________ and ________.
2. We need not select key symbols to represent the sounds of ________ and ________, because they duplicate the sounds of other vowels.
3. Indicate whether the *w* and the *y* in these words are consonants or vowels by writing C or V following each word:

yet	________	*type*	________	*play*	________
wide	________	*draw*	________	*when*	________

4. The *w* in *white* is part of a ________ (consonant, vowel) ________ (blend, digraph).
5. There are ________ (fewer, more) vowel phonemes than there are vowel letters.
6. How many vowel phonemes will we need to identify?

See the Answers to the Reviews section for the answers to Review 13, page 234.

Short Vowel Sounds

	ă (apple) ĕ (edge) ĭ (igloo) ŏ (ox) ŭ (umbrella)
a ă ăpple *e ĕ ĕdge* *i ĭ ĭgloo* *o ŏ ŏx* *u ŭ ŭmbrella*	**1.** One set of phonemes represented by single vowel letters includes those that stand for "short" vowel sounds. The **breve** is a diacritical mark used to indicate the specific pronunciation of each vowel in this group. Its linguistic relationship to "short" can be noted in such words as *abbreviate* and *brevity.* It is the custom, in phonics, to call the vowel sound whose key symbol contains a breve a **short** vowel sound. **1 2 3** *a ă apple* *e ĕ edge* *i ĭ igloo* *o ŏ ox* *u ŭ umbrella*
short	The vowels in column 3 at the right represent the ________ sounds.
breve	Each key symbol (2) consists of the vowel marked with a ________.
	Mark the initial vowel in each key word.
	2. Because, in actuality, these sounds are not held for a shorter period of time than certain other vowel phonemes, some prefer to call them **unglided phonemes.**
short	If you write "unglided" and this text gives the answer as "________" (or vice versa), you may count your answer correct.

ĭ, ŏ, ŭ phonemes	**3.** The key symbols that identify the vowels when they represent their short sounds are *ă, ĕ,* ______, ______, ______. Reading would be easier if five additional characters representing these ________________ (letters, phonemes) were added to our alphabet.
ox fəj map	**4.** It is important to note that various dictionaries indicate pronunciation in different ways. We must study the pronunciation key of the particular dictionary we use. For example, some dictionaries use the *ä* to represent the short *o* (ŏ), key word ________. Other dictionaries may use the symbol ə to represent the short *u* (ŭ). How would these dictionaries represent the pronunciation of *fudge*? ________ You may find that your dictionary indicates the pronunciation of short vowel sounds with the letter and no diacritical mark. In this case, the pronunciation of *map* is written ___________.
m ă, consonant p apple	**5.** Pronounce the word *map.* Listen for three phonemes: the consonant phoneme represented by ________________, the vowel phoneme represented by ________________, and the ________________ phoneme represented by ________________. Pronounce the vowel sound alone. The same vowel sound is heard in ________________ (*apple, far*).
măp ran, grab, back	**6.** Pronounce the vowel phoneme in *map.* Rewrite *map* using key symbols: ___________ Now pronounce the words below. Check those words in which the vowel phoneme is the same as that heard in *map.* *ran* *all* *car* *above* *grab* *back* *paw*
three hĕn	**7.** There are ________ phonemes in *hen.* Listen for the vowel phoneme as you say *hen* aloud. Rewrite *hen* using key symbols to indicate its pronunciation. ________________
mĕt, hĕm, ĕnd	**8.** Mark with a breve each of the vowels in the words below that represents the same vowel phoneme heard in the key word *edge.* *feed* *met* *her* *hem* *end* *reward* If you find this difficult, pronounce the first vowel phoneme heard in *edge.* Then pronounce each word, substituting that sound for each vowel phoneme.

three *rĕd*	**9.** Read this sentence aloud: *I read a book yesterday.* How many phonemes do you hear when you say *read* in the sentence above? __________ Rewrite *read* using a key symbol to indicate each phoneme. __________ You have written in code. Anyone who knows the code can pronounce *read* correctly without a sentence to clarify it.
pĭn, drĭp, lĭft, thĭk	**10.** Pronounce *igloo.* Now say the first vowel phoneme. Rewrite the following words using key symbols to code each phoneme: *pin* ________ *drip* ________ *lift* ________ *thick* ________
three *ox*	**11.** Pronounce *hot.* It contains __________ (How many?) phonemes. The vowel phoneme sounds the same as that in __________ (*boy, ox*) .
lĭp, tŏp, pŏp, lăp, grăph, pŏd key symbols	**12.** Indicate the pronunciation of each short (unglided) vowel sound by using the correct diacritical mark in each of these words. *lip top note pop lap graph pod home* The vowel letters with the marks you placed above them are the __________ for the phonemes they represent.
breve or *ŭ* *jŭmp, ŭs, dŭk, cŭp, tŭb*	**13.** Pronounce *umbrella.* We use the __________ to indicate that the *u* represents a short (unglided) sound. Now, pronounce the vowel sound alone. Place the correct diacritical marks above all the vowels in the following words that represent the same sound as the first vowel phoneme in the key word *umbrella.* *jump use us duck cup house tub*
short *fĕnce, dŭg*	**14.** Pronounce the vowel phoneme represented by the vowel letter in each of the words below. *an fed pin hot cup* Each vowel represents its __________ phoneme. Now pronounce the vowel phoneme in each of the following words. Place a breve above each vowel in this set of words that represents its unglided sound. Check carefully. *car fence pine cow dug*
hĕd, sĕd *sĕnts, ĕnd*	**15.** Pronounce the words below. Listen carefully for the vowel phonemes. Rewrite each word, using the key symbols that indicate the sounds we associate with the vowel and consonant phonemes. *head* ________ *said* ________ *cents* ________ *end* ________

Answers	Frames
one one two two phoneme	**16.** To obtain a better understanding of the short vowels, we will consider them as they usually occur within the English syllable. A **syllable** is the smallest unit of speech that has one vowel phoneme. When you say the word *mat,* you hear ______ (How many?) vowel phoneme(s). The word *mat* consists of ______ (How many?) syllable(s). When you pronounce *mattress,* you hear ______ (How many?) vowel phoneme(s). *Mattress* has ______ (How many?) syllable(s). A syllable in the English language has only one vowel ______.
vowel, consonant	**17.** **The most common vowel-consonant pattern is that of CVC (consonant-vowel-consonant), in which the V (vowel) represents its short sound.** There are many one-syllable words and many accented syllables in multisyllable words that follow this pattern. These words and syllables are made of an initial consonant, a middle ______, and a final ______.
ring, this, rab bit, big	**18.** The C (consonant) in the pattern may represent a digraph or a blend. Check the syllables (or one-syllable words) that have the CVC pattern. *ring* *this* *rab bit* *be side* *rain* *big*
short (unglided) CVC	**19.** VC, in which the vowel represents the ______ sound as in *an,* is also a common pattern. It functions the same as the ______ pattern.
short (unglided) breve	**20.** **The CVC and the VC patterns give clues to the pronunciation of unknown words. In both cases we would expect the vowel to represent the ______ sound.** To indicate the pronunciation of the vowel, we place a ______ above it.
VC, CVC, CCVC CVCC, CCVCC, CCCVCC	**21.** Study the words below. Indicate the vowel-consonant pattern in each. Use a C to represent each consonant and a *V* for each vowel. *at* ______ *hat* ______ *chat* ______ *fast* ______ *trust* ______ *thrust* ______

one *at* vowel	**22.** The words in frame 21 have __________ vowel letter(s). (How many?) We will use CVC to represent the short vowel spelling pattern. We acknowledge that a consonant may not always precede the vowel letter in a short vowel word, as in ______, and that a CVC word may have more than one consonant preceding or following the single ________.
yes (Blends and digraphs are considered as Cs.) no *sĕt, lŏt*	**23.** Do the vowels in all CVC patterns represent the short sound? Study the words and syllables below. Do all of them have the CVC pattern? ________________ Do all the vowels represent the short sound? ________________ Mark the vowels that represent the short sounds with breves. Work carefully. *far* *long* *set* *lot* *her*
yes *Dăn kĕpt hĭs pŏp gŭn.*	**24.** The key words given at the beginning of this section will help us remember the phoneme for each vowel. A sentence that contains each of the short vowel phonemes may be easier to remember. Would the sentence below furnish a key word for each of the short vowel phonemes? ________________ (Check each word with the set at the beginning of this section.) Mark the vowels with breves. *Dan kept his pop gun.*
4 *Năn's pĕt ĭs nŏt fŭn.* *Săm's nĕt ĭs nŏt cŭt.* *Săd Tĕd ĭn hŏt hŭt.* *All mĕn ĭn hŏt bŭs.*	**25.** Look at the groups of words below. In each group, mark the vowels that represent the short sound. Number ________________ is not a good key phrase. (1) *Nan's pet is not fun.* (2) *Sam's net is not cut.* (3) *Sad Ted in hot hut.* (4) *All men in hot bus.*
    chim *can* *wish* *men* *sun* *wing* *gin*	**26.** We often find the vowel phoneme in a closed syllable to be short. **A closed syllable ends with a consonant phoneme.** Study the words below. Check the closed syllables, including closed one-syllable words. *chim ney* *tree* *can* *wish* *men* *sun* *win dow* *begin*

short

don't, bird

27. One vowel in a closed syllable (or in a closed one-syllable word) usually represents its __________ sound. With your key sentence in mind (frame 24), check the vowel phonemes in the following words. Which words do not have the short vowel phoneme?

clap *don't* *skin* *sick* *trust* *fed* *bend* *bird*

---

yes

chick en, pen cil

yes

28. Study the words below carefully.

chick en *pen cil*

Is each syllable a closed syllable? __________ Write the closed syllables here: __________

Is there a single vowel in each syllable? __________

---

unaccented

29. We might expect that we can properly indicate the pronunciation of each of the vowels in *chicken* and *pencil* with a breve. If you pronounce the words too carefully—that is, artificially—you might indicate their pronunciations that way.

Say a sentence aloud containing the word *chicken* and then one with *pencil.*

You will notice that the vowel in the __________ syllable represents
(accented, unaccented)

more of an "uh" sound and not the phonemes you hear in the words *ox* and *igloo.*

---

closed

closed

30. Syllables with the CVC pattern are __________ syllables; those
(closed, open)

with the VC pattern (such as *ant*) are __________ syllables.
(closed, open)

---

lĕm băn hŏp

31. The generalization for the short vowel phoneme is most useful when it is stated:

A single vowel in an accented closed syllable usually represents the short sound of the vowel.

Indicate the pronunciation of the syllables that follow this generalization:

re pay *lem on* *ban jo* *hop per*

---

vowel

short, *i*

32. We have noted the sounds represented by *a, e, i, o, u.* How about the *y?*

gym *sys tem* *sym bol*

Study the words above. Each contains a __________ *y* within the
(consonant, vowel)

syllable. The *y* represents the __________ sound of the letter ______.
(long, short)

(Any errors? Recheck the sound!) *păn, pĕg* *fĭt, stŏp*	**33.** Let us review the short sounds of the vowels. Check the words below against the key words you have learned. Place a breve above each of the vowels that represents the short sound of that vowel. *date* *want* *pan* *peg* *put* *fit* *stop* *cute*
short	**34.** We can expect that single vowels in closed accented syllables will usually represent ________________ sounds. Remember that all one-syllable words are considered accented syllables.
short *shelve, glance, fence, rinse*	**35.** There are many words in which the vowel is followed by two consonants and a final *e* (VCCe). Note that in words ending with a vowel that is followed by two consonants and a final *e,* the first vowel phoneme is usually ________________. (short, long) Which words have the VCCe pattern? *shelve* *glance* *fence* *ride* *rinse* *smile*
e **consonants** **short (unglided), silent**	**36.** Study the words below. *dance* *wedge* *rinse* *fence* *bronze* *lapse* *bridge* *smudge* We can make a generalization concerning these words. **When a word (or syllable) has two vowels, one of which is a final ________________, and the two vowels are separated by two ________________, the first vowel often represents the ________________ sound and the final *e* is ________________.**
VCCe	**37.** The generalization is applied to words that have the ending pattern of VCCe (with exceptions, of course!). The word *lapse* is an example of the VCCe pattern: vowel-consonant-consonant-final *e.* **When a word (or a syllable) has two vowels, one of which is a final *e*, and the two vowels are separated by two consonants, the final *e* is silent and the first vowel often represents its short sound.** *Since* and *judge* end with the ________________ pattern.
chance, ridge, since *sense, prince*	**38.** Check the words below that end with the VCCe pattern. *chance* *ridge* *telephone* *since* *could* *shape* *tree* *sense* *toy* *prince*

Study Guide

Short Vowels

Short Vowel	Key Symbol	Key Word
a	*ă*	*apple*
e	*ĕ*	*edge*
i	*ĭ*	*igloo*
o	*ŏ*	*ox*
u	*ŭ*	*umbrella*

***Breve* (˘)** The breve (˘) is the diacritical mark used to indicate the specific pronunciation of the short vowels. *Unglided* is another term that refers to the short vowel phonemes. Some dictionaries indicate pronunciation in different ways. Your dictionary may indicate the pronunciation of short vowel sounds with the letter and no diacritical mark. You may also find that your dictionary uses the ə to represent the short /*u*/ or that the symbol *ä* is used to represent the short *o*. Note that in these dictionaries, ə*m brel* ə represents the pronunciation of the key word *umbrella,* and *äks* represents the pronunciation of the key word *ox.*

CVC Pattern The most common vowel-consonant pattern is that of the CVC (consonant-vowel-consonant) in which the V (vowel) represents its short (unglided) sound (*pat, pet, pig, pot, puff*).

VC Pattern The V (vowel) in the VC pattern represents the short sound (*ant, etch, itch, odd, up*). The VC pattern functions the same as the CVC pattern.

VCCe Pattern When a word or a syllable has two vowels, one of which is a final *e,* and the two vowels are separated by two consonants, the first vowel often represents the short sound and the final *e* is silent (*dance, fence, since, dodge, fudge*).

Closed Syllable A closed syllable ends with a consonant phoneme (*at*). A single vowel in an accented, closed syllable usually represents the short (unglided) sound of the vowel.

Ww as a Vowel As a vowel, the *w* represents no distinct phoneme of its own. The vowel *w* always follows another vowel in English words and is used in combination with the other vowel (*new, cow, saw*).

Yy as a Vowel As a vowel, *y* represents no distinct phoneme of its own. When *y* is a vowel, its pronunciation is shown by the key symbols we associate with the *i* and the *e.* The vowel *y* is often silent (*play*).

short	**39.** Study the words below. *bridge* *dodge* *smudge* *wedge* Note that in words ending with *-dge,* the first vowel phoneme is usually ________________. (short, long)

Answer	Frame
no	**40.** Now consider the following words. *fence* *range* *paste* *hinge* *prance* Is the VCCe pattern completely reliable? ________________
bed *pin*	**41.** Now take time to study your own dictionary. Look up *bed.* Does the breve appear above the *e* in the pronunciation guide? Since the unglided vowel sound is so common, many dictionaries indicate the pronunciation of all short sounds with the letter alone (no diacritical mark). How would the pronunciation of *bed* be shown in these dictionaries? ________________ Of *pin?* ________________
ă ĕ ĭ ŏ ŭ *ăpple, ĕdge, ĭgloo* *ŏx, ŭmbrella*	**42.** Write the key symbols we are using in this text to represent the short vowel phonemes. ________ ________ ________ ________ ________ Write the key word for each short vowel. Mark the initial vowel in each key word. Pronounce the short vowel phonemes. Can you say them rapidly? Practice them. Since they are so common, you should be familiar with them.

Review 14

1. What is the major generalization concerning short vowel sounds?
   a. Write the generalization that applies to the words *pet* and *in.*
   b. Write the generalization that applies to the vowel–consonant ending pattern in the words *since* and *dance.*
2. We are studying the vowel phonemes that are represented by single letters. We have learned to associate 5 of the 19 vowel phonemes with their key pronunciation symbols. Mark the vowels to indicate their pronunciations.

   bed *next* *lot* *cat* *trip* *skin* *mop* *us* *send* *bug*
3. Write the vowel-consonant pattern for each of the following words.

   up *hat* *lapse* *tub* *ad* *rinse*
4. We expect the single letter *g* to represent its hard sound, except when it is followed by ______________, ______________, or ______________.

See the Answers to the Reviews section for the answers to Review 14, page 235.

Long Vowel Sounds

breves	ā (*apron*) ē (*eraser*) ī (*ice*) ō (*overalls*) ū (*unicorn*) **1.** This section introduces the long vowel sounds as shown above. Thus far we have identified five other vowel sounds. We call them "short" or unglided sounds. We distinguish the short vowels (as in the dictionary) from other vowel sounds by placing ________ over them.
a ā *apron* *e* ē *eraser* *i* ī *ice* *o* ō *overalls* *u* ū *unicorn* name	ā (*apron*) ē (*eraser*) ī (*ice*) ō (*overalls*) ū (*unicorn*) **2.** One set of phonemes represented by single vowel letters is those that "say their own names." The key symbol for these vowel phonemes is a **macron** (-). Pronounce the first word at the right. Make the sound represented by the underlined vowel; then say the name of the underlined vowel. **1** / **2** / **3** *a* / ā / *apron* ____ / ____ / *eraser* ____ / ____ / *ice* ____ / ____ / *overalls* ____ / ____ / *unicorn* The sound represented by the vowel is the same as the ________ of the vowel. Pronounce the rest of the key words (3), vowel phonemes (key symbols) (2), and letter names (1) the same way. Complete the table. (Many dictionaries are now using an equivalent symbol, the *yōō*, to indicate the *ū*. Check your dictionary.)
ē, ī, ō, ū	**3.** The key symbol, as found in the dictionary, for the *a* in *apron* is *ā*. What would the key symbol be for each of the other underlined vowels in frame 2? ________ ________ ________ ________
pine	**4.** "Macron" contains the word element *macro,* which means "long" or "great." It has been the custom, in phonics, to call the vowel sound whose key symbol is a macron over the vowel letter a "long vowel sound." Therefore, we would say the *i* in ________ (*pin, pine*) represents a long vowel sound.
long	**5.** It would seem that in the normal pronunciation of words, we would hold long vowel sounds for a greater length of time than short vowel sounds. This is not necessarily true. Some texts now use the term **glided sound** rather than ________ (long, short) to indicate the sound of a vowel that "says its own name." We will use these terms interchangeably.

Answers	Frames
tāke, gō, fīne, bē, sāme (If you had any incorrect, study them carefully. Does the *a* in *many* "say its own name"?)	**6.** Place a macron above each of the vowels that represents a long (glided) sound in these words. Be sure the vowel "says its own name." *take go many fine once all be same*
yo͞o is not *o͞o*	**7.** Though we will use the macron (*ū*), we will briefly consider the use of the *yo͞o* and the *o͞o* to indicate the long *ū*. Some teachers' manuals use the *yo͞o* to indicate the pronunciation of the long *ū* in *cube* and the *o͞o* to indicate the pronunciation of the long *ū* in *tune.* Say *cube* and *tune.* Listen carefully. You may hear different pronunciations of the long *u* in *cube* and *tune.* A /*y*/ precedes the /*oo*/ in *cube.* This long vowel sound is therefore represented by ______________ (*yo͞o, o͞o*), . The sound that the *u* represents in *tune* ________________ (is, is not) preceded by /*y*/. We would expect this sound to be represented by a(n) ______________ (*yo͞o, o͞o*). (Consult your teacher's manual for the symbols that are used to represent the long *ū*.)
cake, be, time *home, huge*	**8.** These five vowel phonemes are represented by the key symbols *ā, ē, ī, ō, ū.* Select a word from the list below that illustrates each. *ā* ______________ *ē* ______________ *ī* ______________ *ō* ______________ *ū* ______________ *be up cake home huge time run*
nāmȩ, thēsȩ, cūtȩ, bōnȩ *tōȩ, pīnȩ*	**9.** Study the words below. Indicate those vowels that represent their long (glided) sounds by placing macrons above them. Put a diagonal line (/) through each vowel that is silent. *name these cute bone toe pine*
e, e **long (glided)**	**10.** There are many one-syllable words with two vowels in which *e* is the second vowel as well as the final letter of the word. We can make a generalization concerning these words. Study the words *name* and *pine;* then complete this generalization: **When a one-syllable word has two vowels, one of which is a final __________, the __________ is silent and the first vowel usually represents its __________ sound.**

VCe yes	**11.** This generalization most often applies to words that have the ending pattern of VCe. The word *use* is an example of VCe: vowel-consonant-final vowel *e.* *Time* and *plate* have the ending pattern of ________________. Does this generalization apply to them? ________________ **When a one-syllable word has two vowels, one of which is the final *e*, the *e* is silent and the first vowel usually represents its long sound.**
VCe	**12.** The C in the vowel-consonant-final vowel *e* (VCe) pattern may signify a single consonant letter or a consonant digraph but only one consonant phoneme. Since *ph* represents a single-consonant phoneme, the nonsense word *sophe* has an ending pattern ________________.
dīne̸, hōpe̸, fāce̸, rīde̸, cūbe̸, phōne̸ VCe	**13.** Mark each vowel in the following words with the proper diacritical mark. Put a slash (/) through each silent letter. *dine hope face ride cube phone* All of the above have the vowel-consonant ending pattern ______________.
When a one-syllable word has two vowels, one of which is the final *e*, the *e* is silent and the first vowel usually represents its long sound.	**14.** Write the generalization concerning vowel sounds illustrated by the words: *ate game ice*
come, some, there	**15.** It is well to remember that the generalization is very helpful but not infallible. Check the words in the following set that **do not** follow the generalization. (Is the final *e* silent? Does the first vowel "say its own name"?) *come place these some there late clothe same*
dance pāste fence VCCe VCCe VCCe *wāste rinse* VCCe VCCe	**16.** This generalization is of little value in helping to determine the vowel sounds in words ending with the vowel-consonant pattern of VCCe, even when such words are of one syllable. Study the words below. Indicate the vowels that represent the long sound by using the macron. Write the ending pattern (begin with the vowel) under each of the words. *dance paste fence waste rinse* ________ ________ ________ ________ ________

dăns, rīd, sāf
brĭj, kāk, fĕns
long (glided)
short (unglided)
silent

17. Write each word below to show pronunciation, using the key symbols we associate with each vowel and consonant letter. Omit each silent letter.

dance	________	*ride*	________	*safe*	________
bridge	________	*cake*	________	*fence*	________

We can see that in one-syllable words that end with the pattern of VCe, the first vowel is usually ______________; in one-syllable words that end with the pattern of VCCe, the first vowel is usually ______________. The final *e* in both patterns (VCe and VCCe) is usually ______________.

---

cīse
tāke
tĭve
pōse
pēde
mīre

18. Study the two-syllable words below in column 1. The syllable division and accent placement for each word is shown in column 2. Mark the vowel in the last syllable in each word to show pronunciation.

1	2
concise	*con cise'*
mistake	*mis take'*
native	*na' tive*
compose	*com pose'*
stampede	*stam pede'*
admire	*ad mire'*

With these words in mind, our generalization might be extended to read:

When a word or an accented syllable has two vowels, one of which is the final *e*, the *e* is silent and the first vowel usually represents the long (glided) sound.

Follow	**Do Not Follow**
stove	*come*
cone	*one*
throne	*none*
globe	*some*

19. Let us consider an exception. Say the words below. Listen carefully to the sound that the vowel *o* represents.

stove	*cone*	*come*	*one*
throne	*none*	*globe*	*some*

Arrange the words in two columns: (1) those in which the ending pattern **VCe** is of value in determining the pronunciation of the vowel and (2) those in which the ending pattern **VCe** does not help us determine the pronunciation of the vowel.

Words do not follow the generalization when the vowel letter *o* is pronounced like the sound of "uh" in the word *done.*

BOX 3.1

Final E Solves Four Spelling Problems

Before spelling was finalized in the 17th century, early writers used the final *e* to solve several tricky spelling problems. We will consider four ways in which the final *e* came to the rescue:

1. English words ending with a /*v*/ or a /*z*/ phoneme presented a sticky spelling problem for early writers. Although English words can end with a /*v*/ or /*z*/ phoneme (*groove, breeze*), spelling conventions did not provide for a single *v* or *z* to be the final letter (*groov, breez*). The inventive writers added a final *e* to avoid ending words with a final *v* or *z* grapheme (e.g., *starve, swerve, bronze, snooze*).
2. Early writers needed a way to indicate when the *th* is voiced (*teethe*) and when it is unvoiced (*teeth*). In solving their problem, the inventive writers once again used the final *e,* adding it to words such as *teethe* and *clothe* so as to avoid confusion with words such as *teeth* and *cloth.*
3. The final *e* also came in handy when spelling words that end in /*s*/. Sometimes the /*s*/ is part of the word (*dense*); sometimes it is part of a suffix (*dens*). In using the final *e,* the writers of yesteryear generously provided the reader with a helpful visual cue for sorting out when the letter *s* is part of a root word (*tens* + *e* = *tense, brows* + *e* = *browse*) and when the final *s* is part of a suffix (*horse* + *s* = *horses; lapse* + *s* = *lapses*).
4. Thanks to the final *e,* it is clear when to use the soft *c* (*key word: sun*) and *g* (*key word: jeep*) in words such as *choice* and *damage.* Without the final *e,* the reader might be tempted to pronounce *choic* (choice) as /*choik*/ and *damag* (damage) as /*damag*/.

English is a dynamic and evolving language in which spelling changes occur over relatively long periods of time. Will the final *e* eventually drop away from words in which the *e* neither contributes to pronunciation nor gives the reader an important visual clue? No one knows—but we might speculate. Generally speaking, American spelling changes make words simpler, such as dropping the *u* from the British *colour* and substituting the trendy *nite* for *night.* So perhaps the writers in some future century will spell *groove* and *breeze* as *groov* and *breez.*

long (or glided)	**20.** We have identified five vowel phonemes that represent the ____________ sounds of the letters.
(All words below must have a silent, final *e.*)	We have also learned one generalization that gives a clue to that sound. Select one word for each of the five vowels to illustrate this generalization. Place a macron above the vowels selected.
rōle, remāke	*rattle* *one* *role* *piece* *remake*
extrēme, prīce, cūbe	*extreme* *come* *price* *cube* *dance*

consonant long (glided) VCe	**21.** We have noted that when we see a word or an accented syllable with the pattern of a single vowel followed by a single ________________ and final *e*, the single vowel is likely to represent its ________________ sound. The vowel-consonant ending pattern we expect to see is ________________.
short *pīne, rāte, kīte, hāte* *cūte, strīpe, pāle, āte* long	**22.** All the vowels in the words below represent the ______________ sound. Check each one to make sure. Then add a silent *e* to the end of each word to see what happens. To show the new pronunciation, mark the first vowel in each of the new words you've made with the appropriate diacritical mark. *pin* *rat* *kit* *hat* *cut* *strip* *pal* *at* The vowels now represent their ________________ sounds.
e pronunciation (or sound)	**23.** We can see from words such as *cut* and *cute* that the silent _________ at the end of a word has a purpose. It changes the meaning of the word as well as the ______________ of the word.
  <u>go</u>, <u>so</u> <u>lo</u>, <u>me</u> *<u>fe</u> ver, <u>ti</u> ger, <u>pa</u> per*	**24.** Another situation in which we often find the vowel to be long is that of the open syllable. **An open syllable ends with a vowel <u>phoneme</u>.** Study the words below. Underline the open syllables, including open one-syllable words. *go* *so lo* *pine* *me* *sup pose* *fe ver* *ti ger* *pa per*
  CV open	**25.** This generalization most often applies to words and syllables that have the vowel-consonant pattern of CV. Study the words and the underlined syllables below. *me* *<u>be</u> long* *<u>ma</u> ple* *so* The words and the underlined syllables have the vowel-consonant pattern of ______________. Each of the above words and underlined syllables is a(n) ______________ syllable. (open, closed)

consonant phoneme silent	**26.** The first syllable of *sup pose* ends with a ________________ phoneme. The second syllable of *sup pose* is not an open syllable because it does not end with a vowel ________________. The last letter is a vowel, but it (letter, phoneme) is ________________.
yes *ē* CV no *r*	**27.** Is the first syllable of *fe ver* an open syllable? ________________ What key symbol represents the final phoneme of the first syllable? ____________ The first syllable in *fe ver* has the vowel-consonant pattern of ____________. Is the second syllable an open syllable? ________________ What key symbol represents the final phoneme? ________________
  long	**28.** Study these words: *hel lo* *be* *me ter* *ti ger* The underlined vowels represent their ________________ sounds. (long, short)
  fā, hē, sī, tō, hū **open** **long (or glided)** **CV**	**29.** In the words below, place a macron above each vowel (*a, e, i, o, u*) that represents its long (or glided) sound. *fa vor* *he* *si lent* *to tal* *hu man* We might generalize: **A single vowel in an ________________ syllable often represents its ________________ sound. The vowel-consonant pattern for an open syllable is ____________.**
  shē, bē long, dī graph, hā lō, hel lō, do	**30.** Study the words below. Draw lines under the single vowels in the open syllables. Place macrons above those vowels you underlined that represent long sounds. Work carefully. You may find exceptions. *she* *be long* *di graph* *ha lo* *hel lo* *do*
e open	**31.** Although the *a* in *about* and the ____________ in *debate* are single vowel letters in ________________ syllables, they do not represent long sounds. (closed, open) **We tend to shorten the vowel sounds in unaccented syllables.**

long (glided)	**32.** The generalization has more application when we limit it to accented syllables: A single vowel in an open accented syllable usually represents its ____________ sound. We will study this more fully later.
lō *lō*	**33.** We should note, however, that sometimes single vowel letters in open unaccented syllables do represent the long sounds. Consider these words: *so' lo* *ha' lo* Two syllables from these words that illustrate this are ________ from *solo* and ________ from *halo.* Mark the vowels in these unaccented syllables.
<u>*pa*</u> *pa,* <u>*to*</u>	**34.** We should also note that not all vowels in open accented syllables represent long sounds. (Exceptions, exceptions!) In the words below, underline the syllables that are exceptions to the generalization: **Single vowel letters in open accented syllables usually represent their long sounds.** *no* *pa' pa* *to* *she*
short no long, silent	**35.** We will now consider long vowel exceptions to the closed syllable generalization. We expect that single vowels in closed syllables—the CVC and VC patterns—will usually represent ____________ sounds. (long, short) Do the words below follow the closed syllable generalization? ________ *sight* *high* *right* *sigh* **An exception to the closed syllable generalization is found in words in which the *i* is followed by *gh*.** The *i* represents the ____________ sound and the *gh* is ____________ (long, short) in such words.
ld	**36.** The words below represent another exception to the closed syllable generalization. *child* *wild* *mild* *sold* *told* *hold* We can summarize: **When *i* or *o* is followed by ____________, the vowel usually represents the long sound.**

closed closed open phoneme	**37.** Let us review. Syllables with the CVC pattern are ________ (closed, open) syllables; those with the VC pattern (such as *ant*) are ________ (closed, open) syllables. Syllables that have the CV pattern are ________ (closed, open) syllables. An open syllable ends with a vowel ________. (phoneme, letter)
a, e, i, o, u	**38.** The previous frames in this section contain examples of the five vowels, ______, ______, ______, ______, and ______, in which they represent their long sounds.
vowel	**39.** We have learned that the vowel *w* always appears with another __________ letter. Therefore, there would be no instances in which we could apply the single-vowel open syllable generalization to the *w.*

BOX 3.2

The Extra E

Exception words such as *gone* and *done,* which we expect to be pronounced with a long *o,* are a consequence of the quirky way in which the English spelling system developed. Before the 14th century, the final *e* represented an "uh" that was pronounced at the end of words. To get a sense of how contemporary words would sound with a final "uh," say *gone* and *done,* and then add an extra "uh" to the end—"gonuh" and "donuh." Sometime around the 14th century, the "uh" was dropped from pronunciation, and the final *e* became the silent letter in words spelled with the VCe pattern.

Then something curious happened. For some unknown reason, the early writers began to attach a final *e* to short vowel words that ended in a consonant letter. The writers usually doubled the final consonant, suggesting that they knew that the final *e* in the VCe pattern signaled that the preceding vowel is long. Put into a contemporary context, the word *pit* might be spelled *pitte,* and *pin* as *pinne.*

For some time, English spelling was cluttered with extra consonants and final *e*s. Spelling was eventually untangled in the 17th century when the practice of adding an extra *e* to the end of short vowel words was discontinued. However, some of the words from this earlier period still continue to be spelled with the unnecessary final *e,* which is the reason we have words such as *gone* and *done* in our English language dictionary today.

Study Guide

Long Vowels

Long Vowel	Key Symbol	Key Word
a	*ā*	*apron*
e	*ē*	*eraser*
i	*ī*	*ice*
o	*ō*	*overalls*
u	*ū*	*unicorn*

Macron (-) The macron (-) is the diacritical mark used to indicate the specific pronunciations of the long vowels. *Glided* is another term that refers to the long vowel phonemes.

Long ū Some dictionaries are now using the *(y)*$\overline{oo}$ to indicate the *ū*. Some teachers' manuals use two symbols to indicate the *ū*—the *y*$\overline{oo}$ for the *ū* in *unicorn* and *cube,* and $\overline{oo}$ for the *ū* in *tune* and *true.*

VCe Pattern When a word or an accented syllable has two vowels, one of which is a final *e,* the *e* is silent and the first vowel usually represents the long (glided) sound (*ape, hope*).

o Pronounced as "uh" Exception to the VCe Pattern Words do not follow the VCe generalization when the vowel letter *o* is pronounced like the "uh" in the words *done* and *come.*

Open Syllable An open syllable ends with a vowel phoneme (*be, try*). Single vowel letters in open, accented syllables usually represent their long (glided) sounds (*she*).

Unaccented Syllables We tend to shorten vowel sounds in unaccented syllables (*a bout'*).

CV Pattern The CV pattern is an open syllable in which the vowel usually represents its long sound (*be, tree*).

Yy as a Vowel When *y* is the final letter in a one-syllable word (*my*), it usually represents the sound we associate with long *i* (key word: *ice*). When *y* is the final letter in a two-syllable word (*happy*), it usually represents the long sound of *e* (key word: *eraser*).

igh Exception to the Closed Syllable Generalization When the *i* is followed by *gh* in a word or a syllable, the *i* usually represents the long sound and the *gh* is silent (*light*).

i or o Followed by ld Exception to the Closed Syllable Generalization When *i* or *o* is followed by *ld,* the vowel usually represents the long sound (*wild, fold*).

	40. Let us examine the generalization with respect to the vowel *y*. Look at the words below. Rewrite these words. Use the key symbol we associate with each vowel and consonant phoneme.
bī, mī, whī, flī, krī	*by my why fly cry*
	In each instance the *y* represents the phoneme we associate with the key
ī	symbol ___________.
CV	The vowel-consonant pattern for these words is ___________.
	41. Study the words below, and then complete the generalization:
	When y is the final letter of a two-syllable word, it
long, *e*	**represents the ___________ sound of ___________.**
	happy lucky baby windy
	42. *Y* is not always the final letter in a word. Study the words below. Rewrite them to show the pronunciations of the consonants and of the vowels representing the long sounds.
bī pas, sī pres, pī thon	*by pass* ___________ *cy press* ___________ *py thon* ___________
	43. If *y* represents the long sound of the *e* when it is the final and only vowel in the last syllable of a multisyllabic word, then the open syllable generalization we have been studying applies to *a, e, i, o, u,* and *y.*
cry	The *y* would represent the sound of the long *i* in ______________ and the (*cry, happy*)
lucky	long *e* in ______________ . (*my, lucky*)
A single vowel in an open accented syllable often represents its long sound.	**44.** State the generalization that concerns a single vowel in an open accented syllable.

Review 15

1. We have been studying five phonemes that represent the long sounds of the vowels: *ā*, __________, __________, __________, __________. We can show the pronunciation of each vowel by placing a ____________ (name of diacritical mark) over it.
2. *Y* can represent a long sound also, but it does not have a key symbol: It is a duplication of either the long ____________ (as in *cry*) or the long ____________ (as in *lucky*).
3. We have learned to recognize two patterns that may give clues as to the vowel sound in an unknown word. One is the vowel-consonant-silent ____________ pattern (VCe). State the generalization: ______________.
4. The other is a single-vowel, open syllable pattern: The single vowel in an open, ____________ syllable is often ____________.
5. Another way we can state the same generalization is: When the only vowel in a word or accented syllable comes at the ____________ of the syllable, that vowel usually represents its ____________ sound.
6. The long sounds of the vowels are easiest to recognize in known words because the name of each vowel is the same as the ____________ it represents.
7. Pronounce each of the words below.

   dine *tack* *way* *watch*
   table *go* *tight* *enough*

   a. Place a C above each word that ends with a consonant phoneme.
   b. Place a V above each word that ends with a vowel phoneme.
   c. Indicate the pronunciation of the final phoneme by writing the key symbol. If the word ends with a consonant blend, use only the symbol that represents the final phoneme in the blend.
   d. Underline the words in which the final syllable is an open syllable.
8. We are studying the vowel phonemes that are represented by single letters. We have learned to associate 10 of the 19 vowel phonemes with their key pronunciation symbols. Mark the following vowel graphemes to indicate their pronunciations.

   bite *bit* *can* *cane* *pet* *Pete* *us* *fuse* *mop* *mope*

See the Answers to the Reviews section for the answers to Review 15, page 235.

Schwa (ə)

---

a ə *comma*
e ə *chicken*
i ə *family*
o ə *melon*
u ə *circus*

a, e, i, o, u

1. Say the words at the right aloud. Listen to the phoneme represented by the underlined letter. When you say the words slowly and distinctly (and artificially), they may sound quite different from one another, but when these words are used in ordinary speech, the underlined part represents a very soft "uh."

1	2	3
______	ə	*comma*
______	ə	*chicken*
______	ə	*family*
______	ə	*melon*
______	ə	*circus*

The letters that represent the "uh" sound in the words at the right are ______, ______, ______, ______, ______. Place them properly in column 1.

ə

2. Dictionaries usually indicate the soft vowel sound found in unaccented syllables with a **schwa** (ə).

The pronunciation is shown by the sign ____________ (an inverted *e*).

---

blend

3. How is the word *schwa* pronounced? The *sch* grapheme in *schwa* represents the phoneme we associate with the key symbol *sh.*

The *sh* and the consonant *w* form a ______________ (digraph, blend). The *a* represents an "ah" sound.

---

commə, chickən, gerbəl
melən, circəs

4. Rewrite each of the words below to show the pronunciation of the vowel in the **unaccented** syllable.

com' ma ________ *chick' en* ________ *ger' bil* ________

mel' on ________ *cir' cus* ________

Without the schwa, each of these vowels would need a separate diacritical mark.

---

bā' kən

5. **The schwa is used to indicate the pronunciation of the vowel phoneme in many unaccented syllables.**

Study the word below. Rewrite it, indicating the sound of each letter.

ba' con ______________

---

pĕn səl, lī ən, sĕk ənd, pī lət

a, e, i, o, u

6. Say the words below in a natural manner. Rewrite them, using key symbols to indicate each of the phonemes.

pencil *lion* *second* *pilot*

Check the vowels that can represent the schwa phoneme:

a *e* *i* *o* *u*

unaccented	**7.** The use of the schwa for each vowel that represents the short "uh" sound, along with the frequent use of the short *i* (i), has simplified pronunciation keys greatly. Almost all vowels in ________________ (accented, unaccented) syllables represent one of these two short, soft sounds.
ə *i*	**8.** Let us examine the words *distant* and *village.* The dictionary may indicate the pronunciations as dĭs′ tənt and vĭl′ ĭj. The ________________ and the ________________ indicate the two soft phonemes regardless of spelling.
facet, sicken *banquet, melon*	**9.** The following words are written to show their pronunciations. What are the words? *făs′ ĭt* ____________ *sĭk′ ən* ____________ *băng′ kwĭt* ____________ *mĕl′ ən* ____________
vegetable, postage	**10.** Examine the words below. They are written the way they might appear in your dictionary. What are the words? *vĕj′ tə bəl* ________________ *pōst ĭj* ________________ Note that we pronounce the syllable *ble* as though a very short vowel precedes the *l: bəl.*
er *tī gər*	**11.** Although the word part *er* has only a touch of a vowel sound, the schwa is used with the *r* to indicate the pronunciation of the word part __________. Thus the key symbols for *tiger* are _____________. (Check your dictionary to see how it treats this word part.)
stā′ bəl, mī′ nəs *bal′ ət, dĭf′ ər*	**12.** Rewrite the words below to show pronunciation. Omit the silent letters. *stā′ ble* __________ *mi′ nus* __________ *bal′ lot* __________ *dif′ fer* __________
sō′ fə, plĕzh′ ər *kwĭv′ ər, frē′ kwənt* *kō′ kō, drə mat′ ik*	**13.** Are you ready to code some more difficult words? Rewrite the words below to show pronunciation. They should be written as they might appear in parentheses following the boldface entry word in the dictionary. To avoid artificial pronunciation, check each one by saying it in a sentence. *so′ fa* __________ *pleas′ ure* __________ *quiv′ er* __________ *fre′ quent* __________ *co′ coa* __________ *dra mat′ ic* __________

Study Guide

Schwa

Vowel in an Unaccented Syllable	Key Symbol	Key Word
a	ə	*comma* (soft "uh")
e	ə	*chicken* (soft "uh")
i	ə	*family* (soft "uh")
o	ə	*melon* (soft "uh")
u	ə	*circus* (soft "uh")

Vowels in Unaccented Syllables The vowels in unaccented syllables can reasonably be expected to represent a soft "uh," or the sound we associate with an unglided (short) *ĭ*.

Schwa The dictionary uses a schwa (ə) to indicate the soft "uh" sound found in many unaccented syllables. Without the schwa (ə), the vowels that represent the soft "uh" in unaccented syllables would each need a separate diacritical mark to indicate pronunciation.

Short ĭ The vowels in unaccented syllables may also represent the unglided (short) *ĭ*, such as in *manage* (*măn′ ĭj*). The vowels in unaccented syllables represent the soft "uh," the schwa, more often than the short *ĭ*.

sĭm′ fə nē (or *nĭ*), *lej′ ə bəl* *dĭf′ ə kŭlt (or dĭf′ ĭ kŭlt),* *ăn tēk′*	**14.** Rewrite the words below to show pronunciation. They should be written as they might appear in parentheses following the boldface entry word in the dictionary. To avoid artificial pronunciation, check each one by saying it in a sentence. *sym′ pho ny* ____________ *leg′ i ble* ____________ *dif′ fi cult* ____________ *an tique′* ____________
short *i*	**15.** The first vowel in *decay* represents the __________ phoneme. This use represents the trend toward simplification. It is not *e*. Try it in a sentence to check this. Now try it using *i* as a guide in pronouncing the first syllable.
hăp′ ən (or *hap′ ən*)	**16.** It is necessary to note that various dictionaries indicate pronunciation in different ways. We must study the pronunciation key of the particular dictionary we use. For example, many dictionaries indicate the pronunciations of all short sounds with the letter and no diacritical mark. The pronunciation of *happen* is written ____________.

village, pilot	**17.** Let us review. We have learned that a vowel grapheme in an unaccented syllable could reasonably be expected to represent the sound we associate with the unglided *i* (short *i*) or with the sound represented by the schwa (ə). The *i* would identify the vowel phonemes in the last syllable of ______________. The ə would identify the last syllable of ______________. *(candy, program, village, hotel)* *(pilot, locate, liquid, railroad)*

Review 16

1. The key symbol used to represent many of the vowel phonemes in unaccented syllables is called a ______________ (ə).
2. This symbol is very useful because ______________.
3. The ə*r* is used to indicate the pronunciation of a word part in ______________. (river, erase)
4. The words below are written to show their pronunciations. How are they correctly spelled?

   rē′ gəl   *hănd mād′*   *sĕl′ ə brāt*   *ĕp′ ə sōd*

See the Answers to the Reviews section for the answers to Review 16, page 235.

Other Single Vowels

five schwa, phoneme	**1.** Thus far we have identified 11 vowel phonemes using only ______________ (How many?) vowel letters and a ______________. We can readily tell which ______________ (letter, phoneme) is represented when diacritical marks are used, as in a dictionary, glossary, or other pronunciation guide.
short (unglided)	**2.** We also have examined patterns common to the English language so that we can make a reasonable guess as to the sound of certain vowels. For example, we expect the vowel letter in the pattern CVC to represent its ______________ sound.
apple	**3.** If the vowel in the CVC pattern is *a,* then we would expect *a* to represent the same sound as the vowel phoneme heard in ______________. *(said, car, ball, apple, date, saw)*
glided (long), silent	**4.** We expect the first vowel grapheme in the ending pattern VCe to represent its ______________ sound and the final *e* to be ______________.

---

sew

5. If the first vowel grapheme in the VCe ending pattern is an *o,* then we would expect *o* to represent the same vowel phoneme as that heard in

____________________.
(done, gone, boy, sew)

---

schwa
sofa

6. A vowel in an unaccented syllable could reasonably be expected to represent the sound we associate with the unglided (short) *i* or with the _______________. The ə would identify the vowel phoneme in the last syllable of ____________________ .
(sofa, remit, require, insect)

---

a ä father
a ô ball
a â care
u û fur

graphemes

7. There are still other single-vowel phonemes, as shown in the words at right. Some are influenced by the consonant following the vowel. We will identify these vowel phonemes and suggest a key word by which each can be remembered. However, we commonly use the pronunciation key given in the pronunciation guide of the dictionary for these more difficult phonemes. Each of these phonemes is represented by a variety of spellings—in other words, by a variety of ________________.
(phonemes, graphemes)

1	2	3
a	_____	*father* (*fäthər*)
a	_____	*ball* (*bôl*)
a	_____	*care* (*câre*)
u	_____	*fur* (*fûr*)

Complete the table by filling in the key symbols (2).

We have noted that various dictionaries use different ways to indicate pronunciation. Check the pronunciation guide in your dictionary for key symbols.

---

graphemes (or spellings)

8. Let us begin with the *ä* phoneme. The phoneme that we will identify with the key symbol *ä* and the key word *father* may be confusing because of regional differences in pronunciation. It is represented by many different letters and combinations of letters.

Dictionaries reveal anywhere from 3 to 11 different ______________ that represent this phoneme.

ä

9. Pronounce the words below. If you do not hear the same vowel phoneme as in *father,* your pronunciation reflects a regional difference. You are not wrong.

arm *calm* *hearth* *sergeant* *bazaar*

Now pronounce each word so you can hear the phoneme we represent by the key symbol _________ in each one.

---

a, al, ea, e, aa

10. In the words below, underline the graphemes that represent the phoneme we identify with the key symbol *ä*. Include the silent letters that could be considered a part of the grapheme.

arm *calm* *hearth* *sergeant* *bazaar*

Answers	Frames
fär, täkō, pläzə *käm, gärd, därk*	**11.** If you cannot agree with the pronunciation for each word, use your dictionary. Your pronunciation may reflect that of your region. Use the key symbols to show the pronunciations of these words: *far* ________ *taco* ________ *plaza* ________ *calm* ________ *guard* ________ *dark* ________
r *far, guard, dark*	**12.** Study the vowel phoneme in the word *far.* We can barely separate it from the following consonant phoneme, so we call it a(n) ________ -controlled (*r, l, w*) vowel. Which words in frame 11 include an *r*-controlled vowel? ____________
raw, caught, walk, broad, *fought, tall, coffee*	**13.** Pronounce *ball.* Listen to the vowel phoneme. We will represent this phoneme with the key symbol *ô.* Say the words below. Check those in which you hear the phoneme heard in *ball.* *raw* *caught* *walk* *broad* *bead* *fought* *tall* *coffee* Some of the answers here may also be affected by regional variations in pronunciation. Check your dictionary.
aw, au, al, oa, ou, a, o	**14.** What graphemes in the frame above represent the vowel phoneme heard in *ball?* ______ ______ ______ ______ ______ ______ ______
rô, kôt, wôk, brôd *bēd, fôt, tôl, kôfē*	**15.** Rewrite the words in frame 13, using key symbols to indicate pronunciation. ________ ________ ________ ________ ________ ________ ________ ________
ball *sô, kôl*	**16.** Pronounce *saw.* The *a* represents the vowel phoneme in ________. (*ball, sat*) When *a* is followed by an *l* or *w* in the same syllable, the *a* may represent the sound we associate with the key symbol *ô.* Rewrite the words below to show pronunciation. *saw* ________ *call* ________
shawl, small *false, drawn*	**17.** These words are written to show their pronunciations. What are the words? *shôl* ________ *smôl* ________ *fôls* ________ *drôn* ________

short, port, sport *o* *r, ôr*	**18.** Now let us consider the *r*-controlled *ô*. Say the words below. Check those in which you hear the *r*-controlled *ô* (*ôr*). *short* *shot* *pot* *port* *spot* *sport* The *r*-controlled vowel in these words consists of the letter ______ followed by the letter ______ (*or*). Write *or* to show pronunciation. ______
kôrəs, skôr, shärk *pôrch, bôrdər, krangk*	**19.** Write the words below to show pronunciation. *chorus* ________ *score* ________ *shark* ________ *porch* ________ *border* ________ *crank* ________
crank	**20.** The word in frame 19 that does not contain an *r*-controlled vowel is ________.
yes six	**21.** Now let's examine the vowel phoneme in the chair key word *care.* The key symbol we use to represent this phoneme is *â.* Study the words below. Pronounce each word aloud. Is the vowel phoneme the same in each word? ______ *chair* *share* *their* *there* *bear* *prayer* In these examples, one vowel phoneme is represented by __________ (How many?) graphemes.
ai, a, ei, ea, ay	**22.** In each word below, underline the grapheme that represents the same vowel phoneme heard in *care.* The graphemes represent vowel phonemes, so do not underline the controlling consonants. *chair* *share* *their* *bear* *prayer* You can see that our table in frame 7 is greatly oversimplified. Column 1 should show the six graphemes that, when followed by *r,* represent the vowel phoneme we hear in *care.*
kôr, whâr, fârē *shâr, hâr, bär*	**23.** Rewrite the words below, using the key symbols to indicate the pronunciations of consonants and vowels. Omit silent letters. *core* ________ *where* ________ *fairy* ________ *share* ________ *hair* ________ *bar* ________

  air, anchor, square *pile, scarce, chair* *race, civic, their or there*	**24.** The following words are written as they would appear in a dictionary to show pronunciation. Spell them correctly. *âr* ________ *ăng′ kər* ________ *skwâr* ________ *pīl* ________ *skârs* ________ *châr* ________ *rās* ________ *sĭv′ĭk* ________ *ŧħâr* ________ You can interpret the dictionary code!
 r *i, e, ea, o, u, y*	**25.** Another *r*-controlled vowel phoneme is that heard in *fur.* In fact, it is impossible to separate the vowel phoneme from the ________. What graphemes represent the vowel phoneme heard in *fur* as shown by the words below? Underline each one, taking care to identify only the vowel. *thirst* *germ* *learn* *worm* *purple* *myrtle*
 thûrst, jûrm, lûrn *wûrm, pûrpəl, mûrtəl*	**26.** Rewrite the words in frame 25, using the *û* to show pronunciation. ________ ________ ________ ________ ________ ________
 several different *fur*	**27.** The phoneme that we associate with the key symbol *û* may be represented by ______________________ grapheme(s). Its key word (only one, several different) is ____________.
     wûrkər, wûrkt, snâr	**28.** Note that this phoneme is not the same as that heard in the unaccented syllable of a two-or-more-syllable word, as in *lemon* (*lĕm* ə*n*), or the phoneme heard in a suffix, generally a separate syllable, as in *farmer* (*färm* ə*r*) and *smaller* (*smôl* ə*r*). Rewrite the following words to show pronunciation. *worker* ________ *worked* ________ *snare* ________
kärnāshən, bärnyärd, bâr *pârənt, kāk, hûrt*	**29.** Rewrite these words to show pronunciation. *carnation* ________ *barnyard* ________ *bear* ________ *parent* ________ *cake* ________ *hurt* ________

	30. There are two broad generalizations that may be of some help in determining the pronunciations of these single vowels in unknown words.
	If the only vowel letter in a word or syllable is followed by *r*, the vowel will be affected by that *r*.
	Say the words below.
	car *serve* *curl* *first* *corn* *hair*
short	The vowel sounds are neither long nor ___________. They are almost lost in
r	the consonant letter __________.
precedes	**31.** A vowel ________________ (precedes, follows) the letter *r* in the words in frame 30. Some
	teachers' manuals use *Vr* (Vowel-*r*) to represent this pattern and use the term ***r*-controlled** when referring to this sequence.
	32. Your teacher's manual may indicate five *r*-controlled vowels: the *ar* as in
er, ir, or	*farm*, the _____ as in *her,* the _____ as in *stir,* the _____ as in *shore*, and the
ur	_____ as in *fur.* Write these words using key symbols to show pronunciation.
färm, hûr, stûr	*farm* _________ *her* _________ *stir* _________
shôr, fûr	*shore* _________ *fur* _________
three	The five *r*-controlled vowels represent only ___________ (How many?) pronunciations.
câre	For our study, we acknowledge that *âr,* key word _________ , is an *r*-controlled vowel. Check your teacher's manual to determine the *r*-controlled vowels it identifies for instruction.
	33. Here is another helpful generalization:
	If the only vowel in a word or syllable is followed by *l* or *w*, the vowel will be affected by that *l* or *w*.
	Study the words below.
	draw *saw* *late* *fall* *small* *shawl*
late	Which word does not belong in the list? _________
no	Do any of the others represent the long or short sound of *a*? _________
yes	Does the *a* followed by *l* represent the same sound as the *a* followed *w*? _____
	Again, regional variations in the pronunciations of these words may cause you some difficulty.

Study Guide

Other Single Vowels

Vowel Letter	Key Symbol	Key Word
a	*â*	*care*
u	*û*	*fur*
a	*ä*	*father*
a	*ô*	*ball*

R-Controlled Vowels When the only vowel letter in a word or syllable is followed by *r,* the vowel will be affected by that *r.* When pronouncing a vowel followed by the *r,* the vowel phoneme is almost lost in the consonant.

R-Controlled â(r) It is impossible to separate, in normal pronunciation, the /*â*/ from the /*r*/. Six graphemes represent the *â* when followed by *r: care, hair, heir, wear, where,* and *prayer.*

R-Controlled û(r) It is impossible to separate, in normal pronunciation, the /*û*/ from the /*r*/. Several graphemes represent the *û(r),* as we see in the words *first, germ, learn, worm, purple,* and *myrtle.*

R-Controlled ä(r) The *a,* when preceding the letter *r,* represents an *r*-controlled vowel. Examples of the *r*-controlled *a,* pronounced as /*är*/, may be heard in the words *arm, yard, arch,* and *large.* This phoneme may also be spelled with the *ea* grapheme, as in *hearth,* and the *er,* as in *sergeant.*

R-Controlled ô(r) The *o,* when preceding the letter *r,* represents an *r*-controlled vowel. Examples of the *r*-controlled *o,* pronounced as /*ôr*/, may be heard in the words *more, court,* and *order.*

ä The *ä,* key word *father,* does not always precede the letter *r* in English words. Several graphemes represent the *ä,* as shown in the words *calm, cot, shah,* and *bazaar.*

ô The *ô,* key word *ball,* is heard in *caught* and *broad.* Several graphemes represent the *ô,* as shown in the words *saw, caught, walk, broad, fought,* and *coffee.*

a Before l or w (ô) When the letter *a* is the only vowel in a word or syllable and precedes the letter *l* or the letter *w,* the *a* is affected by the *l* or *w* and is pronounced /*ô*/. Notice the difference in the phonemes that the letter *a* represents in *bald* (*bôld*) and *bad* (*băd*) and in *jaw* (*jô*) and *jam* (*jăm*). Examples include *call, almost, talk, draw, awful,* and *shawl.*

Review 17

1. We have been studying the vowel phonemes that can be represented by single-vowel key symbols. The first group of five (example, apple) we labeled the ________________ vowel phonemes. Write their key symbols: ________________
2. The second group of five (example, *ice*) we labeled ______________ vowel phonemes. Write their key symbols: ______________

3. The third (example, *comma*) was given a key symbol not in the alphabet, called the ______________. This key symbol, ______________ , represents each of the vowels when it has the sound heard in ______________.
(happy, agree)
It is very useful because ______________.

4. That left us with four additional single vowel phonemes, which cannot be grouped except for how they are influenced by the phoneme ______________
(following, preceding)
the vowel. We found that they were affected by phonemes represented by the ______________, ______________, and ______________.

5. The key words for these vowel phonemes can be placed in the following sentences. Fill in the blanks and mark the vowels.
   a. She hit the ______________ over the fence.
   b. The kitten has soft, fluffy ______________.
   c. Tom's ______________ will take Tom on a fishing trip next Saturday.
   d. The mother dog takes good ______________ of her puppies.

See the Answers to the Reviews section for the answers to Review 17, page 236.

Diphthongs

consonant *l*	**1.** We have been studying the vowel phonemes that are represented by single-vowel letters. We will now turn our attention to those that are represented by combinations of letters. Say *oil.* The word *oil* is composed of two phonemes: one vowel and one ______________. They are represented by the graphemes *oi* and ______________.
diphthongs	**2.** The *oi* functions as one phoneme called a **diphthong.** **A diphthong is a single-vowel phoneme, represented by two letters, resembling a glide from one sound to another.** A study of **phonetics** (the science of speech sounds) would show that many single-letter vowels are actually diphthongs. They represent more than a single sound. Note the gliding sound of the *u* in *use.* You may be using "glided" rather than "long" for this vowel phoneme. We will call only the two-letter gliding combinations ______________.

diphthong	**3.** In this study, we have made the arbitrary statement that there are 44 phonemes. It really is not that simple! Say *few.* Is the vowel phoneme equivalent to the phoneme heard at the beginning of *use,* or should we consider *ew* a separate diphthong, not a duplication of any single-vowel phoneme? Our decision is to consider that *few* = *fū*. So we will **not** call *ew* a __________.
oi *ou*	**4.** It seems most helpful to classify only two of the vowel phonemes as diphthongs. These are the vowel sounds heard in *oil* and *house.* The ________ and the ________ then represent 2 of the 44 speech sounds in our language.
boil, boy, coin *enjoy, toy* *oi, oy*	**5.** Examine the words below. Underline the grapheme in each word that represents the diphthong *oi.* *boil* *boy* *coin* *enjoy* *toy* There are two spellings that represent this diphthong: ______ and ______.
boil, boi, koin, ĕnjoi, toi *oi*	**6.** Rewrite the five words in frame 5 using the marks of pronunciation (the diacritical marks). __________ __________ __________ __________ __________ The key word for this diphthong is *oil,* the key symbol ______________.
house, brown, cow *mouse, blouse, owl* *ou, ow*	**7.** The second diphthong is that heard in the key word *house.* The key symbol is *ou.* Read the words below. Underline the diphthongs. *house* *brown* *cow* *mouse* *blouse* *owl* This diphthong is also represented by two spellings: the _____ and the _____.
oi, oy *oi* *oil* *ou, ow* *ou* *house*	**8.** Complete the table at the right with the two spellings of each diphthong (1), key symbols (2), and key words (3). **1** / **2** / **3** *oi,* _______ / *oi* / _______ _______, _______ / _______ / *house*
ou *kloun*	**9.** The key symbol for the vowel phoneme heard in *clown* is _________. Rewrite *clown* to show its pronunciation. ________________

two, two two zero, *ou, oi*	**10.** We are recognizing ________ (How many?) diphthongs. Each has ________ (How many?) spellings. The key symbol for each diphthong is composed of ________ (How many?) letters with with ________ (How many) diacritical marks. These letters will be either ______ (*ou, ow*) or ______ (*oi, oy*) because they are the **key** symbols. We find them used in most dictionaries for pronunciation purposes.
  koi, noiz, broil snō, kou snow	**11.** Study the words below. Rewrite them using key symbols to indicate the pronunciations of all the phonemes. Underline the diphthongs. *coy* ________ *noise* ________ *broil* ________ *snow* ________ *cow* ________ There is no diphthong in ____________.
   powder, proud, how, soil	**12.** Underline the diphthongs in the following words. Work with care. The *ou* and *ow* often represent other phonemes. Be sure you underline only those that have the vowel phonemes found in *oil* and *house.* *powder* *proud* *course* *how* *soil* *courage* *gracious*
 short	**13.** The *-ous* ending, as in *gracious,* is more likely to represent the phonemes we associate with the key symbols __________ (long, short) *u* and *s* (or the schwa and *s*) than with the diphthong *ou* and the *s.* If we do not have the word in our speaking vocabulary, however, it is difficult to determine whether the *ou* (*ow*) is a diphthong.

Review 18

1. Two of the 44 phonemes are classified as diphthongs. What are the key symbols of these two diphthongs? ____________ ____________
2. The diphthongs are ____________ (vowel, consonant) phonemes.
3. Copy each of the following words that contains a diphthong, and write the key symbol of the diphthong following it.

   cough *owl* *grow* *cow* *through* *moist* *oyster*
4. Use key symbols to show the pronunciation of each of the following words; omit silent letters and underline diphthongs.

   house *boy* *ounce* *enjoy* *noise* *brow*

See the Answers to the Reviews section for the answers to Review 18, page 236.

Vowel Digraphs

two one	o͞o *(food)* o͝o *(hook)* **1.** The second category of phonemes represented by two-letter vowels is that of the **vowel digraph.** A digraph is a _______-letter grapheme that represents _______ phoneme(s).
two digraph	**2.** Listen to the vowel sound as you pronounce *food* aloud. Separate the phonemes as you pronounce *food* again: /f/ /oo/ /d/. Say the vowel phoneme aloud. The key symbol we use to identify the vowel sound heard in *food* is o͞o. This is a _______-letter vowel grapheme representing a single phoneme. We call it a vowel ____________.
o͞o, o͞o, ō ō o͞o, ŭ, o͞o ō, ōə or ōĭ, ō	**3.** Write the key symbol to indicate the pronunciations of the vowels in each of the following words. Omit silent letters. Work carefully. *school* _________ *broom* _________ *rowboat* _________ *soon* _________ *flood* _________ *through* _________ *so* _________ *poet* _________ *though* _________
no no *flood*	**4.** Does o͞o represent the same phoneme as ō? _______ When we see *oo* in a word, can we be sure that it has the sound heard in *food?* _______ The word _______________ in frame 3 contains two *o*s but has the sound of a short *u.*
no *through*	**5.** Is the sound indicated by the key symbol o͞o always spelled with two *o*s? _______ Which word in frame 3 contains /o͞o/ but is not spelled with two *o*s? ___________
ou, o͞o, o͞o ō, o͞o, o͞o o͞o, o͞o, *oi* ā, o͞o, o͞o	**6.** Examine the following words carefully. On the line following each, write the key symbol that represents its vowel pair. *mouse* _________ *cool* _________ *kangaroo* _________ *dough* _________ *drew* _________ *due* _________ *glue* _________ *moon* _________ *coil* _________ *main* _________ *soup* _________ *cartoon* _________

Answers	Frames
yes, no breve	**7.** A second digraph that cannot be represented by a single letter is found in the word *hook.* Pronounce *food* and then *hook.* Pronounce the vowel phoneme in each word. Are they spelled the same? ______ Do they sound alike? ______ Since the key symbol for the sound heard in *food* is two *o*s covered by an elongated macron (o͞o), it is logical to represent the short phoneme heard in *hook* with an elongated ________________ over the two *o*s (o͝o).
oo o͞o *food* oo o͝o *hook*	**8.** **A vowel digraph is a two-letter grapheme that represents one vowel phoneme.** Complete the table at the right with the most common spelling of each of each digraph (1), key symbol (2), and key word (3) for each digraph. **1** | **2** | **3** ____________ | o͞o | ____________ ____________ | o͝o | ____________
fo͝ot, go͞ose, to͝ok, lo͝ok, so͞on, po͞ol, wo͝od, to͞oth, lo͞om	**9.** Using *food* and *hook* as key words to aid you, mark the words below to show pronunciation. *foot goose took look soon pool wood tooth loom*
digraph no o͞o, o͝o	**10.** When we see the vowel ________________ *oo* in a word, can we be sure of the phoneme it represents? __________ The double-*o* is most likely to represent the __________ (o͞o, o͝o) in *food* or the __________ (o͞o, o͝o) in *hook.*
goose o͞o	**11.** When you see a double-*o* in an unknown word, the only clue to pronunciation is that it most often represents the o͞o as in ___________ (*goose, book*). You may wish to choose other key words to help you remember the phonemes. *Hook* serves as a good key word for the phoneme we represent by o͝o if we see a resemblance between an elongated breve and a hook! A mental image of the flat surface of a stool may help you remember that the key symbol ______ represents the sound heard in *sto͞ol* (or a *plāte* of *fo͞od!*).
blŭd, sto͝od, zo͞o *flŭd, dro͞op*	**12.** Not all *oo*s represent the sounds heard in *food* and *hook.* Rewrite the words below to show the correct pronunciation of each. *blood* _________ *stood* _________ *zoo* _________ *flood* _________ *droop* _________
phonemes consonant, vowel	**13.** The /o͞o/ and /o͝o/ represent 2 of the 44 ________________ of the American-English language. We now have identified all of the phonemes: 25 ___________ phonemes and 19 ___________ phonemes! However, we must study still another category of vowel combinations.

Review 19

1. What is a digraph?
2. What are the key symbols that identify each of the vowel digraphs?
3. When you see a double-*o* in an unknown word, how will you know what sound it represents?
4. Using key symbols, indicate the pronunciation of each of these words: *tooth, spoon, book, loose, stood, moo, shook.*
5. Show, through the use of key symbols, how you would expect this nonsense word to be pronounced: *clood.*
6. Write the symbols, consonants, and vowels to indicate the pronunciation of each of these words. Omit silent letters.

    boot, fudge, down, toy, shook, cocoa, night, fruit, throw, through, though, thought, quit, book, smooth, fool, breath, breathe, knight

See the Answers to the Reviews section for the answers to Review 19, page 236.

Other Vowel Pairs

grapheme phoneme /o͞o/ /o͝o/	**1.** A digraph is a ______________ composed of two letters that represent one ______________. The *oo* in *food* represents / /. The *oo* in *hook* represents / /.
diphthongs	**2.** We have a special name for the digraphs represented by a "gliding phoneme," as found in *mouse* and *toil.* They are called ______________.
one ā, ē, ā ē, ō, ā	**3.** Now examine the following words. Each has two vowels that represent ________ phoneme(s). What phoneme does each vowel pair represent? Be sure to use the diacritical mark to identify the phoneme. *rain* ________ *heat* ________ *fail* ________ *green* ________ *coat* ________ *say* ________

grapheme, phoneme long	**4.** Each of the words in frame 3 contains a vowel digraph: Each has a two-letter ________ that represents one ________; but each of these vowel pairs represents a sound already studied: the ________ sound (*long, short*) we associate with a single vowel letter. None of these pairs has a distinctive sound of its own. We will call them **vowel pairs** to distinguish them from the digraphs that represent distinctive sounds: o͞o and o͝o. It is important to note, however, that some teachers' manuals use the term **vowel digraph** or **vowel team** to identify two adjacent vowels that represent one long vowel phoneme, as in *feet, coal, nail,* and *leaf.*
rāi̸n three, *r, a, n*	**5.** We need to give further study to this large group of vowel pairs because they form one of the common patterns in the English language. First, examine the word *rain.* Underline the pair of vowels. Indicate the silent vowel by drawing a slash through it. Mark the long vowel. ________ *Rain* has ______ (How many?) phonemes represented by ______, long ______, and ______.
macron silent *tāi̸l, sāy̸, sēa̸t, fēe̸d, cōa̸t*	**6.** Study the words below. Underline the pair of vowels in each word. As you say each word, place a ________ (macron, breve) over the first vowel. Indicate that the second vowel is ________ by drawing a slash through it. *tail say seat feed coat*
long silent	**7.** **A syllable must have only one vowel phoneme.** Many syllables (and one-syllable words) have two vowel letters. Note the words below. *rain feed hue toe* In these cases, the first vowel represents its ________ sound and the second vowel is ________.
two **long** **silent**	**8.** We can make a generalization about the vowel pairs in the words you have studied: **When ________ vowels appear together in a syllable (or one-syllable word), the first usually represents its ________ sound and the second is ________.**

bēa̸ch, plāy̸, māi̸l, ēa̸ch	**9.** Mark each vowel in these words to show the pronunciation. *beach* *play* *mail* *each*
CVVC *i, e* *o, e* *o, a* *e, e*	**10.** Study the words below. The first two follow the pattern VCe, and the last two follow the pattern ________. Place the vowel that represents the long sound in the first column following the word and the silent letter in the second. *pine* ________ ________ *rose* ________ ________ *boat* ________ ________ *jeep* ________ ________
long **silent**	**11.** If the vowel pairs were as regular as those represented by the VCe ending pattern, we could form a generalization to include both types: **When there are two vowel letters in a word or syllable,** **the first usually represents its ________ sound** **and the second is ________.**
diphthong	**12.** The generalization does not apply to *boil* because *oi* is a ________. It has a distinctive sound of its own.
digraph *bro͝ok*	**13.** The generalization does not apply to *brook* because *oo* is a ________ with a distinctive sound. Use the diacritical mark to show pronunciation. ________
sounded	**14.** If the only exceptions to the "first-vowel-long" generalization were the diphthongs and the double-*o* digraphs, we might consider them "phonemes represented by single letters," because in each case only one of the letters is ________. (silent, sounded)
no *pail, toe, snow*	**15.** Study the words below. Can we depend on the "first-vowel-long" generalization for all but vowel diphthongs and double-*o* digraphs? ________ Check the words that follow this generalization: **When two vowels appear together in a word or syllable, the first may represent the long sound and the second is usually silent.** *pail* *said* *auto* *toe* *piece* *snow* *few*

Answers	Frames
i̸ē, i̸ē, i̸ē, e̸ā silent long	**16.** Place diacritical marks on the vowel pairs in the words below. *field* *believe* *niece* *great* In this set, the first vowel is ____________ and the second represents the ____________ sound.
ai, oa, ee, ea, ay	**17.** Although it is true that more words fall under the "first-vowel-long" generalization than any other, there are many exceptions. It can only be used as a clue to the possible pronunciation of a word. However, there are some pairs that follow the generalization more consistently than others. Those that are most consistent appear in these words: *rain, boat, keep, each, play.* The pairs that follow the generalization a greater percentage of the time are ________, ________, ________, ________, ________.
sĕd, hĕd	**18.** However, even these are not without exception. One of the most common sets (*ai*) appears in said. Another pair, the *ea,* occurs in *head.* Rewrite *said* and *head* using diacritical marks to show pronunciation. *said* ____________ *head* ____________
nā bər, bâr *ôt, brĕd* *sô, pēs* *grōn, gro͞o* *lăf, oul* *fo͝ot, fēl*	**19.** Indicate the pronunciations of all the vowels and consonants in the words below by using the key symbols. A part of a dictionary key is given below to provide a bit of assistance. *neighbor* ________ *bear* ________ *ought* ________ *bread* ________ *saw* ________ *peace* ________ *grown* ________ *grew* ________ *laugh* ________ *owl* ________ *foot* ________ *feel* ________

Dictionary Key

â care ä father ô ball, order û fur

o͞o food o͝o hook

Answers	Frames
no *thro͞o, t̸hō, bou* *rŭf, kôf*	**20.** Examine the spellings of the words below. They look as though they should rhyme. Do they? ________ To show the inconsistencies in our language, indicate the pronunciations of all the graphemes in these words. *through* ________ *though* ________ *bough* ________ *rough* ________ *cough* ________

Study Guide

Diphthongs, Vowel Digraphs, and Other Vowel Pairs

Vowel Diphthongs

Diphthong	Key Symbol	Key Word
oi, oy	*oi*	*oil*
ou, ow	*ou*	*house*

A **diphthong** is a single vowel phoneme, represented by two letters, resembling a glide from one sound to another. Examples of vowel diphthongs include *coin, boy, mouse,* and *how.*

Vowel Digraphs

Vowel Digraph	Key Symbol	Key Word
oo	*o͞o*	*food*
oo	*o͝o*	*hook*

A **vowel digraph** is a two-letter grapheme that represents one vowel phoneme. The key symbol represents the sound heard in *food* and *school,* while the key symbol o͝o represents the sound heard in *hook* and *book.*

Other Vowel Pairs

Vowel Pair	Key Symbol	Key Word
ai (rain)	*ā*	*apron*
ay (play)	*ā*	*apron*
ea (each)	*ē*	*eraser*
ee (keep)	*ē*	*eraser*
oa (boat)	*ō*	*overalls*

When two vowels appear together in a word or syllable, the first may represent the long (glided) sound and the second is usually silent. Some vowel pairs follow the generalization more consistently than others. Pairs that are the most consistent appear in the words *rain, play, boat, each, keep,* and *pie.*

no	**21.** The words below seem to consist of rhyming couplets. Say the words in set 1 aloud; in set 2; set 3. Do they rhyme? ________________ Indicate the pronunciations of all the graphemes in these words. Work set by set.
	1 **2** **3**
brāk, brĕd, sho͞o	*break* __________ *bread* __________ *shoe* __________
frēk, bēd, tō	*freak* __________ *bead* __________ *toe* __________

no *kou, kōm, pād* *lō, tōōm, sĕd* *bŏm*	**22.** Do these sets consist of rhyming words? ________________ Show their pronunciations. **1** — *cow* ________ *low* ________ **2** — *comb* ________ *tomb* ________ *bomb* ________ **3** — *paid* ________ *said* ________
20: *though* 21: *freak, bead, toe* 22: *low, paid*	**23.** List the words in the last **three** frames (20–22) that follow the "first-vowel-long" generalization.
diphthong, digraph dictionary hearing	**24.** We have been working with words you know to help you to get a background. But in your reading, if you come across an unknown word with a two-vowel combination, you might first check for *ou, oi, oo,* and so forth to see if it might be a ________________ or a double-*o* ________________. Next, try the "first-vowel-long" generalization, since it is the most common. If that doesn't give you a clue, use your reference book, the ____________. For phonics to be of help, the word must be in your ____________ vocabulary. (writing, hearing)

Review 20

1. Many vowel pairs follow a pattern: a ________________ has a gliding sound as ______________ (key symbol) in *oil* and ______________ in ______________; a ______________ in which the ________________ represents the vowel sound in *food* and ________________ in ________________.
2. Then there are pairs that do not have distinguishing key symbols because they represent single vowels that already have key symbols—for example, *boat, lean, chain.* These words contain vowel pairs that often follow the generalization: ________________.
3. The vowels may be separated, as in the pattern VCe. What is the generalization?
4. A syllable may have more than one vowel ________________ but only one vowel ________________.

See the Answers to the Reviews section for the answers to Review 20, page 237.

Recap II

Answers	Frames
phonemes digraphs phonemes	**1.** We have been studying 44 ________________ (sound units) of the American-English language. The consonants fell into two groups: the 18 represented by single letters and the 7 ________________. The 19 vowel ________________ also fall into groups, 15 represented by single vowel letters and 4 by two-letter combinations.
short, long	**2.** We put our greatest emphasis on the five ___________ sounds (as in *hop*) and the five ___________ sounds (as in *hope*). (As you work through these frames, complete the outline at the right. Write the diacritical marks for the short vowels in I.A and the diacritical marks for the long vowels in I.B.)
ə unaccented schwa	**3.** We use a nonletter symbol (_____) to designate the soft sound heard in the ___________ syllable of many two- or three-syllable words. We call it the ____________. (Fill in C.1.)
r *câre, ärm, ôt, hûrt*	**4.** There are four other single-letter phonemes that are often controlled by the letter following them, generally *l, w,* or __________. These phonemes represent a large variety of graphemes (e.g., â may represent *ai, a, ei, e, ea, ay*) in various words. Mark the four key symbols in this sentence: *Take care of your arm, you ought not hurt it.* (Fill in C.2–C.5.)
diphthongs, *oi* *ou, house*	**5.** We also studied four vowel phonemes represented by two vowel letters. Two of these are gliding sounds called _________. They are represented by _________ in *oil* and _________ in _________. (Fill in II.A.)

Vowel phonemes represented by

I. Single letter symbols
   A. Short
      1. ă
      2.
      3.
      4.
      5.
   B. Long
      1.
      2. ē
      3.
      4.
      5.
   C. Other
      1. ə
      2.
      3.
      4.
      5.

II. Double letter symbols
   A. Diphthongs
      1.
      2.
   B. Digraphs
      1.
      2.

digraphs o͞o, o͝o	**6.** The other two-letter combinations with distinctive sounds needed to complete the 19 vowel phonemes are called __________. They are found in ________ as in *food* and ________ as in *hook.* (Fill in II.B.) You have now completed the outline of the key symbols that represent the vowel phonemes. Turn to pages 142–147 to check your answers. You have mastered all the phonemes!
symbols ōa̸, ēe̸, ēa̸, āi̸ ō, ē, ē, ā long, silent	**7.** Other vowel pairs do not have distinguishing key __________ because they represent single vowels with their own phonemes—for example, *coat, fleet, dean, main.* What vowel phoneme is represented in each of these? ________ ________ ________ ________ Mark the vowels in each word. ________ ________ ________ ________ In general, the first vowel represents its __________ sound and the second of the pair is __________.
  ō, ŏ ə, ô, û y, ĭ silent, *a* e, *e* istening	**8.** Vowel letters are not very reliable. **A.** A letter may represent more than one phoneme: For example, an *o* may represent _______ as in *hope,* _______ as in *hop,* _______ as in *mammoth,* _______ as in *ought,* or _______ as in *worm.* **B.** A phoneme may be represented by more than one vowel letter: The *ĭ* may be represented by _______ in *myth or* _______ in *fin.* **C.** A letter may represent no phoneme. It may be ________as the _______ in *roam,* the _______ in *race,* or the _______ in *doe.* Although vowels are not very reliable, the use of certain generalizations will help us to identify words already in our ______________ vocabulary. (reading, writing, listening) (Of course, there are exceptions to the generalizations, too!)
  long **silent**	**9.** Some of these generalizations have been referred to previously, and others follow. **When a one-syllable word or accented syllable contains two vowels, one of which is the final *e,* the first vowel usually represents its __________ sound and the final *e* is __________ (the VCe pattern).**

phoneme *echo, say, though, be* consonant *open, thought, rate, once* hearing the final phoneme	**10.** An open syllable ends with a vowel ________________ (the CV pattern). (phoneme, letter) Check the words that end with an open syllable: *echo open say though thought rate be once* A closed syllable ends with a ________________ phoneme (the CVC, VC pattern). Which of the words above have closed syllables? ________________ Whether a syllable is open or closed depends on ____. (hearing the final phoneme, seeing the final letter)
long *he, why* CV	**11.** A single vowel in an open accented syllable often represents its ________________ sound. Which of the following words follow this generalization? *he why pen road do* The vowel-consonant pattern is ________________.
short *pin, sent, cat* CVC	**12.** A single vowel in a closed accented syllable usually represents its ________________ sound. Which of the following words follow this generalization? *pin sent cat hope thought* The vowel-consonant pattern is ________________.
phoneme, vowel	**13.** Although a syllable may have more than one letter, it has only one one vowel ________________. The ________________ has the most influence on the syllable. (vowel, consonant)
accented ə (schwa)	**14.** Vowels behave differently in accented and unaccented syllables. The vowel is most clearly heard in an ________________ syllable. The vowel in most unaccented syllables represents the ____________ or the ĭ.
mē lēpe̸, phā tŏg, rĕl nō, phō, ŏt, drāi̸f, sk͞oos	**15.** The generalizations we have studied in connection with these vowel phonemes should aid in the pronunciation of words we do not recognize. The words below are nonsense words. Take a chance that the vowel phonemes follow the rules even in unaccented syllables or have their most common sound. Mark every vowel in these "words" to show pronunciation: *me lepe pha tog rel no pho ot draif skoos*

Part IV

A Review of the Phonemes

Review of Phonemes

phonemes (or sounds)	**1.** Our written language is not based on pictorial representations of objects or ideas. It is a phonetic language in that there is a relationship between the letters of the alphabet and the ________________ of the spoken language.
consonants	**2.** In fact, many of the ________________ are fairly reliable as to sound. (consonants, vowels)
phonemes letter	**3.** However, there are so many inconsistencies in the sound–letter relationship that the English language is not an easy one to learn to read. If it were a consistent, strictly phonetic language, then: (1) there would be one and only one letter to represent each of the ______________ of the spoken language, and (2) there would be only one phoneme represented by each ______________ of the alphabet.

	4. The truth of the matter is:
	(1) A letter may represent more than one sound.
26	For example, each vowel represents several sounds. Our alphabet has _______
phonemes	letters (and some of them are useless) to represent the 44 ________________.
	(2) The same sound may be represented by more than one letter.
phonemes	The 44 ________________ are represented by 251 different graphemes. For example, we spell the first consonant phoneme we hear in *chute* (key
sh	symbol: _______) in 14 different ways!
	(3) A letter may represent no sound.
silent	Almost any letter may, at some time or another, be _________________.
spoken	**5.** We have identified the 44 phonemes that, for all practical purposes in the teaching of reading, make up the sounds of our ____________ language. (spoken, written)
	6. We have designated a key symbol for each of these phonemes to serve as our pronunciation guide.
symbol	These key pronunciation symbols, then, provide us with a one-to-one correspondence between sound and _________________. For example,
j	we use the _______ to symbolize the sound heard in *jam,* even though it may be represented by *g* as in *gentle, d* as in *graduate,* or *dg* as in *judgment.*
key symbol	**7.** Let us review, through the following outline, the 44 phonemes we have identified and the ____________________ we have designated for each.
	Study and make responses as indicated. When choices appear in parentheses, underline the correct answer. For example, there are 44 (<u>phonemes,</u> graphemes).

Review Outline

		Key Symbol
	I. CONSONANT PHONEMES	
	A. Represented by a single consonant letter	1. *b*
boat	*b* as in _________________ (pages 35–38). (*boat, comb*)	
	Complete this generalization:	
silent, *m*	*b* is usually ______________ when it follows _________ (*comb*) or precedes	
t	_________ (*doubt*) in the same syllable.	
syllable	The *b* in *submit* is not silent because it is not in the same ___________.	

one	Say *rabbit* aloud. How many phonemes do these two like consonants represent? ____________
consonants one	Complete this generalization: Two like ______________ appearing together in a word or syllable generally represent ____________ phoneme (pages 37, 40). (How many?)
les~~s~~on, bet~~t~~er, ham~~m~~er hap~~p~~en, pud~~d~~le, puf~~f~~	Make a slash through the second like consonant in each word to depict the silent letter. *lesson* _________ *better* _________ *hammer* _________ *happen* _________ *puddle* _________ *puff* _________
symbol, word	*c* has no key ________________ or ________________.
a, o, u end letter	*c* usually represents the sound we associate with the *k* when it is followed by ________ (*cat*), ________ (*coat*), or ________ (*cut*) or when it appears at the ________ (*comic*) of a word and when followed by any other ____________ (*clasp*) (pages 54–55).
e, i *y*	*c* usually represents /*s*/ when it is followed by ________ (*cent*), ________ (*city*), or ________ (*cycle*) (pages 54–55).
cabin *cymbal* *cube* *city* *cot* *cell* *close* *mice*	Use the words below to complete the table at the right by selecting words in which *c* represents the hard sound or the soft sound. *cymbal city cabin cube cell cot close mice* **Hard c** / **Soft c** _______ _______ _______ _______ _______ _______ _______ _______
s	*c* can be a silent letter when it follows _________ as in *scene.*
ch	We could replace the letter *c* with *k* and *s* were it not for the _______ digraph.
dog	*d* as in ________________ is fairly dependable. 2. *d* (key word)
ladder, /*t*/	*d* may be silent as in _____________ or it may represent ____________ when part of the *-ed* suffix. (*ladder, laden*) (/*f*/, /*t*/)
dg *ld*	*d* also represents /*j*/ as part of the combination _________ (*bridge*), and _________ (*soldier*) (pages 45–46).
/*v*/	*f* as in *fish* is a fairly reliable letter, with the notable exception in the word *of,* in which the letter *f* represents _________ (page 43). 3. *f*
gh, ph	This phoneme is sometimes spelled _________, as in *enough,* or _________, as in *graph* (pages 43–44).

Answers	
goat, hard	*g* as in ________ (*goat, giant*) represents the ________ (hard, soft) sound. **4. *g***
a	This sound is usually heard when *g* is followed by the vowel ____ (*game*),
o, u	____ (*goat*), or ____ (*gum*) and when followed by any other
letter, end	_____ (*glad*) or appearing at the _____ of a word (*drag*) (page 51).
soft	*g* usually represents a ________ (hard, soft) sound when it is followed by the
e, i, y	vowel _____ (*gerbil*), _____ (*giant*), or _____ (*gym*) (page 52).
gift	The word _____ (*gym, gift*) does not follow this generalization.
	Study the words below. For each set, choose a word from the six at the right in which *g* represents the same phoneme as the other underlined letters in the set and has the same vowel following it. *gypsy, good, gentle, guard, ginger, gate*
1. *gate* 2. *gentle* 3. *ginger* 4. *good* 5. *guard* 6. *gypsy*	**1:** *game, gave* ____ **2:** *gent, germ* ____ **3:** *giant, margin* ____ **4:** *goal, gold* ____ **5:** *gulp, guess* ____ **6:** *gym, gyrate* ____
hat	*h* as in ________ (*ghost, hat, honor*). **5. *h***
end	*h* is never heard at the ________ (*oh*) of a word or syllable.
beginning	Sometimes *h* is silent (*honor*) at the ________ of a word.
g	The *h* is silent when it follows the consonant _____ (*ghost*),
k, r	_____ (*khaki*), or _____ (*rhyme*) (pages 38–39).
vowel	*h* is also silent when it follows a _______ (*oh*) in a word or syllable.
	Put a slash through each silent *h*.
~~h~~onor, o~~h~~, hurra~~h~~, r~~h~~yme	*honor* ____ *oh* ____ *hurrah* ____ *rhyme* ____
habit, poo~~h~~, g~~h~~ost, k~~h~~aki	*habit* ____ *pooh* ____ *ghost* ____ *khaki* ____
	j as in jeep. **6. *j***
e	The /j/ phoneme is often represented by a *g* followed by the vowel _____,
i, y	_____, or _____ (pages 44–45).
ld	The /j/ phoneme may also be represented by _____ (*soldier*) and
dg	_____ (*fudge*).

king	*k* as in __________________. (key word)	7. *k*
silent	*k* is ______________ (*knight*) at the beginning of a word or syllable when	
n	followed by _________ (pages 33–35).	
	Put a slash through each silent *k*.	
k̸not, k̸now	*knot* *key* *know* *keep*	
lion	*l* as in __________________. (*lion, calm*)	8. *l*
	The letter *l* is sometimes silent when followed, in the same syllable, by	
m, k, d	_________ (*calm*), _________ (*chalk*), or _________ (*should*) (page 40).	
moon, reliable	*m,* as in __________________, is a __________________ letter. (key word) (reliable, unreliable)	9. *m*
nut	*n* as in __________________. (*nut, condemn*)	10. *n*
m	*n* can be silent when preceded by _________ (*autumn*) (page 47).	
/*ng*/	*n* generally represents _________ when it is followed by *g* (*sing*) or *k* (*thank*).	
	p as in *pig.*	11. *p*
reliable	As a single letter, *p* is __________________. (reliable, unreliable)	
s, t	When *p* is followed by _________ (*pseudo*), _________ (*pterodactyl*), or	
n, silent	_________ (*pneumonia*), it is usually ___________ (pages 40, 42).	
symbol	*q* has no key ______________.	
k	The dictionary uses a ________ to indicate its pronunciation.	
	The *que* at the end of a word (*antique*) represents the phoneme we	
k	associate with ________. The letter *q* is almost always followed by the letter (*k, s*)	
u, silent	________. The *u* may be ________ or represent the sound we associate	
w	with the key symbol ________ (pages 33–35).	
plak, kwēn, kwit	Rewrite *plaque, queen,* and *quit* to show pronunciation.	

	r as in *ring.*	12. *r*
reliable *r*	*r* is very ________________. When we see *r,* we can be sure that it represents (reliable, unreliable) the sound we associate with the key symbol _________ (page 33).	
sun /s/, /z/ /sh/ /zh/	*s* as in ________________. (*his, sure, sun*) Except when acting as a plural at the end of a word, *s* represents the phonemes we associate with _________ (*miss*) and _________ (*his*) with about equal frequency. *s* also represents the phoneme _________ (*sugar*) and occasionally stands for _________ (*treasure*) (page 62).	13. *s*
table *s, f* *ch* *ch* *sh,* silent *mother*	*t* as in ________________. (*table, than*) *t* may be silent when it follows the letter _________ (*listen*) or _________ (*soften*) and when it precedes _________ (*catch*). In connection with a vowel, *t* may represent _________ (*future*) or _________ (*station*) (page 64). *t* may be ________________ in a words adopted from the French language (*ballet*). *t* is often part of the consonant digraph *th* as in ________________, in which (*mother, fast*) case the /*t*/ is not heard.	14. *t*
van	*v* as in ________________ is very reliable (page 33). (*van, off*)	15. *v*
wagon consonant vowel, follows silent blend (or cluster), digraph silent	*w* as in __________________________ (page 58). (*two, why, wagon, who*) *w* serves as a ________________ and as a vowel. As a consonant, it precedes the ________________ (*was*). As a vowel, *w* ________________ the vowel (*snow*). Sometimes *w* is ________________ (*wrote*). *w* may also be part of a consonant ________________ (*dwell*) or ________________ (*which*). Occasionally, *w* appears to be part of a digraph (*wh*) but is ________________ (*who*).	16. *w*

	x has no phoneme of its own (page 61).
/ks/, /gz/, /z/	It represents the _________ in *six,* the _________ in *exam,* and the _________
/gz/	in *xylophone.* We are more apt to use _________ when *x* appears between two vowel phonemes (*exam*).
yo-yo	*y* as in _______________ (page 58). (*day, yo-yo*) 17. *y*
vowel	*y* serves as a consonant and as a _______________.
	y at the beginning of a word or syllable represents the sound we associate
/y/, silent	with _________. *y* within a syllable acts as a vowel and may be ___________ (*day*) or may represent a vowel sound (*rhyme*).
zipper	*z* as in _______________ (page 48). (*quartz, zipper*) 18. *z*
/s/, /zh/	Occasionally, *z* represents _________ (*waltz*) or _________ (*azure*).
	B. Represented by consonant digraphs
chair	*ch* as in _____________________. (*choir, chair, machine*) 19. *ch*
is not, /ch/	*ch* ___________ (is, is not) reliable. *ch* may represent the _________ in *change,* the
/k/, /sh/	_________ in *choir,* or the _________ in *chiffon* (page 71).
	dg represents no phoneme of its own. It often represents the key symbol
/j/	_________ (*fudge*) (page 45).
	gh represents no phoneme of its own.
silent	*gh* is usually ______________ (*bright*) when it precedes *t* in a syllable.
/f/	*gh* is silent (*through*) or represents _________ (*enough*) when it follows the vowel in a word or syllable (page 44). When it appears at the beginning of
h	a word or syllable, the _________ (*ghost*) is silent.
king	*ng* as in _______________ (page 77). (*king, congest*) 20. *ng*
beginning	*ng* is never heard at the _______________ of a syllable, and it always follows
/ng/ thangk	a vowel. The letter *n* may also represent _________ when it is followed by a *g* or *k* (*bring, blank*). Write *thank* to show pronunciation.
	ph has no phoneme of its own (page 44).
f	The key symbol _________ commonly represents the sound, as in *phone.*

ship	*sh* as in ______________ (page 72). (*ship, division*)	21. *sh*
thumb voiceless	*th* as in ______________ (page 73). (*that, thumb*) The /*th*/ in *thin* is ______________. (voiceless, voiced)	22. *th*
that voiced *their* *thaw* *these* *thief* *this* *theme* *those* *thing*	*th̸* as in ______________ (page 74). (*that, thumb*) *th̸* is ______________ (page 74). (voiceless, voiced) Pronounce the words at the right. Write the words in which the *th* is voiced in Column 1 below. Write the words in which the *th* is voiceless in Column 2. **Column 1 Voiced** **Column 2 Voiceless** ______________ ______________ ______________ ______________ ______________ ______________ ______________ ______________	23. *th* *thaw* *their* *thief* *theme* *these* *this* *thing* *those*
whale vowel	*wh* as in ______________ (page 74). (*who, whale*) *wh* appears at the beginning of a word or syllable and is followed by a ______________ (*which*).	24. *wh*
treasure *s* *g, z*	*zh* as in ______________ (page 72). (*treasure, edge*) The /*zh*/ is never represented in a word with the grapheme *zh*. The /*zh*/ may be represented by the __________ (*pleasure*), the __________ (*collage*), or the __________ (*seizure*).	25. *zh*
  a, e, i, o, u *w, y*	**II. VOWEL PHONEMES** **A. Represented by single vowel letters** The letters ________, ________, ________, ________, ________, and sometimes ________ and ________ are classified as vowels (page 87).	

sounds, *y* *w*	Two of the seven vowels are not represented by key symbols because they do not represent __________ of their own. These are the ________ and the ________ (page 88).
i, *e* silent	*y* as a vowel represents no sound of its own. When *y* is a vowel, its pronunciation is shown by the key symbols we associate with the ________ or the ________ (page 88). The vowel *y* is often __________ (*play*).
vowel	As a vowel, *w* is always used in combination with a preceding __________ (*threw*) (page 88).
 apple *edge* *igloo* *ox* *umbrella*	**1. Short sounds** *a* as in ______________ (page 90). (*date, apple, all*) 26. *ă* *e* as in ______________ (page 90). (*edge, even*) 27. *ĕ* *i* as in ______________ (page 90). (*ice, igloo*) 28. *ĭ* *o* as in ______________ (page 90). (*over, ox*) 29. *ŏ* *u* as in ______________ (page 90). (*umbrella, use*) 30. *ŭ*
 short *wĕt, kăt* *hit, hat*	**Breve** The breve (˘) is the diacritical mark used to indicate the pronunciations of ______________ vowels (page 90). Write *wet* and *cat* to show pronunciation. Many dictionaries indicate the pronunciations of the short vowel sounds with the letter alone. How would the pronunciations of *hit* and *hat* be indicated in these dictionaries?
 consonant short hid	**Closed syllable** The closed syllable ends in a ________________ phoneme (page 94). (consonant, vowel) The vowel in a closed syllable usually represents its ______________ sound, (long, short) as in ________________. (*hid, hide*)

CVC	**CVC pattern** The most common vowel-consonant pattern is that of the __________ (consonant-vowel-consonant), in which the V (vowel) represents its short (unglided) sound (page 93).
consonant	The CVC (or VC) syllable ends with a __________ phoneme. (consonant, vowel)
single short	Complete this generalization: A __________ vowel in an accented, closed syllable usually represents the __________ sound of the vowel (page 95).
two silent, first short	**VCCe pattern** Complete this generalization: When a word or syllable has __________ vowels, one of which is a final *e*, and the two vowels are separated by two consonants, the final *e* is __________ and the __________ vowel usually represents its __________ sound (page 96).
apron *eraser* *ice* *overalls* *unicorn* ī ĭ, ē	**2. Long sounds** *a* as in __________ (page 99). (*apron, ant*) 31. *ā* *e* as in __________ (page 99). (*every, eraser*) 32. *ē* *i* as in __________ (page 99). (*ice, itch*) 33. *ī* *o* as in __________ (page 99). (*overalls, over*) 34. *ō* *u* as in __________ (page 99). (*up, unicorn*) 35. *ū* *y* has no vowel phoneme of its own. Its key symbol can be the ________ as in *my,* the ______ as in *myth,* and the ______ as in *happy* (page 109).
long yo͞o o͞o	We use a macron (¯) to indicate the pronunciation of __________ vowel sounds (page 99). Some dictionaries and teachers' manuals use the ________ to indicate the pronunciation of the long *u* in *cube* and the ________ to represent the pronunciation of the long *u* in *tune.*

	Open syllable
vowel	An open syllable ends in a _______________ phoneme (page 104). (consonant, vowel)
long, *hide*	We hear a _______________ vowel phoneme, as in _______________. (short, long) (*hid, hide*)
	CV pattern
	The open syllable generalization most often applies to words and
CV	syllables that have the _______________ vowel-consonant pattern, as
no	in _______________ (page 105). (*no, not*)
	VCe pattern
	Complete this generalization:
two	When a one-syllable word or accented syllable has _______________
silent	vowels, one of which is a final *e,* the *e* is _______________ and the first
long	vowel usually represents its _______________ sound (page 101).
	Mark each vowel in the following words with the proper diacritical mark. Put a slash through each silent letter.
mīc~~e~~, bōn~~e~~, māk~~e~~, hīd~~e~~	*mice* *bone* *make* *hide*
	CVVC pattern
	Complete this generalization:
two	When _______________ vowels appear together in a word or syllable, the (How many?)
long	the first usually represents its _______________ sound and the second is
silent	_______________ (page 128).
	The pairs that follow the generalization a greater percentage of the time are
ai, oa, ee	__________ (*rain*), __________ (*boat*), __________ (*street*),
ea, ay	____________ (*beach*), and _______________ (*play*) (page 129).

	3. Other vowel sounds	36. ə
	Schwa	
a *e, i* *o, u*	ə represents the soft, unaccented sound of the vowel ______ in *comma,* ______ in *chicken,* ______ in *family,* ______ in *apron,* and ______ in *circus* (page 111).	
care *care, chair, there*	*â* is the vowel phoneme we associate with the key word ______ (page 115). Underline the portion(s) of the words *care, chair,* and *there* that, when combined with *r,* represent this phoneme.	37. *â*
fur *hurt, term, courage*	*û* is the vowel phoneme we associate with the key word ______ (page 115). Underline the portion(s) of *hurt, term,* and *courage* that, when combined with *r,* represent this phoneme.	38. *û*
vowel *l, w*	Complete these generalizations: If the only vowel in a word or syllable is followed by *r,* the ______ is affected by that *r,* as in *car, hurt,* and *orbit* (page 119). If the only vowel in a word or syllable is an *a* followed by *l* or *w,* the *a* is affected by that ______ or ______, as in *saw* and *fall* (page 119).	
father *heart, taco, plaza*	*ä* is the vowel phoneme we associate with the key word ______ (page 115). Underline the portion(s) of *heart, taco,* and *plaza* that represent this phoneme.	39. *ä*
ball *caution, tall, cost*	*ô* is the vowel phoneme we associate with the key word ______ (page 115). Underline the portion(s) of *caution, tall,* and *cost* that represent this phoneme.	40. *ô*
	B. Vowel sounds represented by vowel combinations	41. *oi* 42. *ou*
	1. Diphthongs	
oil *oy* *house* *ow*	*oi* as in ______. This phoneme is also represented by the letters ______ (page 122). *ou* as in ______. This phoneme is also represented by the by the vowels ______ (page 122).	

	2. Vowel digraphs 43. o͞o 44. o͝o
food	o͞o as in ________________ (page 125). (food, flood)
hook	o͝o as in ________________ (page 125). (food, flood, hook)
	3. Other vowel pairs (teams) The key symbols for other vowel pairs—*ai, oa, ee, ea,* and *ay*—have already been given.

Part V

Onsets and Rimes

Onsets and Rimes

26, 44 vowels, consonants	**1.** Thus far we have been studying the ________ letters and _______ phonemes of the American-English language. We have learned that the arrangement of __________ and __________ within the syllable affects the pronunciation.
   consonant begins	**2.** We will now turn our attention to the consonant(s) at the beginning of the syllable and the vowel and the consonant(s) that follow it at the end of the syllable. The **onset** is the ________________ letter(s) that precede(s) the vowel in a syllable. The dictionary defines an onset as a "beginning or commencement." Therefore, a syllable ________________ with an onset. (begins, ends)
  single consonant blend digraph	**3.** The onset is the single consonant, consonant blend, or consonant digraph that begins a syllable. Study these words: *bat, street, thorn.* The onset in *bat* is a ________________________. (single consonant, consonant blend) The onset in *street* is a consonant ________________. (blend, digraph) The onset in *thorn* is a consonant ________________. (blend, digraph)
pig, smile, chip, wish, splash, bold, strain, pill	**4.** Underline the onset in each one-syllable word below. Count the letters in each of the onsets you underline. *pig smile chip wish splash bold strain pill*

	5. Complete the table by filling in the onset (1) and key symbol (2) for each one-syllable word (3).
	1 **2** **3**
c, k, cat	____ ____ *cat*
kn, n, knight	____ ____ *knight*
bl, bl, black	____ ____ *black*
gh, g, ghost	____ ____ *ghost*
ph, f, phone	____ ____ *phone*
wh, wh, white	____ ____ *white*
sk, sk, skin	____ ____ *skin*
p, p, pink	____ ____ *pink*
consonant	An onset may consist of one or more __________ letters. (vowel, consonant)
	6. There are many syllables and one-syllable words in the English language that do not begin with an onset. Examine the one-syllable word *at.* Does *at*
no	begin with an onset? __________
consonant	*At* does not begin with an onset because there is no __________ letter preceding the vowel. Does the one-syllable word *chat* begin with an onset?
yes	__________ The onset in the word *chat* is the consonant digraph
ch	__________.
	7. We have noted that a word or syllable may not always begin with an onset. Mark the one-syllable words below that **do not** begin with an onset.
off, it, add, out, up, elf	*off* *show* *it* *add* *out* *split* *up* *elf* *queen*
	8. Study the two-syllable words below. Write the onset that begins each syllable.
	thir teen *pump kin* *gar den* *mag ic*
th t, p k, g d, m	__ __ __ __ __ __ __ __
ic	Which syllable in the words above does not begin with an onset? ______
consonant	**9.** We have learned that an onset is the __________ letter(s) that
precedes	begin(s) the syllable. We have also learned that an onset __________ (precedes, follows)
	the vowel in a syllable. Do we expect every syllable to begin with an onset?
no	__________

Answers	Frame
vowel, consonant(s)	**10.** We call the vowel and the consonant(s) that follows it at the end of the syllable the **rime.** *Rime* is a variation in the spelling of the word *rhyme.* The dictionary defines *rhyme* as "the agreement among the ending vowel and consonant sounds in words." Therefore, the rime consists of the ________________ and the final ________________ in a syllable.
spend, beg, strut, drink, stop, flat one	**11.** Study the one-syllable words below. Underline the rime in each word. *spend* *beg* *strut* *drink* *stop* *flat* How many vowel phonemes do you hear in each one-syllable word? ________________
2, 1, 2, 1, 3, 2 3, 3, 2, 1, 1, 3 rime	**12.** Use the numbers of the rimes below to indicate the rimes in the words at the bottom of the frame. **1.** *ug* **2.** *ant* **3.** *op* *plant* _____ *bug* _____ *slant* _____ *dug* _____ *top* _____ *grant* _____ *drop* _____ *hop* _____ *chant* _____ *plug* _____ *rug* _____ *mop* _____ You can see that our written language has many words that contain the same ________________.
can, match, kept, tent, ham, salt, trust	**13.** Study the rimes in the words below to see if each rime always consists of one consonant that follows the vowel phoneme. Underline the rime in each one-syllable word. *can* *match* *kept* *tent* *ham* *salt* *trust*
consonant *lamp, swift, push, call, thought, sold*	**14.** We can see from the words in frame 13 that a rime may have more than one ________________ letter following the vowel phoneme. Mark the rimes in the one-syllable words below. *lamp* *swift* *push* *call* *thought* *sold*
amb one silent	**15.** The rime in the one-syllable word *lamb* is ____________. This rime consists of one vowel, *a,* and two consonant letters, *m* and *b.* Say *lamb* out loud. How many consonant phonemes do you hear in this rime? ________________ The last consonant letter is ________________.
look, sleep, mouse, write, blame, train, ride no yes	**16.** Study the rimes in the words below. Underline the rime in each one-syllable word. *look* *sleep* *mouse* *write* *blame* *train* *ride* Does the rime always consist of one vowel letter? ______ Does each rime consist of one vowel phoneme? ______

two one	**17.** There are many rimes in written English that have more than one vowel letter. Say the one-syllable words below aloud. *boat* *made* *store* *seed* The rimes in the words above consist of ________ vowel letters. (How many?) How many vowel phonemes do you hear in each rime? ________
sure, dance, store, home, leave, mouse	**18.** Underline the rime in each word below. Then pronounce the words aloud. Notice that you hear only one vowel phoneme. *sure* *dance* *store* *home* *leave* *mouse*
rime consonant *ore, our, ent, aste* *ain, ar, arve, oint*	**19.** We have noted that there is one ________ in each syllable. The rime consists of the vowel and the ________ letter(s) at the end of the syllable. Write the rime in each one-syllable word below. Work carefully. (If you correctly identify all the rimes, you are really thinking!) *more* ____ *our* ____ *cent* ____ *taste* ____ *rain* ____ *star* ____ *starve* ____ *point* ____
yes yes	**20.** **Phonogram** is another term for the rime in a syllable. Study the words below. Do the words rhyme? ____ *bat* *hat* *cat* Are the words spelled with the same rime? ____ Therefore, in the teaching of reading, phonograms are words with a common rime and rhyming sound.
ad, eed, un, old	**21.** Indicate the phonogram (rime) in each group below. *had* *seed* *fun* *cold* *bad* *need* *run* *bold* *mad* *feed* *sun* *hold* __ __ __ __
four	**22.** In the teaching of reading, we also use the term **word family** to describe words that share a common rime and a common rhyming sound. How many word families are in frame 21? ________

    bed, red, led *fan, man, ran* *run, sun, fun*	**23.** Group the words below into word families. *bed* *fan* *run* *man* *red* *led* *sun* *fun* *ran* **Family 1** ________ ________ ________ **Family 2** ________ ________ ________ **Family 3** ________ ________ ________
consistently	**24.** Study the word families in frame 23. The rime in each word family ____________________ represents the same sounds. (consistently, inconsistently)
rime, yes yes	**25.** *Cat* and *mat* contain the same ________. Do *cat* and *mat* rhyme? ________ Do *cat* and *mat* belong in the same word family? ________
yes no no	**26.** Now let us consider *bed* and *head.* Do *bed* and *head* rhyme? ______ Are *bed* and *head* spelled with the same rime? ______ Do *bed* and *head* belong in the same word family? ______
rhyme	**27.** We have noted that when words have the same rime, the words may also __________, as in *bug* and *dug.* There are exceptions (of course!), as we see in *cough* and *bough.*
 fish, wish *deed, feed* yes no	**28.** Now pronounce the sets of words below to see if the words that rhyme also contain the same rime. Mark the sets of words that have the same rime. *fish* *joke* *pail* *deed* *wish* *oak* *stale* *feed* Does each set of words rhyme? ________________ Does each set of words have the same rime? ________________
rhymes phonemes rime	**29.** Each set of words in frame 28 ________________. That is, in each set there is agreement among the ending vowel and the consonant sounds. We have learned that the same ________________ may be represented by different graphemes. Therefore, words that rhyme may not always consist of the same ________________.

en el, ase all *am age, ump in* one	**30.** Write the rime in each of the two-syllable words below. *ken nel* ___ ___ *base ball* ___ ___ *dam age* ___ ___ *pump kin* ___ ___ Each rime consists of ________________ vowel phoneme(s). (How many?)
two one	**31.** There are many rimes in written English that have more than one vowel letter. Say the one-syllable words below aloud. *boat* *made* *store* *seed* The rimes in the words above consist of ______________ vowel letters. (How many?) How many vowel phonemes do you hear in each rime? ____________
vowel phoneme rime	**32.** We have seen that the rime consists of one ________________ phoneme and the consonant(s) that follow(s) the vowel phoneme in the syllable. We have learned that each syllable contains one vowel ________________. Therefore, each syllable must contain one and only one ________________. (onset, rime)
two two	**33.** Say the two-syllable words below aloud. *ti ger* *pic nic* *in tense* *blan ket* How many vowel sounds do you hear in each word? ________________ Each word has ________________ rimes.
two syllables rimes	**34.** If you hear two vowel phonemes in a word, you can be sure that the word has ________________ rimes. You can also be sure that a word (How many?) with two rimes has two ________________. Therefore, the number of ________________ in a word is equal to the number of syllables in a word.

Answers	Frame			
	35. Pronounce the one-syllable words below. Complete the table by filling in the onset (1) and the rime (2) for each word (3).			
		1	**2**	**3**
r *ight*		_____	_____	*right*
s *ave*		_____	_____	*save*
s *at*		_____	_____	*sat*
l *ook*		_____	_____	*look*
d *ish*		_____	_____	*dish*
f *ind*		_____	_____	*find*
b *ig*		_____	_____	*big*
gr *een*		_____	_____	*green*

Answers	Frame
consonant(s) vowel consonant(s) onset rime, vowel consonant	**36.** Let us review. We have learned that the onset is the ________________ at the beginning of the syllable (*boat*), and the rime is the ________________ and ________________ that follow(s) it at the end of the syllable (*boat*). A word or a syllable may not have an ________________ (*oat*). However, the syllable must have a ________________. The rime has one ________________ phoneme and may have more than one ________________ letter that follows the vowel (*dish*).

Answers	Frame					
	37. Now use your knowledge to combine the onset (1) with the rime (2) and write the one-syllable word (3) on the line below.					
		1	**+**	**2**	**=**	**3**
scratch		*scr*	+	*atch*	=	_____
bird		*b*	+	*ird*	=	_____
street		*str*	+	*eet*	=	_____
am			+	*am*	=	_____
twig		*tw*	+	*ig*	=	_____
shrine		*shr*	+	*ine*	=	_____
chick		*ch*	+	*ick*	=	_____

Study Guide

Onsets and Rimes and 50 Common Rimes

Onset

The **onset** is the consonant that precedes the vowel in a syllable. The onset may have more than one consonant letter.

Rime

The **rime** consists of a vowel and the final consonant(s) in the syllable. The rime may have more than one vowel letter but only one vowel phoneme (*reach*).

Rhyme

Rhyme is the agreement among the ending vowel and consonant phonemes in words (*rain, train* or *head, bed*). Words that share a rime (*rain, train*) may rhyme. Words that rhyme may not always share the same rime (*head, bed*). Furthermore, words that share the same rime may not always share the same ending vowel and consonant sounds (*head, bead*).

50 Common Rimes

Rime	Examples	Rime	Examples
ab	*cab, grab, lab, tab*	*ell*	*bell, fell, sell, tell*
ace	*face, place, race, space*	*en*	*den, hen, men, pen*
ack	*back, black, sack, track*	*ent*	*bent, sent, tent, went*
ad	*bad, had, mad, sad*	*est*	*best, rest, test, west*
ade	*grade, made, shade, trade*	*et*	*bet, set, pet, wet*
ag	*bag, flag, rag, tag*	*ice*	*dice, mice, nice, twice*
ail	*fail, mail, sail, tail*	*ick*	*brick, lick, quick, trick*
ain	*gain, main, pain, train*	*ide*	*bride, side, tide, wide*
air	*chair, fair, pair, stair*	*ig*	*big, dig, pig, wig*
ake	*bake, make, take, wake*	*ight*	*fight, night, right, sight*
all	*ball, call, fall, tall*	*ill*	*bill, fill, hill, pill*
am	*clam, ham, ram, slam*	*in*	*fin, pin, thin, win*
ame	*came, game, name, same*	*ing*	*king, ring, sing, sting*
amp	*camp, damp, lamp, stamp*	*ink*	*link, pink, sink, wink*
an	*can, fan, man, tan*	*ip*	*dip, hip, ship, slip*
and	*band, hand, land, sand*	*it*	*hit, pit, sit, slit*
ang	*bang, hang, rang, sang*	*ock*	*block, rock, sock, stock*
ank	*blank, drank, rank, sank*	*og*	*dog, frog, hog, log*
ap	*cap, lap, map, nap*	*old*	*cold, fold, hold, told*
at	*cat, fat, hat, sat*	*op*	*hop, mop, pop, stop*
ate	*date, gate, late, rate*	*ot*	*dot, hot, got, lot*
eam	*beam, cream, dream, team*	*ug*	*bug, dug, hug, tug*
eat	*beat, meat, neat, seat*	*ump*	*bump, dump, hump, pump*
ed	*bed, fed, led, red*	*un*	*bun, fun, run, sun*
eed	*deed, feed, need, seed*	*ut*	*but, cut, nut, shut*

Review 21

1. Write the onset for each of the one-syllable words below.

   wrong *could* *shop* *high* *stay*
   sun *bowl* *school* *stage* *goat*

2. Which of the one-syllable words below do **not** begin with an onset?

   ask *loss* *fan* *ouch* *am*
   blue *green* *leave* *old* *if*

3. The rime consists of one ____________ phoneme and the ____________ that follows in the syllable.

4. Write the rime for each of the one-syllable words below.

   train *sent* *mice* *swamp* *flour*
   child *bought* *since* *house* *trip*

5. Which of the one-syllable words above have rimes that include more than one vowel letter?

See the Answers to the Reviews section for the answers to Review 21, page 237.

Part VI

Syllabication and Accents

Introduction

pronunciation	**1. The syllable is the unit of pronunciation.** It is convenient to use one-syllable words to illustrate the vowel and consonant phonemes because a one-syllable word is, in itself, one unit of ________________.
syllable	**2.** The generalizations that apply to a one-syllable word may apply to each syllable of a two-or-more-syllable word and generally apply to the accented ________________ of a word.
syllable	**3. There is one vowel phoneme in each unit of pronunciation,** that is, in each ______________.
vowel two	**4.** Each syllable contains only one ______________ phoneme. If you hear two vowel phonemes, you may be sure the word has ______________ syllables.
phoneme *pine ī, boy oi, right ī, pause ô* (If you missed *pause ô*, reread the frame.)	**5.** Each syllable may have more than one vowel letter but only one vowel ________________. The word *cause* (*kôz*) has one vowel phoneme: *ô*. Underline the vowel letters in the words below. Write the key symbol that represents the vowel phoneme in the space following each word; mark it to show pronunciation. pine ________ boy ________ right ________ pause ________

syllables 1 ĕ 1 ŭ 2 ō, ĭ (or ə) 2 ā, ĭ 1 *ou*	**6.** How many units of pronunciation (or ____________) are there in each of these words? What is the vowel phoneme in each syllable? Mark the vowel(s) in the space at the right to show pronunciation. **No. of Syllables** **Vowel Phoneme(s)** *red* ____________ ____________ *jumped* ____________ ____________ *broken* ____________ ____________ *raining* ____________ ____________ *house* ____________ ____________
syllable	**7. One syllable in a two-or-more-syllable word receives more emphasis or greater stress than the other syllables.** We indicate this accented ____________ by placing an accent mark (′) at the end of the accented syllable.
accent (or stresss)	**8. In multisyllabic words, more than one syllable may be stressed.** There will be one primary __________ (shown by ′) and one or more secondary accents. The secondary accent is shown by ′.
vowel	**9.** We have already noted that the accent, or stress point, affects ____________ sounds. (vowel, consonant)
accented	**10. The vowel phoneme is the most prominent part of the syllable. Vowels behave differently in accented and unaccented syllables.** The vowel is most clearly heard in the ____________ syllable.
schwa	**11.** Many syllables, when pronounced carefully in isolation, appear to follow the generalizations we have noted. In normal speech, however, we have a tendency to give most vowels in the unaccented syllables the soft, short, indistinct ____________ sound.
ŏ ə	**12.** We can clearly see this behavior of vowels in accented and unaccented syllables in words that are spelled alike but accented differently. Read these sentences: *Your conduct is exemplary.* (*k* _______ *n′dukt*) *I will conduct you through the factory.* (*k* _______ *n dukt′*) Show the pronunciation of the vowel in each of the first syllables above.

kŏn' kən kəm kŏm'	**13.** Write the first syllable of each of the underlined words to show its pronunciation. If the first syllable is the stressed syllable, include the accent mark. *I signed the contract.* ________ *"Can't" is a contraction.* ________ *The work is complete.* ________ *You are competent!* ________
phoneme letter	**14.** Each syllable has only one vowel ________ (phoneme, letter). It may have more than one vowel ________ (phoneme, letter).
yes yes yes oi, diphthong	**15.** Is *boy* a one-syllable word? ________ Does it have more than one vowel letter? ________ Does it have one vowel phoneme? ________ What key symbol represents this phoneme? ________ This vowel phoneme is called a ________.
accent	**16.** To decode a word not known at sight, we need to have some idea of where to place the accent. There are some clues to where the ________ may be found in unknown words.

Clues to Placement of Accents

accent	**1.** Obviously, it is necessary to have some understanding of where to expect to find the accented syllable. **First, we consider one-syllable words to have a primary ________.**
yes (They are one-syllable words; therefore, they are the accented syllable.)	**2.** The vowel phoneme in the accented syllable tends to follow the generalizations we have studied concerning its sound. Would you expect the words below to conform to these generalizations? ________ *met* *rain* *rate* *cat* *hope* *boy*

accented	**3.** Dictionaries, in showing pronunciation, do not place accent marks on one-syllable words. It is taken for granted that they are ________________.
ex chang' ing, play' ful *slow' ly, cold' est*	**4.** **In general, prefixes and suffixes (affixes) form separate syllables. The accent usually falls on or within the root word.** Place the accents in these words. *ex chang ing* *play ful* *slow ly* *cold est*
suffix	**5.** The root word is more likely to be accented than the prefix or __________.
pre cook', un bend' able *move' ment, re wrote'*	**6.** Show the syllabic division and place the accent for each word below. *precook* *unbendable* *movement* *rewrote*
accent *snow'man, some'thing, cow' boy*	**7.** **In compound words, the primary ______________ usually falls on or within the first "word."** Rewrite these compound words to show the syllables; place the accents. snowman __________ something __________ cowboy__________
black', bird' *black' bird*	**8.** Accents within sentences will not be considered here. However, note that a change in accent in each of the following sentences changes the meaning. Place the accent on *black* or *bird* in each sentence: *I see a black bird; I think it is a crow.* *The blackbird built its nest in the marsh.*
root, first	**9.** We have noted that (1) one-syllable words are accented; (2) accents usually fall on or within the _________ word rather than on an affix; (3) the ________ "word" in a compound word is usually the accented one.
first second first second	**10.** **The placement of the accent may differentiate between a noun and a verb in words that are spelled alike. The accent usually falls on the first syllable of a noun.** Study the sentences below. Write *first* or *second* to show the syllable on which the accent falls in each of the underlined words. *What is this <u>object</u>?* ________________ *Do you <u>object</u>?* ________________ *This is a <u>present</u> for you.* ________________ *Please <u>present</u> this to your friend.* ________________

Answers	Frames
bet' ter, thun' der, trum' pet	**11.** **When there is a double consonant within a word, the accent usually falls on the syllable that closes with the first letter of the double consonant:** *splen' did, din' ner* Place the accent in each of these words. *bet ter* *thun der* *trum pet*
tim' ber, pen' sion, shel' ter, rab' bit	**12.** Place the accents in the words below. *tim ber* *pen sion* *shel ter* *rab bit*
ex ten' sion, mag net' ic, men' tion	**13.** **In most multisyllabic words ending in the suffix *-tion, -sion,* or *-ic,* the primary accent falls on the syllable preceding the suffix.** Place the accent in these words. *ex ten sion* *mag net ic* *men tion*
na' tion, car na' tion, no mad' ic, an gel' ic	**14.** Mark the primary accent in each word below. *na tion* *car na tion* *no mad ic* *an gel ic*
nā' shən, kär nā' shən nō măd' ĭk, ăn jĕl' ĭk	**15.** Pronounce the words in frame 14. Using your knowledge of phonemes, rewrite the words to show pronunciation. *na tion* ________ *car na tion* ________ *no mad ic* ________ *an gel ic* ________
preceding first preceding	**16.** We expect the primary accent in a multisyllabic word ending in the suffix *-tion, -sion,* or *-ic* to fall on the syllable ______________ the suffix. Pronounce the words below aloud. *poet* *nomad* *donate* *concept* *poetic* *nomadic* *donation* *conception* The accent is on the ______________ syllable of the root word. When a word ends in *-tion, -sion,* or *-ic,* the accent is on the syllable ______________ the suffix.
main tain', be neath', ex plain'	**17.** Let us make another generalization: **When the vowel phoneme in the last and closed syllable of a word is composed of two vowel letters, that syllable is *most often* accented.** Mark the accents in these words. *main tain* *be neath* *ex plain*

ex ceed', con ceal' *de cay', com plain'*	**18.** Divide the words below into syllables and mark the accents. *exceed* ________ *conceal* ________ *decay* ________ *complain* ________
CV CVVC', VC CVVCC' CVC CVVC', V CCVVC'	**19.** Mark the accent in the "words" below. CV CVVC VC CVVCC CVC CVVC V CCVVC
When the vowel phoneme in the last and closed syllable of a two-syllable word is composed of two vowel letters, that syllable is most often accented.	**20.** State the generalization that applies to the "words" in frame 19.
first consonant vowel *-tion, -sion, ic*	**21.** We have noted that (1) when a word is used as different parts of speech, the accent is usually on the ________ syllable of the noun; (2) the accent usually falls on the syllable that closes with the first letter of a double ________; (3) when the last (and closed) syllable of a word has two ________ letters, that syllable is most often accented; and (4) the accent falls on the syllable preceding the ________ suffix ending(s).
fin' ish, prac' tice, scoun' drel *cen' ter, mon' key lis' ten*	**22.** **When there is no other clue, note that the accent most often falls on the first syllable of a two-syllable word.** Study these words to see if they follow this generalization. Place the accents. *fin ish* *prac tice* *scoun drel* *cen ter* *mon key* *lis ten*
accented	**23.** Let us review all the generalizations concerning the placement of the accent. Consider the word *day.* A one-syllable word is considered to be ________. (accented, unaccented)
sun' set compound first	**24.** Rewrite the word *sunset* and place the accent. ________ In ________ words, the accent usually falls on the ________ "word."

catch' ing root prefix	**25.** Rewrite the word *catching* and place the accent ____________ The accent usually falls on the ____________ word rather than on the suffix or ____________.
un faith' ful root	**26.** Consider this word: *unfaithful.* Place the accent. ____________ Sometimes a root word has more than one affix, or the word has so many syllables that two or more syllables are stressed. The primary accent, then, usually falls on or within the ____________ word.
 reb'el noun	**27.** Consider the word *rebel* in the sentence: *He is a rebel.* Place the accent. ____________. Certain words that are spelled the same sometimes function as different parts of speech. The accent on the first syllable generally indicates that it is a ____________.
noun verb *con tent'*	**28.** The word *con' tent* is a ____________. The word *con tent'* is a ____________. How would you place the accent in this sentence? *After many revisions, the novelist was finally <u>content</u> with the manuscript.*
glit' ter consonant closes consonant	**29.** Consider this word: *glitter.* Place the accent. ____________ When there is a double ____________ within a word, the accent usually falls on the syllable that ____________ with the first letter of the (closes, opens) double____________.
ob tain' last	**30.** Consider this word: *obtain.* Place the accent. ____________ When two vowel letters appear within the last and closed syllable of a two-syllable word, the ____________ syllable is most often accented. (first, last)
or gan' ic *at ten' tion* ***-tion*** ***-sion, -ic***	**31.** Divide the words *organic* and *attention* into syllables. Use what you have learned thus far to place the accent. Complete the generalization: **In most multisyllabic words ending in the suffix ________,** **________, or ________, the primary accent falls on the syllable that precedes the suffix.**

Study Guide

Syllable Accents

Syllable Defined

The **syllable** is the unit of pronunciation. There is one vowel phoneme in each syllable (unit of pronunciation). Each syllable may have more than one vowel letter but only one vowel phoneme (*boy, pause*).

Accent or Stress

One syllable in a two-or-more-syllable word receives more emphasis or greater stress than the other syllables. The accent, or stress point, affects the vowel sound.

Accent Marks

An accent mark indicates the primary stress (*ti′ ger*). In multisyllabic words, more than one syllable may be stressed. The secondary accent is shown by (′) (*cen′ ti pede′*).

Vowels in Accented Syllables

Vowels behave differently in accented and unaccented syllables. The vowel is most clearly heard in the accented syllable (*pa′ per, plan′ et*).

Vowels in Unaccented Syllables

We have a tendency to give most vowels in unaccented syllables the soft, short, indistinct *schwa* sound (*pen′ cil, pĕn′ səl*) or the short *i* (*bracelet, brās′ lĭt*).

Clues to Placement of Accent

One-Syllable Words We consider one-syllable words to have a primary accent (*bed′, boy′*).

Prefixes and Suffixes In general, prefixes and suffixes (affixes) form separate syllables. The accent usually falls on or within the root word (*play′ ful, slow′ ly*).

Compound Words In compound words, the primary accent usually falls on or within the first "word" (*cup′ cake, snow′ man*).

Nouns and Verbs The placement of the accent may differentiate between a noun and a verb in words that are spelled alike. The accent usually falls on the first syllable of a noun (*ob′ ject*) and the second syllable of a verb (*ob ject′*). (*His con′ duct was excellent. He will con duct′ the tour.*)

Double Consonants When there is a double consonant within a word, the accent usually falls on the syllable that closes the first letter of the double consonant (*let′ ter, trum′ pet*).

Words Ending with *-tion, -sion,* or *-ic* In most polysyllabic words ending in the suffix *-tion, -sion,* or *-ic,* the primary accent falls on the syllable preceding the suffix.

Two Vowels in the Final Syllable When the vowel phoneme in the last syllable of a word is composed of two vowel letters, that syllable is most often accented (*ex plain′, be neath′*).

When There Is No Clue to Accent When there is no other clue, the accent most often falls on the first syllable of a two-syllable word (*fin′ ish, prac′ tice*).

for get' ting, con' tract, de mand' ed, ap pear' ance, o' pen ing, can teen', show' boat	**32.** Using what information you have and remembering that it is not customary to place accent marks on one-syllable words, place accent marks in all the appropriate places in the following: *I was for get ting my con tract which de mand ed my ap pear ance at the o pen ing of the can teen on the show boat.*

Review 22

1. The unit of pronunciation is the ________________.
2. The basic speech sound, or the smallest sound-bearing unit, is the ________________.
3. Can there be more than one vowel letter in a syllable?
4. Can there be more than one vowel sound in a syllable?
5. The vowel phoneme is most clearly heard in the ________________ syllable.
6. We studied several generalizations concerning the placement of accent marks. State the generalization that applies to each of these words. Place the primary accent in each word.

   a. *in ter change a ble*
   b. *cow boy*
   c. *fast*
   d. *con vict* (noun)
   e. *na tion*
   f. *dol lar*
   g. *con ceal*
   h. *pa per*

See the Answers to the Reviews section for the answers to Review 22, page 237.

Clues to Syllable Division

A single vowel in a closed syllable generally represents its short sound.	**1.** We have established some guidelines to help us decide on which syllable an accent might fall. We still have this problem: Where do the syllabic divisions occur? There are generalizations to help, but with many exceptions. First, we need to review two generalizations concerning vowel phonemes. State the generalization that applies to the vowel sound of *met.*
A single vowel in an open syllable generally represents its long sound.	**2.** State the generalization that applies to the vowel sounds of *me* and *so.*

short (unglided)	**3.** Let us attempt to syllabicate the word *pupil.* If you divided it *pup il,* the first vowel would be expected to have its ________________ sound.
long (glided), open	**4.** If you divided it *pu pil,* the first vowel would be expected to have its ________________ sound: It is in a(n) ________________ syllable. (open, closed)
last (unaccented), *pū' pəl*	**5.** Write the correct pronunciation of *pupil,* placing the accent and using the *schwa* in the ________________ syllable. ________________
When there is no other clue in a two-syllable word, the accent most often falls on the first syllable.	**6.** Which generalization concerning the placement of accent would seem to apply?
le gal, (lē' gəl)	**7.** Now write *legal* as it would appear in the dictionary. The entry word should show syllabication only. Follow this by rewriting the word to show pronunciation, using the key symbols and omitting silent letters (if any). ________________ ________________
vowel	**8.** Let us make a generalization: **If the first vowel in a two-syllable word is followed by a single consonant, that consonant often begins the second syllable.** In other words, the syllable division is between the single ______________ and the single consonant.
si lent, (sī' lənt) *ti ger, (tī' gər)* *lo cal, (lō' kəl)*	**9.** Follow the above generalization and write these words as they would appear in the dictionary entry word followed by pronunciation. *silent* __________ __________ *tiger* __________ __________ *local* __________ __________
open CV' CVC	**10.** We have designated CV to represent an open syllable (page 104). But how might we represent the open syllable clue to syllabic division? We will use CV/CV to indicate the open syllable clue. The first syllable in the word *pupil* (*pu pil*) is a(n) ______________ syllable. Using C to represent consonant and V to represent vowel, we might represent *pupil* as CV' CVC. Show the syllabic division, mark the accent, and indicate the consonants and vowels in *bagel.* ______________

si' lo, CV' CV *ba' con*, CV' CVC *do' nut*, CV' CVC *sea' son*, CVV' CVC	**11.** Show the syllabic division and indicate the vowels and consonants in the words below. *silo* ________ ________ *bacon* ________ ________ *donut* ________ ________ *season* ________ ________ Key: C is consonant. V is vowel.
vowel open, closed	**12.** Study the words in frame 11. We can see that CV/CV indicates that the first syllable is an open syllable. The open syllable ends with a ________ phoneme. The second, unaccented syllable may be ________ (*co la*) or ________ (*ba con*).
co' la, CV' CV *ba' con*, CV' CVC	**13.** Place the accents and indicate the vowels and consonants in *cola* and *bacon.*
silent	**14.** Let us review another generalization: **When two consonants apear together, the second is generally ____________ (*rattle*).**
short (unglided) long (glided) short (unglided)	**15.** Examine the word *puppet.* If we divide it *pup pet,* we would expect the first vowel to have its ____________ sound. If we divide it *pu ppet,* we would expect the *u* to be ____________. The *u* in the word *puppet* should be ____________.
closed *pŭp pet*	**16.** For the *u* to have the correct sound in the word *puppet,* it should appear in a(n) ____________ (closed, open) syllable. Write the word *puppet,* dividing it correctly. Mark the *u.* ____________
pup pet *p* *pŭp' ət* or *pŭp' ĭt* short	**17.** Now write *puppet* as it would appear in the dictionary—first the entry word, using syllabication but the correct spelling. __________ Follow this with the correct pronunciation. Omit the second ________. __________ Sometimes in an unaccented syllable, the vowel is not a *schwa* but rather a related sound, the soft ____________ (short, long) *i.*

consonants **consonants**	**18.** We can make a generalization: **When two vowel letters are separated by two ____________,** **the syllable division is generally between the ____________.**
closed short (unglided) VC/CV	**19.** The first syllable in *after* (*af ter*) is ______________ (open, closed). Therefore, we expect the vowel sound in this syllable to be ________________. We will use _______________ (CV/CV, VC/CV) to represent the closed syllable generalization for syllabic division.
closed consonants VC/CV	**20.** The closed syllable generalization (expressed VC/CV) gives us a clue for syllabic division. Study the words below. *normal* *better* *bandit* *hammer* The first syllable is ______________ (open, closed). We divide the syllable between the two adjacent __________. How do we represent the closed syllable generalization to syllabic division? ____________
mat' ter, sig' nal *shel' ter, gos' sip*	**21.** Observing the open and closed syllable generalizations, divide the words below into syllables and place the accents. *matter* __________ *signal* __________ *shelter* __________ *gossip* __________
cri' sis, CCV' CVC *chi' na,* CCV' CV *pen' guin,* CVC' CVVC	**22.** Study the words at the right. Divide each word into syllables and place the accent (2), and indicate the vowels and consonants (3). **1** / **2** / **3** *panda* / *pan' da* / CVC' CV *crisis* / ______ / ______ *china* / ______ / ______ *penguin* / ______ / ______
CV/CV vowel VC/CV consonants	**23.** Let us review: We can use __________ to represent the open-syllable generalization for syllabic division. The syllable division is between the single __________ and the single consonant. We can use __________ to represent the closed-syllable generalization for syllabic division. The syllable division is between the two ____________.

 open long (glided), first	**24.** Note the relationship among the sounds of the vowels, the syllabication, and the accent. When we divide the word *diner,* the first syllable is a(n) ______________ (open, closed) syllable with the division between the vowel and the consonant. The vowel has its ________________ sound, and the accent is on the ________________ syllable.
 closed short (unglided) first	**25.** When we divide *dinner,* the first two letters are the same, but the pronunciation is different: The first syllable is __________________, the sound represented by the first vowel is __________________, and the accent is on the __________________ syllable.
 closed short (unglided)	**26.** The syllabic division between consonants is more dependable than the division between the single vowel and single consonant. There are many words in which the first single consonant ends the first syllable: *ex it, nov ice, hon or, fac et.* In these words, the first syllable is __________________ (open, closed) and the vowel has its __________________ sound.
  second	**27.** When in doubt, however, try this generalization first: **If the first vowel in a two-syllable word is followed by a single consonant, that consonant often begins the _____________ syllable,** as in *di ner.*
tī ger yes	**28.** Divide *tiger* into syllables: _____________. Mark the vowel in the first syllable to show pronunciation. If *tiger* were spelled with two *g*'s, would it be expected to rhyme with *bigger?* __________________
yes yes yes *lĕt' ter, nŭm' ber* *ĕf' fort, măt' ter*	**29.** Study the words below. Is each a two-or-more-syllable word? _______ Is there a single vowel in the first syllable? _______ Is the single vowel followed by two consonants? _______ If so, divide the words between the consonants. Mark the first vowel in each to show its pronunciation. Mark the accent. *letter* __________ *number* __________ *effort* __________ *matter* __________

If the first vowel in a two-syllable word is followed by a single consonant, that consonant often begins the second syllable.	**30.** State the generalization for the syllabication of *meter.*
When two vowels are separated by two consonants, generally the word is divided between the consonants.	**31.** State the generalization for the syllabication of *member.*
  hōpe̸, hŏp, hŏp′ p̸ĭng long (unglided)	**32.** Show the pronunciations of these words by dividing them into syllables, marking the vowels, placing the accents, and drawing slashes through silent letters. *hope* __________ *hop* __________ *hopping* __________ If we did not double the *p* to form *hopping,* we might expect the last letter of the first syllable to represent a __________ (long, short) *o.* This would not be our intention.
  sun shine	**33.** Let us make a generalization: **Divide a compound word between the two "words" that form the compound, as in cowboy (cow boy).** Divide *sunshine* into syllables. __________
compound two two	**34.** The words below are __________ words. *sunshine* *seashore* *backyard* *seahorse* Each compound word consists of __________ (How many?) one-syllable words. Therefore, each of these compound words has __________ (How many?) syllables.
  two *bat tle* one three	**35.** We expect each "word" in a compound word to represent one or more syllables. Now let us consider the compound word *battleship.* How many syllables do you identify in *battle?* __________ Divide *battle* into syllables. __________ How many syllables do you identify in *ship?* __________ Therefore, *battleship* consists of __________ (How many?) syllables.

match' book, rain' drop fire' crack er, pan' cake	**36.** Use the compound word generalization and other generalizations to divide the words below into syllables. Place the accents. *matchbook* ________ *raindrop* ________ *firecracker* ________ *pancake* ________
th	**37.** Remember that a two-letter grapheme, a digraph, acts as a single letter. **Generally, do not syllabicate between the letters of a digraph.** The word *together* is not *to get her* because the digraph ________ is not to be divided.
dol' phin, kitch' en pan' ther, cash' ew	**38.** Show the syllables and mark the accent in the words below. *dolphin* ________ *kitchen* ________ *panther* ________ *cashew* ________
cluster	**39.** Consonant clusters represent phonemes that are blended together when pronounced. **Consonant clusters are often in the same syllable.** The word *secret* is not *sec ret* because the consonant ____________ generally is not divided.
con stant, lob ster sis ter, com plete sister	**40.** Divide the words below into syllables. *constant* ________ *lobster* ________ *sister* ________ *complete* ________ The word ______________ is an exception. The syllables in *sister* are divided between the consonants in the cluster.
clusters	**41.** Let us summarize. **We generally do not syllabicate between the letters in a consonant digraph or consonant cluster,** as in *dolphin* (*dol phin*) and *complete* (*com plete*). Consonant digraphs are more reliable clues to syllabic division than consonant ______________.
go' pher, ar' cher, mar' shal, bush' el	**42.** Observing the consonant digraph, consonant cluster, and other generalizations, divide the words below into syllables. Mark the accented syllable. *gopher* *archer* *marshal* *bushel*

phoneme phoneme	**43.** Remember that vowel pairs, also known as vowel digraphs or vowel teams, represent one ________________ (*freedom, train, boat, day, green, seat*). We generally do not divide syllables between vowel letters that represent one ________________.
do not	**44.** A vowel diphthong represents a glide from one sound to another (*announce*). Therefore, we ______________ divide syllables between the (do, do not) letters in a diphthong.
	45. We can make another generalization: **We generally do not syllabicate between the letters in a diphthong or vowel pair that represent one phoneme,** as in *royal* (*roy al*) and *freedom* (*free dom*).
chee tah *voy age* We generally do not syllabicate between the letters in a diphthong or vowel pair that represent one phoneme.	**46.** How would we divide the word *cheetah* into syllables? ________ How would we divide *voyage* into syllables? _____________ State the generalization for the syllabication of letters in a vowel digraph or diphthong.
slŭg′ gish, măm′ mal *mē′ ter, lā′ ter* *mō′ tive, lăt′ ter* yes	**47.** We are studying generalizations that pertain to syllabication. In this study we are using words we already know. Now pretend you do not know the words below. Divide them into syllables following the "open-syllable, long" and "closed-syllable, short" generalizations. Mark the vowel in the first syllable to show pronunciation. Place the accent. *sluggish* _________ *mammal* _________ *meter* _________ *later* _________ *motive* _________ *latter* _________ Are all of these words marked the way they really are pronounced? _________
pī′ rət (or ĭt), păn′ thər *grā′ vē, hăp′ pən*	**48.** Pretend you do not know the words below. Syllabicate them according to the generalizations we've been studying. Mark the vowels to show pronunciation. Place the accents. Follow the directions carefully. *pirate* _________ *panther* _________ *gravy* _________ *happen* _________

yes	**49.** Reread the words in frame 48. Are they all marked the way they are really pronounced? ________. If any are not, correctly divide them into syllables and mark the vowel in the first syllable.
often	**50.** If the first vowel is followed by a single consonant, that consonant ________ (always, often) begins the second syllable. (Take time to check your results. Are you getting them all correct? Are you applying what you have learned? Do you complete a frame, writing all the answers before you move the mask down? You should be able to see the results of your study. May you have a great feeling of self-satisfaction!)
root syllables	**51.** We have observed that the accent is generally on the ______ word rather than on the prefix or suffix. It is natural, then, to expect prefixes and suffixes to form ________ separate from the root word.
un fold, re lent less, re o pen ing	**52.** **Prefixes and suffixes usually form separate syllables from the root word.** Divide the words below into syllables. *unfold* ________ *relentless* ________ *reopening* ________
d, t *loaded, dieted, gated*	**53.** Most prefixes and suffixes form separate syllables from the root word. We have learned that *-ed* forms a separate syllable when it is added to root words that end in a ________ or a ________ phoneme (page 46). Indicate the words in which *-ed* forms a separate syllable. *loaded* *laughed* *traveled* *dieted* *gated*
sī' dər, sō' də, stā' shən *ŭn tīm' lē, wĭn' dō*	**54.** Observing the generalizations, divide the words below into syllables and mark them to show pronunciation. Place the accents. *cider* ________ *soda* ________ *station* ________ *untimely* ________ *window* ________
two *ble, cle, ble*	**55.** Examine the words *table, circle, marble.* Each of these words has ________ syllables. Write the last syllable in each word. We can show the pronunciations of these syllables as *bəl* and *kəl.* *ta* ________ *cir* ________ *mar* ________
consonant	**56.** A helpful generalization is: **If the last syllable of a word ends in *le* preceded by a ________, that consonant usually begins the last syllable.**

Answers	Frames
pur ple, can dle, mar ble *cir cle, ta ble*	**57.** Divide the words below into syllables. *purple* ________ *candle* ________ *marble* ________ *circle* ________ *table* ________
consonant, unaccented *schwa*	**58.** Study the words in frame 57. The final syllable in each word consists of a ____________ and *le* (C + *le*). This syllable is ____________. (accented, unaccented) The vowel sound in the C + *le* syllable is a ____________.
ga ble (*gā' bəl*)	**59.** Write the complete pronunciation of *gable* as it would appear in the dictionary. ____________ (____________)
pronunciation (or meaning)	**60.** Now let us examine a word that is the same as *gable* except for an *m* that precedes the *ble.* Read this sentence: *Do not gamble with your health.* The letter *m* affects the ____________ of the word.
b *gam ble*	**61.** The last syllable in *gamble* ends with *le* preceded by the consonant ______. Show how we would divide the word. (Note that other generalizations correctly apply to these words.) ____________
gam ble (*găm' bəl*)	**62.** Now write *gamble* as it would appear in the dictionary. ____________ (____________)
consonants consonant root compound before diphthong blend (cluster)	**63.** The syllable divisions are most commonly made in the cases: **A.** between two __________ (as in *ladder*) **B.** between a single vowel and a single __________ (as in *paper*) **C.** between prefixes, suffixes, and ____________ words (unhelpful) **D.** between words that form a ____________ word (*snowman*) **E.** ____________ the C + *le* (as in *stable*) (before, after) They are not made between letters representing a single phoneme, that is, between letters in a digraph or a ____________ (as in *app<u>oi</u>nt*). They generally are not made between the letters in a consonant ____________ (as in *secret*).

syllable are not	**64.** We have seen that syllables are units of pronunciation. The arrangement of vowels and consonants within the ________________ affects the pronunciation. We have noted that generalizations about syllabication are helpful but ________________ infallible. (are, are not)
ā' bəl *change a ble* *chānj' ə bəl*	**65.** Sounds may change with the lengthening of the word: Divide *able* into syllables. Mark it to show pronunciation. ________________ Divide *changeable* into syllables. ________________ Rewrite it to show pronunciation. ________________
long *schwa* unaccented	**66.** In *able,* the *a* represents the ________________ sound. In *changeable,* the second *a* represents the ________________ sound; it is now in the ________________ syllable. (accented, unaccented)
CV̆C CV̆ph v̆C Cv̆C blv̄ Cv̄ Cv̆ph Cv̄phe̸ Did you succeed?	**67.** To check our understanding, let us use symbols. Study the key below. Divide the following "words" into syllables, marking the vowels as they would be found most commonly and as though all syllables were accented. Key: C is consonant V is vowel (other than *e*) e̸ is silent *e* ph is digraph bl is cluster which is blended C v C C v ph __________ v C C v C __________ bl v C v __________ C v ph C v ph e̸ __________

Study Guide

Syllable Division

Four Clues to Pronunciation

The four important clues to the pronunciation of a given word are (1) the vowel phonemes, (2) the consonant phonemes, (3) the position of the vowel in the syllable, and (4) the accented syllable.

First Vowel Followed by a Single Consonant

If the first vowel in a two-syllable word is followed by a single consonant, that consonant often begins the second syllable (*tī′ ger, sī′ lent*).

Two Vowels Separated by Two Consonants

When two vowels are separated by two consonants, the syllable division is generally between the consonants (*pup′ pet, mag′ net*). Syllable division between consonants is more dependable than the division between the single vowel and single consonant.

Prefixes and Suffixes

In general, prefixes and suffixes form separate syllables from the root word (*play′ ful, un smil′ ing*).

***Last Syllable* le**

If the last syllable of a word ends in *le* preceded by a consonant, that consonant usually begins the last syllable (*tā′ ble, han′ dle*).

Compound Words

Divide compound words between the "words" that form the compound (*check′ list, moon′ light*).

Consonant Digraphs and Consonant Clusters

In general, do not syllabicate between consonant digraphs (*cash′ ew, pan′ ther*) and consonant clusters (*sē′ cret, vī′ brate*).

Vowel Digraphs (Pairs) and Vowel Dipthongs That Represent One Phoneme

In general, do not syllabicate between the letters in a vowel digraph (*ex′ ceed, free′ dom*) or diphthong (*trow′ el, thou′ sand*).

Review 23

1. Examine the following consonant-vowel word patterns. In each one, place a slash where the syllable division would most likely occur. Make sure that there is a vowel in each syllable. Give the reason you divided the word as you did. There are no digraphs in these words.
   - **a.** CVCVCC
   - **b.** CVCCVC
   - **c.** CVCCV
   - **d.** CCVCVCC
2. How would you expect the following words to be divided? Why? (Pretend that you do not know the words; then you cannot say "I can hear the pronunciation unit.")
   - **a.** *playful*
   - **b.** *capable*
   - **c.** *father*

See the Answers to the Reviews section for the answers to Review 23, page 238.

Recap III

26 consonants phonemes	**1. Phonics** is the study of the relationship of letters and letter combinations to the sounds they represent. There are ______ letters in our alphabet, classified as vowels and ______________. These letters and combinations represent the 44 sounds, or ________________, used in the American-English language. (This is oversimplified but adequate in this step of the process of teaching children to read.)
phoneme phoneme 44 phonemes	**2.** How easy the development of independence in decoding would be if each letter represented only one ________________ and each phoneme was represented by only one letter! You know that is not the case; however, you have gained an understanding of the patterns within the inconsistencies. You have also developed a one-to-one correspondence between grapheme and ________________ by selecting a key symbol to represent each of the ________________ ________________ of the language.

pronunciation phoneme accented accented vowel vowel *i (ĭ), ə (schwa)*	**3.** Another relationship is that of the syllable to the word. A **syllable** is a unit of ________________. Each syllable must have one and only one vowel ________________. Each word has one syllable that receives the greatest amount of stress. We call this the ________________ syllable. If a word has only one syllable, that is the ________________ syllable. There is a strong relationship between the ________________ (vowel, consonant) and the accented syllable. The ________________ in the unaccented syllable often is represented by the soft, short sound of _____ or by the ____________.
syllables accented	**4.** You have become acquainted with the clues that help you (1) to divide a word into ________________ and (2) to determine which syllable is ________________. The following frames present specific words, selected to illustrate your knowledge of the syllable–accent generalizations as well as to review other learnings.
      see-saw, see′ saw, (sē′ sô) compound first, compound	**5.** On the blanks after each word, (1) rewrite it as an entry word in the dictionary (useful for end-of-the-line hyphenation); (2) rewrite, adding the accent; and (3) in parentheses, using all your knowledge of phonemes, rewrite the word showing pronunciation. To make this study more effective, as you work, say the generalizations of syllables, accents, and other understandings to yourself. Also fill in the other blanks as indicated. *seesaw* ________________ ________________ ________________ Using the word *seesaw* as an example, say to yourself "*Seesaw* is a ________________ word; the syllabic division comes between the words of which it is composed." (Fill in the first blank.) "The accent usually falls on or within the ________________ word of a ________________ word." (Fill in blank two.) On blank three, mark the word for pronunciation.

s, two one long, silent *ē* *ô* *ball* *(sē′ sô)*	**6.** Continue your conversation about *seesaw:* "We represent the consonant phonemes in *seesaw* with ________. The first syllable has ________ vowel letters. We know that each syllable can have only ________ vowel phoneme. When there are two vowel letters in a syllable, generally the first is ________ and the second is ________. So the phoneme in the first syllable is represented by ________. In the second 'word' the vowel phoneme is *w*-controlled. The key symbol is ________; the key word is ________." (But maybe you prefer to use *ought* (*ôt*) as the key word. Do you?) The third blank, frame 5, reads ________. Examine the footnote. Turn to page 242. Read items V 10 and 9. Did you use them in your conversation? How about S 1 and A 2 on page 243? V 10, V 9, S 1, A 2*
s *i* *cit-rus, cit′ rus,* *(sĭt′ rəs)*	**7.** The second word in your study is *citrus.* (Caution: Although you can achieve correct results immediately, don't do it that way. This is your opportunity to review by yourself your understandings of the generalizations: syllables, accents, and so on, including "*c* usually represents the ________ phoneme when followed by ________.") Selected references to Appendix A are given. Check your "conversation" after each frame. Did you include these generalizations? Also note irregularities in consonant and vowel phonemes. *citrus* ________ ________ ________ C 2, V 3, V 14, S 5, A 5*
un but ton ing, *un but′ ton ing,* (*ŭn bŭt′ ən ĭng*) or (*ən bŭt′ ən ĭŋ*)	**8.** Continue with the words as given in each of the following frames. *unbuttoning* ________ ________ ________ V 3, V 14, S 2, S 5, A 2*
ad mi ra tion, *ad mi ra′tion,* *(ăd mə rā′ shən)*	**9.** *admiration* ________ ________ ________ S 2, A 6*
wrin kle, wring′ kle, *(ring′ kəl)*	**10.** *wrinkle* ________ ________ ________ C 1a.n, S 3, A 8*

*Key to generalizations (Appendix A): C: Consonants, p. 241; V: Vowels, p. 242; S: Syllabic Division, p. 243; A: Accent Clues, p. 243.

1. *an nex, an nex′,* (ə *nĕks′*) 2. *an nex, an′ nex,* (*ăn′ ĕks*)	**11.** We will (1) *annex* the land on which the new (2) *annex* was built. (1) ______ ______ ______ (2) ______ ______ ______ A 4*
ti ger, ti′ ger, (*tī′ gər*)	**12.** *tiger* ______ ______ ______ S 4*
weath er, weath′er, (*wĕṯh′ ər*)	**13.** *weather* ______ ______ ______ S 6*
con tain, con tain′, (*kən tān′*)	**14.** *contain* ______ ______ ______ C 2, V 10, A 7*
yel low, yel′ low, (*yel′ ō*) consonant	**15.** *yellow* ______ ______ ______ Is this *y* a vowel or a consonant? ______ C 6, S 5, A 5*
reading (Children should know the words at the hearing level.)	**16.** Turn to Appendix A. Restudy the generalizations to check your thinking. I hope you are saying "I did very well." ("perfect"—?) The problem we face is that you know these words. If you were attacking words not in your ______ (reading, listening) vocabulary, you would have a better test of your phonics ability.
onset, rime consonant phoneme, follow(s)	**17.** Another way to analyze the syllable is to divide it into the ______ and the ______. You know that the **onset** is the ______ letter(s) that begins the syllable, and the **rime** is the vowel ______ and the consonant letter(s) that ______ the vowel phoneme.

*Key to generalizations (Appendix A): C: Consonants, p. 241; V: Vowels, p. 242; S: Syllabic Division, p. 243; A: Accent Clues, p. 243.

	18. Using your knowledge of the onset and the rime in the syllable, divide the word *pencil* into syllables. Then analyze the two syllables as the onset and rime.
pen, cil	The word *pencil* consists of the two syllables __________ and __________.
p	The first syllable, *pen,* consists of the onset __________ and the rime
en	__________.
c	The second syllable, *cil,* consists of the onset __________ and the rime
il	__________.
	19. Now continue to identify the onset and the rime in each of the syllables in the following words.
sur, prise	The word *surprise* consists of the two syllables __________ and __________.
s, ur	The first syllable, *sur,* consists of the onset ______ and the rime ______.
pr, ise	The second syllable, *prise,* consists of the onset ______ and the rime ______.
lav, en, der	The word *lavender* consists of the three syllables ______, ______, and ______ .
l, av	The first syllable, *lav,* consists of the onset ______ and the rime ______.
en	The second syllable, *en,* consists of the rime ______.
d, er	The third syllable, *der,* consists of the onset ______ and the rime ______.
	20. You have studied the relationship of letters and letter combinations to the
sounds (phonemes)	________________ they represent and have built a depth of understanding
phonics	in the content of ________________. You will use that content to help those learning to read to develop skill in the recognition and identification of words.
	It must be pointed out that the use of phonics is the basis of **one** of the word-attack skills (skills needed to attain independence in reading) and that the
reading	mastery of the total ________________ process requires the development of still other sets of skills, including the understanding of the material read. Reading is a complicated process!

*Key to generalizations (Appendix A): C: Consonants, p. 241; V: Vowels, p. 242; S: Syllabic Division, p. 243; A: Accent Clues, p. 243.

Part VII

Structural Analysis

Morphemes, Prefixes, Suffixes, Contractions, and Compound Words

Introduction

phonemes	**1.** The graphemes we have studied thus far represent _________. Now we will turn our attention to groups of graphemes that represent sound and meaning.
re *place, ment* meaning	**2. Structural analysis** is a word identification skill. For the purpose of illustrating this skill, let us assume that *replacement* is an unfamiliar word. You might logically divide *replacement* into three meaningful units: _________, _________, and _________. Now pronounce *replacement.* Consider the contribution each unit makes to the ___________ of *replacement.* You have now successfully used structural analysis.
yes	**3.** **Structural analysis is a word identification skill that involves the use of prefixes, suffixes, root words, the "words" in compound words, and the apostrophes in contractions to identify unfamiliar words.** Would you expect the reader to use structural analysis to identify the word *unusually?* ______

Answer	Frame
structural analysis	**4.** In frame 2, you determined that *replacement* consists of three meaningful units. Therefore, ________________ is a useful tool for the identification of *replacement.*
cannot	Now consider *train.* We __________ (can, cannot) divide *train* into smaller, meaningful
phonics	units. We might use __________ to associate phonemes with graphemes, or
onset, rime	we might use knowledge of __________ and __________ to associate phonemes with *tr* and *ain.*
meaning	We can see that structural analysis is suitable for the identification of words that consist of more than one unit of __________.
meaning	**5.** We will begin our study with the **morpheme.** *Morph* means form or shape. We learned in Part I that *pheme* refers to voice or sound. Therefore, a morpheme is a unit of ________ (*morph* + *pheme*) in the English language. **A morpheme is the smallest unit of meaning.**
free	**6.** We will study two types of morphemes: free morphemes and bound morphemes. A **free morpheme** can stand alone as a single word. We cannot divide a free morpheme into smaller units without affecting meaning. **A free morpheme can exist on its own.** *Paint* is a _______ morpheme. We cannot divide *paint* into smaller, meaningful units.
-ing	**7.** A **bound morpheme** cannot stand alone. This morpheme is always attached to another morpheme. The bound morpheme in *playing* is _______. **A bound morpheme must be added to another morpheme.**
free	**8.** We will use *unlocked* as an illustration. *Lock* is a __________ (free, bound) morpheme. *Lock* has meaning in and of itself. We cannot divide *lock* into smaller units and still retain its meaning.
bound	*Un-* and *-ed* are ______________ (free, bound) morphemes. *Un-* and *-ed* must be added to other free morphemes.

one, one *chew* *-able* *chewable*	**9.** Recognizing that we are oversimplifying the situation, we will consider an English word to be a free morpheme, or a free morpheme to which one or more bound morphemes are attached. *Chewable* consists of ________ (How many?) free morpheme(s) and ________ (How many?) bound morpheme(s). Write the free morpheme in *chewable.* ________ Now write the bound morpheme. ________ The bound morpheme and the free morpheme together form the word ________.
free, bound	**10.** We will continue our study by examining the word *reopening.* *Open* is a ________ morpheme. The *re-* and *-ing* are ________ morphemes. Therefore, a word may consist of a free morpheme (*open*) or a free morpheme with one or more bound morphemes (*reopening*).
free **bound** no	**11.** Let us restate our definition of an English word: **For the purposes of teaching reading, a word may consist of a ________ morpheme (a morpheme that can stand alone), such as *jump,* or a free morpheme and one or more ________ morphemes (morphemes that must be added to another morpheme), like the *-ing* in *jumping.* (A word may also contain one or more word parts borrowed from other languages.)** Therefore, we will consider *jump, jumped,* and *jumping* to be words. Do we consider *-ing* to be a word? ______
meaning	**12.** The task of the reader is to identify a familiar word or free morpheme, as well as any bound morphemes. We will use *unlikely* to illustrate this process. **A.** The reader must recognize the word (free morpheme)—*like.* **B.** The reader must also identify the prefix and the suffix (bound morphemes)—*un-* and *-ly.* **C.** Last, the reader identifies the entire word—*unlikely*—and understands how the prefix and the suffix affect its ________.
one	**13.** We have defined a word from the perspective of the teacher of reading. Some teachers' manuals use **root word** as a synonym for a free morpheme. Other manuals use **base word.** We will use root word in our study. Consult your teacher's manual. You may use either term—root word or base word—in your answers. *Lately* consists of ________ (How many?) root word(s).

sadly, restore, powerful, misstep, unfairly, shipment	**14.** Study the words below. *sadly* *restore* *powerful* *misstep* *unfairly* *shipment* Each word consists of a root word (free morpheme) and one or more bound morphemes. Draw a single line under the root word and a double line under the bound morpheme in each word.

Review 24

1. We have defined a morpheme as ________________.

2. *Cat* is a free morpheme because ________________.

3. Circle the free morphemes in the list below.

dog *-ing* *desk* *pre-* *hat* *-ly* *dis-* *table*

4. For the purposes of teaching reading, we define an English word as

____________________________.

5. Underline the bound morphemes in the words below:

collectible *untimely* *enact* *unneeded* *childish*

6. **a.** A bound morpheme must be attached to another ___________.

b. A bound morpheme ____________ stand alone.
(can, cannot)

See the Answers to the Reviews section for the answers to Review 24, page 238.

Prefixes and Suffixes, Contractions, and Compound Words

beginning	**1.** Bound morphemes are divided into two groups: prefixes and suffixes. *Pre-* means before. Therefore, a **prefix** is placed at the ________________ of a (beginning, end) root word (free morpheme). **A prefix is placed before a root word.**
not, not	**2.** A prefix may change the meaning of a root word (free morpheme) or make its meaning more specific. The prefix *il-* denotes "not," therefore, *illegal* means "_______ legal." *Illogical* means "_______ logical."
fill again root word (or free morpheme) bound	**3.** *Re-* means "again." Therefore, *refill* means "to ____________." *Fill* is a _______________. *Fill* has meaning in and of itself. *Re-* is a ________ morpheme. *Re-* must be added to another morpheme (root word).

Answers	Frames
prefix	**4.** Study the words below. Each word consists of a __________ and a root word (free morpheme). Write the prefixes. It is common practice to add a trailing hyphen to a prefix when it is not attached to a root word (*mis-*).
un-, re-, pre-	*uncut* __________ *remove* __________ *prepay* __________
de-, dis, in-	*derail* __________ *disapprove* __________ *invalid* __________
unusual, reopen, midweek, misfit, precondition	**5.** Place a check beside each word below that contains a prefix. *unusual* *union* *reopen* *midweek* *misfit* *precondition*
union	**6.** Which word in frame 5 does not contain a prefix? ________
is not	**7.** The *un* in *union* _________ a prefix. *Union* is the smallest meaningful unit. (is, is not)
is	The *un-* in *unusual* ___________ a prefix. Therefore, we can conclude that (is, is not)
root words (or free morphemes)	*union* and *usual* are ____________________.
	8. Now add the indicated prefix to each root word below. Write the new word at the right.

Answer	Prefix	Prefix Meaning	Root Word	New Word
misuse	*mis-*	bad, wrong	*use*	____________
immobile	*im-*	not	*mobile*	____________
midweek	*mid-*	middle	*week*	____________
recall	*re-*	again, back	*call*	____________
disagree	*dis-*	not	*agree*	____________
defrost	*de-*	do the opposite	*frost*	____________

Answers	Frames
	9. Complete the following:
prefix	**A _________ is placed before a root word to change its meaning or to make its meaning more specific.**
end	**10.** A **suffix** is placed at the _______ of a root word (free morpheme). Write
-ment, bound	the suffix in *encouragement.* ___________ A suffix is a _______________ morpheme. (free, bound)
	A suffix is placed at the end of a root word (free morpheme).

happy, no
un-, -ly, -est, -er

11. We will use the word **affixes** to refer to both prefixes and suffixes or to more than one prefix or suffix in a word (*restlessness*).

Consider *unhappily, happiest,* and *happier.* The root word (free morpheme) is ________. Do these words have the same meaning? ________

Write the affixes in the following words:

unhappily ________ *happiest* ________ *happier* ________

---

cover, 2, re-, -ed
mature, 1, im-
fail, 3, un-, -ing, -ly
magnet, 2, non-, -ic
align, 2, mis-, -ed
judge, 2, pre-, -ed
affix

12. A root word (free morpheme) may have more than one affix. Study the words below. Count the affixes in each one. Write the root word, the number of affixes, and the affix or affixes on the lines below.

	Root Word	**Number of Affixes**	**Affix(es)**
recovered	________	________	________
immature	________	________	________
unfailingly	________	________	________
nonmagnetic	________	________	________
misaligned	________	________	________
prejudged	________	________	________

We can see that more than one ______ may be added to a single root word.

---

number

13. We will recognize two types of suffixes: inflectional suffixes and derivational suffixes.

An inflectional suffix changes number, affects verb tense, indicates comparison, or denotes possession.

The -*s* in *raindrops* is an inflectional suffix. The -*s* denotes a change in __________.

---

number
verb tense
possession
comparison

14. Use the following terms to fill in the blanks below.

comparison *number* *verb tense* *possession*

The -*s* in *bicycles* denotes a change in ____________.

The -*en* in *eaten* indicates a change in ____________.

The ’*s* in John’s indicates ____________.

The -*est* in *tallest* denotes ____________.

Sam's, softest *warmer, books* *sewing, laughed* number, verb tense possession, comparison	**15.** Rewrite the words below, adding the inflectional suffix. *Sam + 's =* __________ *soft + est =* __________ *warm + er =* __________ *book + s =* __________ *sew + ing =* __________ *laugh + ed =* __________ These suffixes change ____________ (*books*), affect ____________ (*sewing, laughed*), indicate ____________ (*Sam's*), and show ____________ (*warmer*).
   derivational	**16.** **A derivational suffix affects meaning and may change grammatical category.** The -*able* in *breakable* changes a verb (*break*) into an adjective (*breakable*). Therefore, the suffix -*able* is a ____________ suffix.
noticeable, dirty, massive, fitness, joyous, historic	**17.** Study the words below. Underline the suffix in each one. *noticeable* *dirty* *massive* *fitness* *joyous* *historic*
 yes derivational	**18.** Do the suffixes in frame 17 affect meaning and change the grammatical category? _________ Given this, we can conclude that these word endings are ________________ suffixes.
   inflectional derivational	**19.** How can we distinguish between inflectional suffixes and derivational suffixes? An inflectional suffix adds meaning to a root word but does not change its grammatical category. Note that the -*er* in *nicer* changes the word's meaning by indicating a comparison. Therefore, the -*er* is a(n) ________________ suffix. (inflectional, derivational) Adding -*ic* to *history,* a noun, changes it into *historic,* an adjective. Therefore, -*ic* is a(n) ________________ suffix. (inflectional, derivational)

20. We have established that affixes affect the meanings of root words and may also change their grammatical categories. Match each word in column 1 with the correct definition in column 2.

Answer		Column 1	Column 2
e	________	1. *fearless*	a. not legal
a	________	2. *illegal*	b. full of danger
i	________	3. *highest*	c. before dawn
c	________	4. *predawn*	d. matched incorrectly
b	________	5. *dangerous*	e. without fear
d	________	6. *mismatched*	f. full of fear
h	________	7. *impolite*	g. capable of knowing
g	________	8. *knowable*	h. not polite
j	________	9. *clouds*	i. having the greatest height
f	________	10. *fearful*	j. more than one cloud

21. Let us now consider contractions.

A **contraction** is a shortened form of two or more words.

Two or more words are combined into a single word. An apostrophe denotes one or more missing letters—for instance, *is not* becomes *isn't*. Word meaning ____________ change.
(does, does not)

Answer: does not

22. Each of the word pairs below may be combined to form a common contraction. Write the contraction.

we are ________	*was not* ________	*I have* ________
she would ________	*they will* ________	*let us* ________

Answer: *we're, wasn't, I've*
she'd, they'll, let's

23. **A compound word consists of two or more root words that when combined form an entirely new word.**

How many "words" are joined together to form the compound word *lamppost*? ______

Answer: two

Do the spellings of the "words" change when they are part of a compound word? ______

Answer: no

searchlight, pineapple
buttercup, limelight
lamppost, mousetrap
backpack, sandman

24. Combine each set of words below to form a compound word.

search + light =	___________	*pine + apple =*	___________
butter + cup =	___________	*lime + light =*	___________
lamp + post =	___________	*mouse + trap =*	___________
back + pack =	___________	*sand + man =*	___________

searchlight *pineapple*
lamppost *buttercup*
mousetrap *limelight*
backpack *sandman*

25. Group the compound words in the frame above into two categories:

(1) compounds in which the general meanings of the "words" are relatively unchanged and

(2) compounds in which the meanings of the "words" have little or nothing to do with the meaning of the compound itself.

Group 1: Meanings are relatively unchanged	**Group 2: Meanings have little or nothing to do with meaning of compound**
___________	___________
___________	___________
___________	___________
___________	___________

krôswôk, īs īt
kôrnbrĕd, lăndlŏkt
trĕdmĭl, hōlsāl

26. Rewrite the compound words below to show pronunciation.

crosswalk	___________	*eyesight*	___________
cornbread	___________	*landlocked*	___________
treadmill	___________	*wholesale*	___________

Study Guide

Prefixes for Word Study

Prefix	Prefix Meaning	Examples
anti-	against	*antibiotic, antitrust*
de-	away from	*defrost, debug*
*dis-**	opposite of, lack of	*displace, disagree*
em-, im-, in-	into, in	*empower, imbed, inbound*
en-	cause to be, on, put into	*enable, enlarge*
fore-	front, before	*forefoot, forefather*
il-, im-, in-, ir	not	*illegal, imperfect, inaccurate, irrelevant*
inter-	between	*interstate, interact*
*mid-**	middle	*midday, midline*
*mis-**	wrong, bad	*misfortune, miscue*
*non-**	not	*nonstop, nonfat*
*out-**	more	*outdo, outperform*
*over-**	too much	*overdue, overweight*
*pre-**	before	*preview, prepay*
pro-	forward, before	*proactive*
*re-**	again	*rewrite, reread*
semi-	half, partly	*semicircle, semifinal*
*sub-**	under	*subway, substandard*
*super-**	above, exceeding the norm	*superhighway, supertanker*
trans-	across	*transatlantic, transplant*
*un-**	not	*unfair, unsafe*
under-	in a lower place	*underpay, underrate*

The most frequently used prefixes are *un-* (*unlucky*), *re-* (*remove*), *in-* (meaning "not," as in *incomplete*), and *dis-* (*dislike*).

* These prefixes are often taught in elementary school. Check your teacher's manual or curriculum guide to identify other prefixes to include in your literacy program.

Study Guide

Suffixes for Word Study

Suffix	Suffix Meaning	Examples
-able, -ible	capable of, quality of	*breakable, collectible*
-age	act of, state of	*storage, leakage*
-al	relating to	*coastal, tropical*
-ance	act of, quality of	*assistance, acceptance*
-ed	past	*played, cried*
-en	relating to	*frozen, strengthen*
-ence	act of, quality of	*patience, dependence*
-er	more	*bigger, nearer*
-er, -or	one who	*actor, baker*
-ess	female	*waitress, actress*
-est	most	*kindest, farthest*
-ful	quality of	*beautiful, helpful*
-hood	state of	*parenthood, childhood*
-ian, -ant, -ent	a person who	*historian, assistant, student*
-ic	of, having to do with	*heroic, historic*
-ing	act of, instance of	*jumping, writing*
-ish	something like	*babyish, ticklish*
-ism	doctrine, practice, condition	*heroism, formalism*
-ist	someone who	*cyclist, biologist*
-ive	being able to, having	*active, negative*
-ize	having the nature of	*materialize, motorize*
-less	without	*careless, fruitless*
-like	similar to	*childlike, lifelike*
-ly	manner of	*neatly, totally*
-ment	result, product	*agreement, improvement*
-ness	quality of	*darkness, happiness*
-ous	full of, state of	*dangerous, famous*
-s, -es	plural	*swings, matches*
-ship	showing status	*membership, flagship*
-sion, -tion	act, state of	*action, celebration*
-ty	state of, characteristic	*ability, validity*
-ure	act of, process of	*closure, legislature*
-ward	in the direction of	*northward, backward*
-y	quality of, condition	*easy, rainy*

These suffixes are often taught in elementary school. Check in your curriculum guide or teacher's manual.

Study Guide

Contractions for Word Study

not	***is***	***will***
aren't (are not)	*he's (he is)*	*he'll (he will)*
can't (cannot)	*here's (here is)*	*I'll (I will)*
couldn't (could not)	*how's (how is)*	*it'll (it will)*
didn't (did not)	*it's (it is)*	*she'll (she will)*
doesn't (does not)	*she's (she is)*	*they'll (they will)*
don't (do not)	*that's (that is)*	*you'll (you will)*
hadn't (had not)	*there's (there is)*	*we'll (we will)*
hasn't (has not)	*what's (what is)*	*what'll (what will)*
haven't (have not)	*when's (when is)*	*where'll (where will)*
isn't (is not)	*where's (where is)*	
mustn't (must not)	*who's (who is)*	
needn't (need not)		
shouldn't (should not)		
wasn't (was not)		
weren't (were not)		
won't (will not)		
wouldn't (would not)		

have	***had***	***would***
could've (could have)	*he'd (he had)*	*he'd (he would)*
I've (I have)	*I'd (I had)*	*I'd (I would)*
might've (might have)	*she'd (she had)*	*it'd (it would)*
should've (should have)	*they'd (they had)*	*she'd (she would)*
they've (they have)		*they'd (they would)*
we've (we have)		*we'd (we would)*
would've (would have)		
you've (you have)		

are	***has***	***Other Contractions***
they're (they are)	*he's (he has)*	*I'm (I am)*
we're (we are)	*it's (it has)*	*let's (let us)*
who're (who are)	*she's (she has)*	*o'clock (of the clock)*
you're (you are)		*t'was (it was)*

	27. Let us review what we have learned thus far:
meaning	**A.** A morpheme is the smallest unit of ________.
free yes no	**B.** A ________ morpheme can stand alone. It has meaning in and of itself. Is *drink* a free morpheme? ________ Is *-ing* a free morpheme? ________
root	**C.** We will call the free morphemes ________ words. *Dog* is an example of a root word.
bound	**D.** A ________ morpheme cannot exist alone. It must be attached to another morpheme. *Re-* and *-ous* are bound morphemes.
beginning	**E.** A prefix is placed at the ________ (beginning, end) of a root word (free morpheme).
end	**F.** A suffix is placed at the ________ (beginning, end) of a root word (free morpheme).
Inflectional	**G.** ________ (Inflectional, Derivational) suffixes change number, affect verb tense, indicate possession, or denote comparison.
Derivational	**H.** ________ (Inflectional, Derivational) suffixes affect meaning and may change grammatical category.
contraction apostrophe	**I.** A ________ combines two words into a single word; a(n) ________ denotes one or more missing letters.
compound word	**J.** A ________ consists of two or more root words that when combined form an entirely new word.

Review 25

1. A ________ is placed at the beginning of a root word.
2. A ________ is placed at the end of a root word.
3. The term ________ refers to both prefixes and suffixes.
4. Draw a single line under the affix or affixes (bound morphemes) in each word below.

climbing	*likeable*	*prehistoric*	*impolite*
previewed	*treatment*	*illogical*	*uncovered*

5. Underline the prefix in each word below.

distrust	*midsized*	*impure*	*unsafe*
nonstop	*subplot*	*rebooted*	*demerit*

6. Underline the suffix or suffixes in each word below. Work carefully, and refer to the Study Guide. Some root words have more than one suffix.

parenthood	*joyous*	*motorists*	*heroism*
actor	*massive*	*musician*	*uselessly*

7. Write an *I* beside each word that contains an inflectional suffix and a *D* beside each word that contains a derivational suffix.

furious ____	*attracting* _____	*wolves* _____
sculptor ____	*penniless* _____	*boyish* _____

8. Most contractions are shortened forms of words in which an ________ denotes one or more missing letters. Does a contraction have the same meaning as the words written separately? Write the contraction for each word pair below:

could have	________	*where is*	________
do not	________	*they are*	________
we will	________	*what will*	________
he had	________	*we would*	________

See the Answers to the Reviews section for the answers to Review 25, page 238.

Spelling Generalizations for Adding Prefixes and Suffixes to Words

	1. *mismatched* *reapplied*
match, apply	The root words in the words above are ________ and ________.
no	Do *mis-* and *-ed* affect the spelling of *match*? _____
yes	Do *re-* and *-ed* affect the spelling of *apply*? _____
	How do we know when adding an affix will affect the spelling of a word? Fortunately, there are guidelines to help us spell words with prefixes and suffixes.
	2. We will begin our study with affixes that usually do not affect root word spelling. Study the words below. Write the prefix for each one.
dis-, mis-	*dishonest* ________ *misfit* ________
im-, pre-	*impatient* ________ *preschool* ________
ir-, in-	*irregular* ________ *indirect* ________
no	Do the prefixes affect the spellings of these root words? ________

Answers	Frames
does not	**3.** We can make a generalization: **Adding a prefix ____________ affect the spelling of the root word.** (does, does not)
shipment, harmful, friendly *kindness, cordless*	**4.** Consider the words below. Underline the suffix in each one. *shipment* *harmful* *friendly* *kindness* *cordless*
consonant consonant no	**5.** Each of the suffixes in frame 4 begins with a ________________. Note, (consonant, vowel) too, that each root word ends with a ________________. (consonant, vowel) Do the spellings of these root words change? ________
consonant	**6.** Complete this generalization: **The spelling of a root word often does not change when we add a suffix that begins with a __________ to a root word that ends in a consonant.**
hats *babies* *bikes* *buses* *plays* *dishes* *balls* *catches* *cars* *boxes* *jumps* *buzzes*	**7.** Next, let's consider generalizations for adding *-s* and *-es* to root words. Rewrite each root word below by adding *-s* or *-es,* as indicated in columns 1 and 2. **Column 1: Root Word + *-s*** / **Column 2: Root Word + *-es*** *hat* ________ *baby* ________ *bike* ________ *bus* ________ *play* ________ *dish* ________ *ball* ________ *catch* ________ *car* ________ *box* ________ *jump* ________ *buzz* ________
babies *buses, dishes, catches* *boxes, buzzes*	**8.** We add an *-s* to most words to form the plural. There are situations, however, that call for adding *-es.* Refer to your answers in the frame above to fill in the blanks below. Add *-es* to a word that ends in a *y* preceded by a consonant (________) or an *s* (________), *sh* (________), *ch* (________), *x* (________), or *z* (________).

leaves, elves, halves *shelves, knives, thieves*	**9.** Now, we will turn our attention to root words that end in *f* or *fe.* Rewrite the words below, adding *-s* or *-es.* *leaf* _______ *elf* _______ *half* _______ *shelf* _______ *knife* _______ *thief* _______
no *surfs, /f/* do not *dwôrfs* *dwôrvz*	**10.** Pronounce the words below: *hooves* *loaves* *strives* *thieves* Notice that we hear the /*v*/ phoneme in each of these words. Does the *f* or *fe* to *v* generalization hold for *puffs*? ______ Words ending in *ff* are exceptions to the generalization. Now add *-s* to *surf.* ________ Do you hear /*f*/ or /*v*/ in *surfs*? ________ We ___________ change the *f* or *fe* to *v* when the plural ends in the (do, do not) phoneme /*f*/. Your dictionary may indicate two pronunciations and two spellings for some root words ending in *f.* For example, the plural of *dwarf* may be *dwarfs* or *dwarves.* Write these two words to show pronunciation: _____________ and _____________. Check your dictionary or spellchecker to verify spelling.
-es *-s*	**11.** Let us summarize the *-s* and *-es* generalizations: **Add ____ to words that end in a *y* preceded by a consonant and to words that end in *s, sh, ch, x,* or *z.* Add _____ to most other words.** **When a root word ends in *f* or *fe* and the plural includes a /*v*/ phoneme, change the *f* or *fe* to a *v* before adding *-es.***
beautiful, busily *happiness, pitiless* *laziness, furious* *tried, worrier*	**12.** Another spelling question is whether to change the final *y* to *i* before adding a suffix. Solve each word "equation" below by adding the indicated suffix. *beauty + ful* = ____________ *busy + ly* = ______________ *happy + ness* = ____________ *pity + less* = ______________ *lazy + ness* = ____________ *fury + ous* = ______________ *try + ed* = ____________ *worry + er* = ______________

yes yes yes	**13.** Let us take a closer look at the root words in frame 12. Do these root words end in a *y*?________ Does a consonant precede the final *y*?________ Does the *y* change to *i* when a suffix is added? ________ **Change the *y* to *i* when a consonant precedes the *y*.**
yes yes no is not	**14.** Study the words below. *stayed* *annoyed* *payment* *joyful* Do the root words end in a *y*? _______ Does a vowel precede the *y*? ________ Does the *y* change to *i*? ______ The spelling of the root word ___________ (is, is not) usually affected when a vowel precedes the final *y*. **Do not change the *y* to *i* when a vowel precedes the *y*.**
annoying, drier *buried, plays* *envious, merciless* *happiness, tried*	**15.** Now apply the *y* to *i* guidelines to solve the word "equations" below. *annoy + ing =* ____________ *dry + er =* ______________ *bury + ed =* ____________ *play + s =* ______________ *envy + ous =* ____________ *mercy + less =* ______________ *happy + nes =* ____________ *try + ed =* ______________
trying, copying, hurrying *applying, emptying, studying*	**16.** Now let us consider *-ing* as a suffix. Rewrite the words below by adding *-ing.* *try* __________ *copy* __________ *hurry* __________ *apply* __________ *empty* __________ *study* __________
yes, no	**17.** Do the words in the frame above end in a *y* preceded by a consonant? _________ Does the *y* change to *i* before adding *-ing*? _______ **Do not change the final *y* to *i* before adding *-ing* to a word that ends in a *y* preceded by a consonant.**

	18. Why do we keep the *y* when adding *-ing* to each word in frame 16? Let us conduct an experiment to investigate this exception.
copiing	Add *-ing* to *copy,* but this time change the *y* to *i.* The new word is ________.
yes	Would you also expect to keep the *y* when adding *-ist* to *copy*? ________
copyist	Write this word. ________
yes, *babyish*	Does this hold for adding *-ish* to *baby*? ________ Write this word. ________
	Keeping the *y* avoids an unnecessary *i* in spelling (*copiing*). Furthermore, keeping the *y* provides a more accurate representation of pronunciation.
	We can restate our exception to the *y* to *i* generalizations accordingly:
	Do not change the final *y* to *i* before adding a suffix that begins with an *i* to a word that ends in a *y* preceded by a consonant.
	19. Let us review the final *y* to *i* generalizations.
consonant	**Change the *y* to *i* before adding a suffix to a word that ends in a *y* preceded by a ____________.**
vowel	**Do not change the *y* to *i* when a word ends in a *y* preceded by a _______.**
consonant	**Do not change the *y* to *i* before adding a suffix that begins with an *i* to a word that ends in a *y* preceded by a _______.**
	20. We have established that the final *y* usually changes to *i* when a root word ends in a *y* preceded by a consonant. But what happens when a word ends in the letter *e*? We shall use *time* as an example.
	Place a check beside each correctly spelled word below.
timer, timing	*timer* *timing* *timeed*
vowel	Dropping the final *e* (*timer, timing, timed*) ensures that we do not add an unnecessary _________.
	21. Solve each word "equation" below by adding the indicated suffix.
baking, hoped	*bake + ing =* __________ *hope + ed =* ____________
closer, saved	*close + er =* __________ *save + ed =* ____________
nicest, latest	*nice + est =* __________ *late + est =* ____________
settled, tumbling	*settle + ed =* __________ *tumble + ing =* ____________

yes yes yes *cyclist*	**22.** Do the suffixes in the frame above all begin with vowels? ________ Do all the words end in a silent *e*? ________ **Drop the final silent *e* before adding a suffix that begins with a vowel.** Should we drop the *e* before adding *-ist* to *cycle*? ________ Write the new word. ________
likely, useless, agreement *nicely, ageless, excitement* *lively, hopeless, movement* *lately, tireless, shipment*	**23.** To better understand the final *e* generalization, we will consider suffixes that begin with consonants. Rewrite each word below by adding the indicated suffix. ***-ly*** ***-less*** ***-ment*** *like* ________ *use* ________ *agree* ________ *nice* ________ *age* ________ *excite* ________ *live* ________ *hope* ________ *move* ________ *late* ________ *tire* ________ *ship* ________
consonant *e*	**24.** Each suffix in frame 23 begins with a ______________. Each root word ends with an ________. **Keep the final *e* when adding a suffix that begins with a consonant.**
noticeable, courageous *replaceable, advantageous* *manageable, outrageous*	**25.** Let's also consider the final *e* generalization as it applies to root words that end in *ce* or *ge.* Rewrite each word below by adding the indicated suffix. ***-able*** ***-ous*** *notice* ________ *courage* ________ *replace* ________ *advantage* ________ *manage* ________ *outrage* ________ When applied to VCe root words, the *-able* and *-ous* suffixes are too irregular to have a final *e* spelling generalization.
soft *s, j* hard, *k, g*	**26.** The final *e* in each word in the frame above indicates that the *c* and the *g* represent ________ (hard, soft) sounds (see Part II, page 55). Write the key symbols for the soft sounds of the *c* ______ and the *g* ______. In the absence of the final *e,* we are inclined to pronounce the *c* and the *g* as ________ (hard, soft) sounds: key symbols ______ and ______.
hazy, shady, wavy, nosy, shiny	**27.** What happens when *-y* is a suffix? Rewrite the words below by adding *-y.* *haze* ______ *shade* ______ *wave* ______ *nose* ______ *shine* ______

long *ē, eraser* vowel	**28.** The *y* in frame 27 represents the __________ vowel phoneme: key (short, long) symbol _______; key word _______. We can conclude that the -*y* acts as a ___________ (see Part III, page 108). Therefore, we would usually expect to drop the final *e* before adding -*y*.
  vowel **consonant**	**29.** We can make these generalizations regarding root words that end in silent *e:* **Drop the final *e* before adding a suffix that begins with a ________.** **Keep the final *e* when adding a suffix that begins with a ________.** **Keep the final *e* when adding -*ous* or -*age* to a root word ending in *ce* or *ge*.**
  hopped, running, dimmer, biggest	**30.** When should the final consonant of a root word be doubled when adding a suffix? Rewrite each word below by adding the indicated suffix. ***-ed*** *hop* _______ ***-ing*** *run* _______ ***-er*** *dim* _______ ***-est*** *big* _______
 short CVC vowel	**31.** Examine the root words in the frame above. Each of these one-syllable words consists of one vowel followed by a single consonant. The vowel phoneme is ___________. (short, long) The vowel-consonant pattern is ___________ (see Part III, page 93). (CVC, CVCe) Each suffix begins with a ________________.
 fla~~t~~ten, ship~~p~~ing, thin~~n~~er *big~~g~~est, hid~~d~~en, hug~~g~~ed*	**32.** Rewrite each word below, by crossing out the silent consonant. *flatten* _________ *shipping* _________ *thinner* _________ *biggest* _________ *hidden* _________ *hugged* _________
 hŏpt, mŏpt, tăpt *hōpt, mōpt, tāpt*	**33.** Study the words below. Pronounce the words in lines 1 and 2. Then write the words to show pronunciation. **Line 1** *hopped* _________ *mopped* _________ *tapped* _________ **Line 2** *hoped* _________ *moped* _________ *taped* _________
short long	**34.** Doubling the final consonant (line 1 in the frame above) indicates that a word has a ____________ vowel phoneme. Not doubling the final consonant (as in line 2) indicates a _____________ vowel pronunciation.

one, one one	**35.** You may wish to use the expression *one-one-one* to help you remember this generalization: **Double the final consonant when a suffix that begins with a vowel is added to a root word that has ________ syllable and ________ vowel and that ends in ________ consonant.** (How many?) (How many?) (How many?)
pin yes yes one, one one	**36.** We will use *pinned* to illustrate one-one-one. The root word is ______. Does the *-ed* begin with a vowel? ______ Is the final consonant doubled? ______ *Pin* has ____________ syllable(s) and ____________ vowel(s), and it ends in (How many?) (How many?) ____________ consonant(s). (How many?)
badly, jobless *madness, fitful* *spotless, sadly*	**37.** What happens when we add a suffix that begins with a consonant? Complete the word "equations" below. *bad + ly =* ____________ *job + less =* ______________ *mad + ness =* ____________ *fit + ful =* ______________ *spot + less =* ____________ *sad + ly =* ______________
vowel	**38.** Let us recap what we have learned so far about the final-consonant-doubling generalization: **Double the final consonant before adding a suffix that begins with a _______ to a root word that ends in a single short vowel followed by a single consonant.**
jumped, fishing, sicker *hunted, resting, helper* *melted, lifting, lender* *limped, farming, camper* *watched, clutching, catcher*	**39.** Continuing our study of the final-consonant-doubling generalization, rewrite each word below by adding the indicated suffix. ***-ed*** ***-ing*** ***-er*** *jump* __________ *fish* __________ *sick* __________ *hunt* __________ *rest* __________ *help* __________ *melt* __________ *lift* __________ *lend* __________ *limp* __________ *farm* __________ *camp* __________ *watch* __________ *clutch* __________ *catch* __________

consonant CVCC	**40.** Study the words in the frame above. Note that each root word ends in more than one ____________. Indicate the vowel-consonant pattern. Use a *C* to represent each consonant and a *V* to represent each vowel. ____________
no *fastest* yes *fattest*	**41.** Would we expect to double the final consonant before adding *-est* to *fast?* __________ Write the new word. __________ Would we expect to double the final consonant before adding *-est* to *fat*? __________ Write the new word. __________ **Do not double the final consonant when a word ends in two or more consonants.**
committed, beginner	**42.** The final-consonant-doubling guideline is most reliable when applied to one-syllable words. Pronounce the two-syllable words below. Rewrite each root word by adding the suffix indicated. *com mit'* *be gin'* *commit + ed =* __________ *begin + er =* __________
CVC last vowel	**43.** Notice that the final syllable in each root word above represents the __________ vowel-consonant pattern. The syllables have one vowel followed by one consonant. The accent, or greatest stress—indicated by '—is placed on the __________ (first, last) syllable. Each suffix begins with a ______________.
covered, opened	**44.** Rewrite each word below by adding the *-ed* suffix. *cov'er* *o' pen* *cover + ed =* __________ *open + er =* __________
first do not	**45.** The accent in *cover* and *open* (frame 44) is placed on the ____________ (first, last) syllable. We usually __________ (do, do not) double the final consonant before adding suffix to a final unaccented syllable.

Study Guide

Spelling Generalizations for Adding Prefixes and Suffixes to Words

Prefixes
The spelling does not change when a prefix is added to the beginning of a root word.

Suffixes Beginning with a Consonant
The spelling of a root word often does not change when adding a suffix that begins with a consonant.

Final y
Change the final *y* to *i* before adding a suffix to a word that ends in a *y* preceded by a consonant (*applies*). Do not change the *y* to *i* before adding a suffix to a word that ends in a *y* preceded by a vowel (*joyful*) or when adding *-ing* (*copying*).

-es and -s
Add *-es* to form the plurals of most words that end in a *y* preceded by a consonant (*babies*) or an *s* (*kisses*), *ch* (*benches*), *sh* (*dishes*), *x* (*boxes*), or *z* (*quizzes*). When a word ends in *f* or *fe* and the plural form includes a /*v*/ phoneme, we often change the *f* to *v* before adding *-es* (*hoof, hooves*). Add *-s* to most other words to form the plurals.

Final e
Drop the final *e* before adding a suffix that begins with a vowel (*timer*). Keep the *e* when adding a suffix that begins with a consonant (*timely*). When applied to VCe root words, the *-able* and *-ous* suffixes are too irregular to have a reliable final *e* spelling generalization.

Final Consonant Doubling
Double the final consonant before adding a suffix to a one-syllable word that ends in a single vowel followed by a single consonant (*hopped*). Do not double the final consonant when adding a suffix to a one-syllable word that ends in more than one consonant or has two vowels (*called, hoped*).

Double the final consonant when the last syllable of a two-or-more-syllable root word receives the greatest stress or accent (*be gin' ner*). Do not double the final consonant when the last syllable of a two-or-more-syllable word is not accented (*o' pen ing*).

canceled or *cancelled*	**46.** Let us consider two-or-more-syllable root words that end in *l*. Solve the word "equation" below: *can' cel + ed =* ________ Would it surprise you to learn that dictionaries may show more than one way to spell some root words when a suffix that begins with a vowel is added to a final unaccented syllable that ends in *l*? It is customary not to double the *l* in American-English spelling (*equaled*). Doubling the *l* is more likely in British-English spelling.
consonant Do not	**47.** Study the two-or-more-syllable words below. Each suffix begins with a ______________. *com mit' + ment = commitment* *for get' + ful = forgetful* __________ double the final consonant before adding a suffix that begins (Do, Do not) with a consonant to a stressed final syllable.
	48. Let us summarize the final-consonant-doubling generalizations. **Double the final consonant before adding a suffix:** **A. that begins with a vowel to a root word that ends in a single short vowel followed by a single consonant** **B. when the last syllable of a two-or-more-syllable root word is accented** **Do not double the final consonant before adding a suffix:** **A. that begins with a consonant** **B. to a word or syllable that ends in more than one consonant** **C. to the final unaccented syllable**
root words (or words) are not	**49.** We have been studying generalizations for the spelling of ___________ to which affixes are attached. These generalizations would be more accurate if each included a cautionary word such as *often, occasionally, sometimes,* or *usually.* For the sake of simplicity, a caution is not explicitly stated for each generalization. However, we acknowledge that the generalizations __________ infallible. We refer to the dictionary or spellchecker when we are in doubt as to the correct spelling. Occasionally, the dictionary may indicate more than one acceptable spelling (*likable, likeable*).

Review 26

1. State the final-consonant-doubling generalization for one-syllable root words.
2. We usually __________ (keep, drop) the final *e* before adding a suffix beginning with a vowel to a word that ends in a silent *e.*
3. Add the indicated suffix to each root word below:

-er		***-ed***		***-est***	
nice	______	*dine*	______	*close*	______
bake	______	*hike*	______	*fine*	______

4. Rewrite each word by adding *-s* or *-es,* as appropriate.

   bird *dish* *toy* *mix* *marry* *boss* *quiz*
5. Complete these generalizations:

   a. Add *-es* to words that end in a *y* preceded by a __________ or with an ______, ______, ______, ______, or ______.

   b. Change the final *f* or *fe* to ______ before adding ______ to root words where the final /f/ changes to /v/. Add ______ to all other words.
6. Solve these word "equations" by adding the indicated suffixes.

   silly + est = ______ *copy + ed =* ______

   deny + ed = ______ *hazy + ness =* ______
7. State the generalization that applies to adding suffixes to the words in problem 6.
8. Solve the word "equations" below:

   camp + ed = ______ *recent + ly =* ______
9. State the generalizations for adding suffixes to the words in problem 8.

See the Answers to the Reviews section for the answers to Review 26, page 239.

Recap IV

	1. We have studied the units of word structure. Let us begin our recap by considering the word *recounted.*
three, free	We recognize __________ (How many?) structural units or parts in *recounted:* one ______
bound, *count*	morpheme and two _______ morphemes. The free morpheme is _______.
re-, -ed	The bound morphemes are _______ and ________.

free	**2.** A free morpheme can exist alone. A bound morpheme cannot exist alone. A bound morpheme must be attached to a ________ morpheme.
beginnings ends	**3.** Bound morphemes can be divided into two groups: prefixes and suffixes. Prefixes are placed at the ______________ of root words; suffixes are placed (beginnings, ends) at the ______________ of root words. (beginnings, ends)
mis-, understood *un-, believe* *-able*	**4.** *Misunderstood* consists of the prefix _______ and the root word _________. *Unbelievable* consists of the prefix _________, the root word _________, and the suffix _________.
D, I, D, D I, D, I	**5.** You have learned that an inflectional suffix changes number, affects verb tense, indicates comparison, or denotes possession. You have also learned that a derivational suffix affects meaning and may change grammatical category. Place an *I* after each word below that includes an inflectional suffix. Place a *D* beside each word that includes a derivational suffix. *angelic* _______ *babies* _______ *studious* _______ *active* _______ *Maria's* _______ *broker* _______ *fastest* _______
	6. Generalizations help us determine how to spell a word when we add a suffix. Use your knowledge to match each of the following words with the correct generalization below. *payable* *attachment* *watches* *staying* *happily* *making* *clapped* *preset*
happily	**A.** _______ Change the *y* to *i* before adding a suffix to a word that ends in a *y* preceded by a consonant.
payable	**B.** _______ Do not change the final *y* to *i* when adding a suffix to a word that ends in a *y* preceded by a vowel.
watches	**C.** _______ Add *-es* to words that end in a *y* preceded by a consonant and to words that end in *s, sh, ch, x,* or *z.*
making	**D.** _______ When a word ends in a silent *e,* drop the *e* when adding a suffix that begins with a vowel.
clapped	**E.** _______ Double the final consonant before adding a suffix to a one-syllable word that ends in a single vowel followed by a single consonant.
attachment	**F.** _______ The spelling of a root word usually does not change when we add a suffix that begins with a consonant to a root word that ends in a consonant.

staying	**G.** ________ Do not change the *y* to *i* when adding a suffix that begins with an *i*.
preset	**H.** ________ The spelling of a root word is not usually affected by a prefix.
contraction compound word	**7.** A ____________ is two words combined into one word; the missing letter (or letters) is (are) replaced by an apostrophe. A _________________ consists of two or more "words" (free morphemes) combined to form a word with a meaning that is different from the two "words" separately.
sea *shore, sea shore* *fire crack er,* three one two	**8.** The compound word *seashore* consists of the "words" _________ and _________. Show the syllable division. _______________ Divide *firecracker* into syllables. ____________ *Firecracker* has ____________ (How many?) syllables. The first "word," *fire,* consists of ____________ (How many?) syllable(s). The second "word," *cracker,* consists of ____________ (How many?) syllable(s).
sounds (phonemes) sound, meaning sound	**9.** You have studied the relationship of letters and letter combinations to the ____________ they represent. You have also studied multiletter groups. The prefix *re-* is an example of a multiletter group that represents both _________ and _________. The *rab* in *rabbit* (*rab' bit*) represents only _________.
phonics structural analysis	**10.** When the reader associates sounds with letters, he or she uses ________ to identify a new word. When the reader recognizes the multiletter groups that represent sound and meaning, he or she uses ____________ to identify a new word.
reading	**11.** You have studied phonics and structural analysis. They form the basis of **two** of the word-attack skills needed to attain independence in __________. Mastery of the total reading process requires the development of still other sets of skills, including the use of context clues and understanding the material read. Reading is a complicated process!

You are now ready for the posttest. Show your mastery of the content of phonics and structural analysis! Best wishes.

Self-Evaluation II

A Posttest

This test is designed to help you evaluate your growth in the field of phonics. Read each item, including all choices. Indicate the answer you consider best by circling the appropriate letter (a, b, c, d, or e) or by marking the appropriate letter on an answer sheet. Please respond to every item. Time: 30 minutes.

I. Multiple Choice. Select the best answer.

1. Which of the following most adequately completes this sentence?

   The consonant phonemes in the English language are represented by

   a. the consonant-vowel combinations.
   b. the distinctive speech sounds we associate with each of the 21 consonant letters of the alphabet.
   c. 18 of the consonant letters of the alphabet plus 7 digraphs.
   d. the single-letter consonants plus their two- and three-letter blends.
   e. The English language is too irregular to represent the consonant phonemes with any degree of accuracy.

2. The second syllable of the nonsense word *omethbin* can be expected to rhyme with

   a. *see.*
   b. *pet.*
   c. *wreath.*
   d. *breath.*
   e. *kin.*

3. The open syllable in the nonsense word *phattoe* can be expected to rhyme with

   a. *fa* of *fatal.*
   b. *day.*
   c. *fat.*
   d. *dough.*
   e. a and b

4. How many phonemes are represented in the nonsense word *ghight*?

a. one
b. two
c. three
d. four
e. six

5. The sound of the *schwa* is represented by

a. the *a* in *carry*.
b. the *e* in *meet*.
c. the *i* in *lighted*.
d. the *o* in *falcon*.
e. the *u* in *rule*.

6. A diphthong is best illustrated by the vowels representing the sound of

a. *oo* in *foot*.
b. *oy* in *employ*.
c *ow* in *low*.
d. *ai* in *said*.
e. All of the above

7. Generally, when two like consonants appear together in a word,

a. one is sounded with the first syllable and the other with the second.
b. both are sounded when the preceding vowel is *e*.
c. both are sounded when the following vowel is *i*.
d. only one is sounded.
e. neither is sounded.

8. A requirement of a syllable is that

a. it contains no more than one vowel letter.
b. it contains no more than one vowel phoneme.
c. it contains at least one consonant phoneme.
d. it contains no more than one phoneme.
e. None of the above

9. An example of a closed syllable is found in the word

a. *low*.
b. *sofa*.
c. *doubt*.
d. All of these
e. None of these

10. The letter *y* is most likely to be a consonant when

a. it follows *o* in a syllable.
b. it has the sound of *i* as in *light*.
c. it is the first letter in a word or syllable.

d. it is the last letter in a word or syllable.
e. None of the above

11. The letter *q* could be removed from the alphabet because it can adequately and without conflict be represented by
    a. *ch* as in *chair.*
    b. *k* as in *kite.*
    c. *cu* as in *cubic.*
    d. All of the above
    e. The idea is foolish; *qu* represents a distinctive consonant phoneme.

12. An example of an open syllable is found in the word
    a. *be.*
    b. *replay.*
    c. *tree.*
    d. All of these
    e. None of these

13. Which of the following has the incorrect diacritical mark?
    a. *băll*
    b. *fĕll*
    c. *wĭsh*
    d. *drŏp*
    e. *cŭt*

14. Which of the following has an incorrect diacritical mark?
    a. *spāde*
    b. *rēady*
    c. *sīde*
    d. *lōne*
    e. *fūse*

15. When *o* and *a* appear together in a syllable, they usually represent the same sound as
    a. the *a* in *bacon.*
    b. the *o* in *done.*
    c. the *o* in *force.*
    d. the *o* in *ghostly.*
    e. the *a* in *camel.*

16. The symbol *s* is used in the dictionary to show the pronunciation of the sound heard in
    a. *should.*
    b. *has.*
    c. *sure.*
    d. *zoo.*
    e. *waltz.*

17. If *e* were the only vowel in an open syllable, that *e* would most likely represent the same sound as

a. the *y* in *by.*
b. the *ea* in *seat.*
c. the *e* in *get.*
d. the *e* in *fine.*
e. None of these

18. A consonant cluster is illustrated by

a. the *ch* in *chin.*
b. the *ng* in *sing.*
c. the *bl* in *black.*
d. the *ph* in *graph.*
e. a, c, and d

19. When the single vowel *i* in an accented syllable is followed by a single consonant and a final *e*, the *i* will most likely have the sound of

a. the *i* in *readily.*
b. the *i* in *active.*
c. the *y* in *cry.*
d. the *e* in *sea.*
e. the *y* in *happy.*

20. If *a* were the single vowel in an accented syllable ending with a consonant, that *a* would most likely represent the same sound as

a. the *ay* in *daylight.*
b. the *a* in *mad.*
c. the *a* in *many.*
d. the *a* in *wall.*
e. the *a* in *car.*

21. When *c* is followed by *i*, it will most likely represent the same sound as

a. the *c* in *cube.*
b. the *c* in *chime.*
c. the *c* in *cello.*
d. *c* followed by *o.*
e. None of these

22. The word *if* ends with the same sound as

a. the *ph* of *phrase.*
b. the *f* in *of.*
c. the *gh* in *cough.*
d. All of the above
e. a and c

23. The symbol *w* is used in the dictionary to show the pronunciation of the sound heard in

a. *want.*
b. *now.*

c. *who.*
d. *two.*
e. a, b, and c

24. When the letter *g* is followed by *a*, it will most likely represent the same sound as

a. the *j* in *jam.*
b. the *g* in *go.*
c. the *g* in *gnat.*
d. the *g* in *bring.*
e. the *g* in *giant.*

25. We usually do not double the final consonant before adding a suffix to a word that

a. ends in a consonant blend.
b. ends in a silent *e.*
c. includes a long vowel phoneme.
d. ends in a consonant digraph.
e. All of these

26. Which underlined item illustrates a free morpheme?

a. *unjust*
b. *dancer*
c. *historic*
d. *nervous*
e. None of these

27. Which word includes a derivational suffix?

a. *diver*
b. *biggest*
c. *books*
d. *faster*
e. *falling*

28. The final *y* to *i* generalization for adding a suffix to a word is illustrated by

a. *paiing.*
b. *buier.*
c. *joyful.*
d. *applies.*
e. c and d.

29. Double the final consonant before adding a suffix to a two-or-more-syllable word in which the

a. last syllable ends in a digraph.
b. last syllable is accented.
c. last syllable ends in a consonant blend.
d. last syllable is unaccented.
e. last syllable has two vowels.

30. The final *e* generalization for adding a suffix to a word is illustrated by

a. *safly.*
b. *gracful.*
c. *finer.*
d. *namless.*
e. a and c

31. Which word includes both a free and a bound morpheme?

a. *happily*
b. *handle*
c. *cowboy*
d. *unison*
e. *level*

32. When adding a plural suffix to a word that ends in *f* or *fe,*

a. just add *-s.*
b. just add *-es.*
c. change the single *f* to *v* and leave the final *fe* unchanged.
d. change the *f* or *fe* to *v* before adding *-es* when you hear a /*v*/ instead of an /*f*/ in the plural form.
e. None of these

33. An inflectional suffix

a. changes the number of the root word.
b. shows comparison.
c. indicates a possessive.
d. None of the above
e. All of the above

34. When adding the *-ing* suffix to a word that ends in the letter *y,* we expect to

a. drop the final *y.*
b. change the *y* to *i.*
c. keep the final *y.*
d. change the *y* to *i* when the *y* is preceded by a vowel.
e. change the *y* to *i* when the *y* is preceded by a consonant.

35. The apostrophe in a contraction denotes

a. possession.
b. one or more missing letters.
c. emphasis placed on a syllable.
d. pronunciation of the vowel.
e. None of the above

36. Which of the words below shows the correct syllable division?

a. *hand' writ ing*
b. *fire' fighter*

c. *re' lation*
d. *choco' late*
e. *qual' ify*

37. A compound word is illustrated by

a. *preteen*
b. *personality*
c. *yardstick*
d. *hit-and-run*
e. *relay*

38. Which word below includes a prefix?

a. *register*
b. *missions*
c. *uncle*
d. *preaches*
e. None of these

39. The contraction *he's* is composed of which of the following two words?

a. *he was*
b. *he will*
c. *he is*
d. *he has*
e. c and d

II. Multiple Choice. Complete each sentence by selecting the word for which the correct pronunciation is indicated.

40. When I picked my vegetables, I dropped a

a. *răd'ĭsh.*
b. *kăr'ŏt.*
c. *kŭ kŭm'bĕr.*
d. *pë.*
e. *kăb'ĭg.*

41. I went to the park for a

a. *kŏn'cûrt.*
b. *rās.*
c. *wôlk.*
d. *pĭk'nək.*
e. *păr'tē.*

42. The wall is

a. *thĭn.*
b. *stŭck'o͞od.*
c. *pĭngk.*
d. *lōu.*
e. *krăk'əd.*

43. The tree we planted was a(n)

a. *fĭr.*
b. *ăzh.*
c. *sprōōs.*
d. *bərtch.*
e. *cē kwoi ə.*

44. I went to the grocery store for

a. *ôr'ĭng əz.*
b. *brēd.*
c. *jăm.*
d. *kōōk'ēz*
e. *kăn'dȳ.*

45. I washed the

a. *wôls.*
b. *wĭnd'ōs.*
c. *kown'tər.*
d. *nīvz.*
e. *sĭnk.*

III. Multiple Choice. There are three words in each item (a, b, c). Select the word in which you hear the same sound as that represented by the underlined part of the word at the top. You may find that the sound is heard in all three words; if so, mark d. If none of the words contains the sound, mark e.

46. ten<u>t</u>

a. missed
b. listen
c. catch
d. All
e. None

47. plea<u>su</u>re

a. vision
b. sabotage
c. rouge
d. All
e. None

48. ta<u>n</u>ker

a. banner
b. singer
c. nose
d. All
e. None

49. gem

a. edge
b. soldier
c. jelly
d. All
e. None

50. that

a. bath
b. theory
c. this
d. All
e. None

51. chill

a. chute
b. chord
c. question
d. All
e. None

52. hook

a. pool
b. moose
c. tooth
d. All
e. None

53. ace

a. bead
b. said
c. lab
d. All
e. None

54. now

a. snow
b. joyous
c. cow
d. All
e. None

55. sock

a. sure
b. sugar
c. city
d. All
e. None

IV. Multiple Choice. Select the letter or letters that represent the onset in each one-syllable word.

56. might

a. mi
b. ight
c. m
d. migh
e. igh

57. scratch

a. scr
b. ch
c. sc
d. scra
e. atch

58. choice

a. oi
b. ce
c. oice
d. ch
e. choi

59. ghost

a. st
b. gh
c. hos
d. ost
e. gho

60. blank

a. ank
b. la
c. lan
d. bla
e. bl

V. Multiple Choice. Select the letter or letters that represent the rime in each one-syllable word.

61. climb

a. cl
b. imb
c. mb
d. limb
e. cli

62. juice

- **a.** ui
- **b.** jui
- **c.** ce
- **d.** uice
- **e.** j

63. shoal

- **a.** oal
- **b.** oa
- **c.** hoa
- **d.** sh
- **e.** al

64. spill

- **a.** ll
- **b.** sp
- **c.** pill
- **d.** spi
- **e.** ill

65. prince

- **a.** nce
- **b.** rince
- **c.** ince
- **d.** ce
- **e.** pr

VI. Multiple Choice. In the following items, where does the accent fall in each word or nonsense word given at the left? Indicate your answer by selecting the last two letters of the accented syllable.

Look at the example: *showboat*. The first "word" in a compound word is generally accented: *show'boat*. Look for the last two letters of *show, ow,* in the row to the right.

You would circle b or mark b on your answer sheet.

Example:

showboat

- **a.** ho
- (**b.**) ow
- **c.** bo
- **d.** at

66. tenlaim

- **a.** te
- **b.** en
- **c.** nl
- **d.** la
- **e.** im

67. grottome

a. ro
b. ot
c. to
d. om
e. me

68. religherly

a. re
b. nl
c. gh
d. er
e. ly

69. pnight

a. pn
b. ni
c. ig
d. gh
e. ht

70. damapantion

a. am
b. ma
c. pa
d. an
e. on

71. present (verb)

a. re
b. es
c. se
d. nt
e. pr

VII. Multiple Choice. Select the word in each row that is **incorrectly** syllabicated.

72. **a.** li ly
b. li lac
c. fa tal
d. ma trix
e. lu rid

73. **a.** fin ger
b. cot ton
c. gamb ol
d. for get
e. pas tel

74. **a.** par don a ble
b. re sist i ble
c. in dent ion
d. in fu sion
e. ex hale

75. **a.** saw dust
b. to get her
c. side walk
d. shark skin
e. loop hole

(See p. 228 for answers to Self-Evaluation II.)

Self-Evaluation II: Number correct ______________

Self-Evaluation I: Number correct ______________

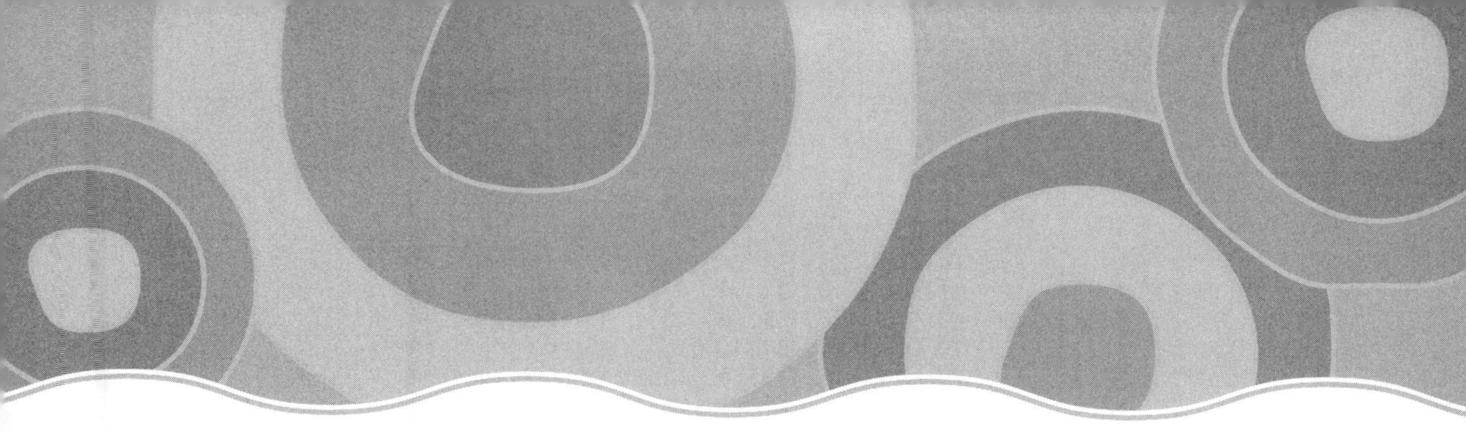

Answers to the Pretest and Posttest

Answers to Self-Evaluation I: Pretest

1. c
2. b
3. a
4. a
5. c
6. d
7. b
8. c
9. c
10. d
11. d
12. a
13. d
14. b
15. d
16. c
17. a
18. e
19. d
20. b
21. a
22. e
23. b
24. a
25. d
26. e
27. e
28. e
29. e
30. c
31. e
32. e
33. c
34. c
35. b
36. a
37. e
38. c
39. b
40. b
41. e
42. d
43. d
44. d
45. d
46. b
47. b
48. c
49. c
50. c
51. d
52. e
53. b
54. b
55. c
56. d
57. a
58. a
59. d
60. e
61. b
62. b
63. a
64. c
65. a
66. b
67. a
68. c
69. d
70. b
71. e
72. e
73. b
74. a
75. c

Answers to Self-Evaluation II: Posttest

1. c
2. d
3. d
4. c
5. d
6. b
7. d
8. b
9. c
10. c
11. b
12. d
13. a
14. b
15. d
16. e
17. b
18. c
19. c
20. b
21. e
22. e
23. a
24. b
25. e
26. e
27. a
28. e
29. b
30. c
31. a
32. d
33. e
34. c
35. b
36. a
37. c
38. e
39. e
40. a
41. b
42. c
43. c
44. c
45. d
46. a
47. d
48. b
49. d
50. c
51. c
52. e
53. e
54. c
55. c
56. c
57. a
58. d
59. b
60. e
61. b
62. d
63. a
64. e
65. c
66. e
67. b
68. c
69. e
70. d
71. d
72. a
73. c
74. c
75. b

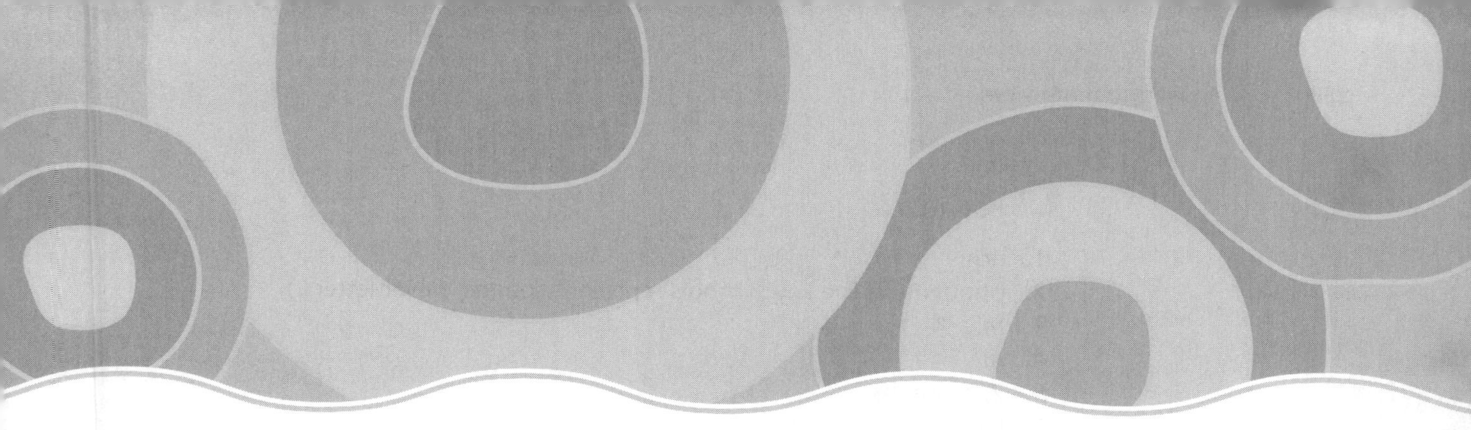

Answers to the Reviews

These reviews give you an indication of your mastery (or lack of mastery) of the material. WORK TO ACHIEVE 100% ON EACH REVIEW! Your success depends largely on your self-motivation. It takes **very** little more effort to achieve mastery than to fail, even while writing each answer. The difference depends on your mind-set. Good luck!

Review 1

1. decode
2. phoneme
3. 44
4. segment (or separate), blend
5. segmenting
6. blending
7. grapheme
8. graphophonic or letter–sound
9. syntactic
10. semantic or meaning

Scores:

Review 2

1. no
2. phonemes (The key symbols represent sounds, never letters.)
3. *m*
4. *m*
5. 2, digraphs
6. letters
7. digraph, one

Scores:

Review 3

1. 5, 5
2. 3, 3
3. digraphs
4. *c, q, x* They are represented by other letters; they have no distinctive phonemes of their own.
5. symbols, words
6. *m, k, r, v*
7. *u,* silent, *w*
8. *m v r, k w v r*
9. When we see a *v* in a word, we know it represents the same sound as that heard at the beginning of *van.*

Scores:

Review 4

1. **a.** *no*
   b. *saf*
   c. *mel*
   d. *plara*
   e. *gaeve*
   f. *lam*
   g. *sim*
   h. *tovom*
   i. *rok*
   j. *rim*
   k. *kwimel*
   l. *klopem*
   m. *vout*
2. digraphs, one

3. We are apt to add a vowel sound.
4. The key symbols represent the sounds of our language. Each sound is represented once. *Q* would be a duplication.

Scores:

If you have missed any items in previous Reviews, retake them now. Write the second score following the first. Do you show improvement?

Review 5

1. **a.** *b* **i.** *j n d r*
   b. *t f* **j.** *h f t*
   c. *h j* **k.** *p l n t d*
   d. *v* **l.** *k w l t*
   e. *f n* **m.** *z r*
   f. *t t* **n.** *s l*
   g. *g s t l* **o.** *k l m*
   h. *s l j r*
2. **a.** *don't, ride, moved*
   b. *fine, graph, photo, off*
   c. *wedge, soldier, Roger*
   d. *knot, stranger*
   e. *his, puzzle, does*

Scores:

If you missed any, turn to the appropriate pages and restudy. Select a previous Review. Write the answers. Did you better your score or maintain a perfect score? Be sure you write your scores for each Review and "review of Reviews."

Review 6

1. A *g* followed by *e, i,* or *y* generally has the sound of */j/*; a *g* followed by *a, o, u,* any consonant, or at the end of a word is */g/* as in *goat*.
2. **a.** *j n t* **h.** *m ch*
   b. *b ng k* **i.** *y l*
   c. *g r l* **j.** *w*
   d. *b g* **k.** *k w k*
   e. *s r k s* **l.** *r t*
   f. *k k* **m.** *y t*
   g. *h* **n.** *n k*
3. *girl*
4. *C* followed by *e, i,* or *y* generally has the sound of */s/; c* followed by *a, o, u,* any consonant, or at the end of a word is */k/.*
5. *ed, d, t*

6. The consonants *w* (as in *wagon*, /*w*/) and *y* (as in *yo-yo*, /*y*/) appear before the vowel in a syllable.
7. a. *g*
   b. *ch*
   c. *j*
   d. *k*
   e. *j*
   f. *k*
   g. *k*
   h. *k*
   i. *k*
   j. *f*
8. digraphs
9. *ranje, ringkle, ransom; manjer, trianggle, lingks*
10. *e, i, y*
11. digraph, *go, j,* silent

Scores:

There were some tricky words in this review. Sincere congratulations if you had them all correct. If you did not, make sure you understand the principle involved. Restudy the appropriate section. Plan to "review this review" soon.

Review 7

1. a. *e, i, y k a, o, u*
   b. *k*
   c. *ks, gz, z*
2. a. hard *a, o, u*
   b. soft *j e, i, y*
3. a. some
   b. *z*
4. *d t*
5. *v*
6. *ch sh*
7. a. *s, sh, z, zh; z; s, zh*
   b. *c, z; z, s, x* (any two)
   c. *k, g, h* silent; *t* silent
8. a. graphemes, phoneme
   b. phonemes, grapheme
   c. phoneme

Scores:

Review 8

1. digraph
2. *k k, h, zh, wh, wh ch, th, th, sh, sh g, w sh, v zh, ng*
3. *weather, which, bring, wish, both, through* (If you omitted the *wh* of *which*, you are correct also.)

4. letter, 7, digraphs, *sh, ch, wh, zh, th, th, t̸h̸, ng*
5. *gh* in tough, *ck* in *luck*, *ph* in *phoneme*
6. *f, k, f*
7. *sungk, fotograf, now* (*no*), *alfabet, feazant, kouf*

Scores:

Continue those reviews of Reviews to improve your scores or maintain perfect scores!

Review 9

1. **a.** *sh v r*
   b. *gz*
   c. *sh r*
   d. *sh r*
   e. *t r zh r*
   f. *k r k t r*
   g. *l zh r*
   h. *th t*
   i. *s k l z*
   j. *g s t s*
   k. *ch r j*
   l. *sh t*
   m. *k w k*
   n. *l sh n*
   o. *d v zh n*
   p. *sh k g*
   q. *s t r ng*
2. The digraph does not appear in a word.

Scores:

Review 10

1. *ng* (*swing*), *wh* (*white*), *zh* (*measure*); *t̸h̸* (*mother*), *sh* (*flash*), *ch* (*porch*)
2. *breath*
3. (1)— (*l* is silent), (2) *yo-yo,* (3) *sun,* (4) *table,* (5) *jeep,* (6)—, (7) *fish,* (8)—, (9) *van,* (10) *goat,* (11)—, (12) *lion,* (13)— (not a consonant), (14) *ring,* (15) *lion,* (16) *ring*
4. is not, does not
5. consonant
6. *this father feather them*
7. *wheel white whip whistle*
8. Each appears at the beginning of a word or syllable and has a vowel following.

Scores:

Review 11

1. **a.** *mang go, man jer, man jy* (The following are spaced only to make them more distinct, not to indicate syllables.) If you get these, you're good!
   b. *pin, pi ng, pi ng k, pi ng-po ng*
   c. *ban, ba ng, ba ng k, ba ng k i ng*
   d. *ran, ra ng, ra ng k, ra ng k i ng*
   e. *ran ch er, ran je, fan sy*
2. **a.** *b, d, f, g, h, j, k, l, m, n, p, r, s, t, v, w, y, z*
   b. digraphs *sh, ch, wh, zh, th, tħ, ng*
3. *C* has no distinctive sound of its own. It is represented by the *s* and *k*.
4. *q, x*
5. *Ph* is represented by *f.*
6. *hole, hi, kwik, gofer, holy, fone, thach, tħat, taut, kom, glisening, dauter, rusle, dout, not, bujet, rap, thingking*

Scores:

Review 12

1. You hear the sounds represented by the letters in the cluster; a digraph represents a new sound.
2. The blends are represented by phonemes we already know.
3. *zh* (*pleasure*), *tħ* (*the*), *ng* (*nearing*), *th* (*through*), *ch* (*changed*), *wh* (*wheel*), *sh* (*shoulder*)
4. *egzit* or *eksit, kuickly (kwikly), sity*
5. */st/, /pl/, /tr/, /dr/, /thr/, /kw/, /sl/.*

Scores:

Review 13

1. *a, e, i, o, u, w, y*
2. *w, y*
3. C, V, V, C, V, C
4. consonant digraph
5. more
6. 19

Scores:

Review 14

1. **a.** When there is a single vowel in a closed accented syllable, that vowel phoneme is usually short.
   b. When a word or a syllable has two vowels, one of which is a final *e,* and the two vowels are separated by two consonants, the first vowel often represents the short sound and the final *e* is silent.
2. *bĕd, nĕxt, lŏt, căt, trĭp, skĭn, mŏp, ŭs, sĕnd, bŭg*
3. VC, CVC, CVCCe (or VCCe), CVC, VC, CVCCe (or VCCe)
4. *e, i, y*

Scores:

Review 15

1. *ē, ī, ō, ū* macron
2. *i, e*
3. *e* When a word or accented syllable has two vowels, one of which is the final *e,* the *e* is silent and the first vowel usually represents its long (glided) sound.
4. accented, long
5. end, long
6. sound (or phoneme)
7. *dine* C *n; tack* C *k;* *<u>way</u>* V *ā; watch* C *ch; table* C *l;* *<u>go</u>* V *ō; tight* C *t; enough* C *f*
8. *bīte, bĭt, căn, cāne, pĕt, Pēte, ŭs, fūse, mŏp, mōpe.*

Scores:

Review 16

1. *schwa*
2. it saves assigning separate diacritical marks to each vowel to indicate a phoneme all share.
3. *river*
4. *regal, handmade* or *handmaid, celebrate, episode*

Scores:

Review 17

1. short or unglided, *ă, ĕ, ĭ, ŏ, ŭ*
2. long or glided, *ā, ē, ī, ō, ū*
3. *schwa, ə, agree* (ə *gre*), it saves assigning separate diacritical marks to each vowel to indicate a phoneme all share.
4. following, *r, l,* and *w*
5. **a.** ball (*bôl*)
   b. fur (*fûr*)
   c. father (*fäthər*)
   d. care (*kâr*)

Scores:

(How did you do? You can feel a *real* sense of accomplishment if you had all of these correct. They are not easy!)

Review 18

1. *oi, ou*
2. vowel
3. *owl-ou, cow-ou, moist-oi, oyster-oi*
4. *hous boi ouns ĕnjoi noiz brou*

Scores:

Review 19

1. A digraph is a two-letter grapheme that represents a single phoneme.
2. *o͞o, o͝o*
3. You cannot tell. The only clue is that it is most often o͞o as in *food.*
4. *to͞oth, spo͞on, bo͝ok, lo͞os, sto͝od, mo͞o, sho͝ok*
5. *klo͞od*
6. *bo͞ot, fŭj, doun, toi, sho͝ok, kō kō, nīt, fro͞ot, thrō, thro͞o, thō, thôt, kwĭt, bo͝ok, smo͞oth, fo͞ol, brĕth, nīt*

Scores:

Review 20

1. diphthong, *oi, ou, house;* digraph, *o͞o, o͝o, ho͝ok*
2. When two vowels appear together in a word or syllable, the first may represent the long sound and the second is usually silent.
3. When a one-syllable word has an ending pattern VCe, the first vowel is generally long and the e is silent.
4. letter, phoneme

Scores:

Review 21

1. *wr, c, sh, h, st, s, b, sch, st, g*
2. *ask, ouch, am, old, if*
3. vowel, consonant(s)
4. *ain, ent, ice, amp, our, ild, ought, ince, ouse, ip*
5. *train, flour, bought, since, house*

Scores:

Review 22

1. syllable
2. phoneme
3. yes
4. no
5. accented
6. **a.** The accent usually falls on or within the root word.
   in ter change′a ble

   b. In compound words, the accent usually falls on the first "word."
   cow′ boy

   c. One-syllable words are accented. *fast′* or *fast*

   d. When a word functions as different parts of speech, the accent is usually on the first syllable of the noun. *con′vict* (noun)

   e. The primary accent is usually on the syllable preceding the *tion* ending.
   na′ tion

   f. The accent usually falls on the syllable that closes with the first letter of a double consonant. *dol′ lar*

   g. When two vowel letters are within the last syllable of a two-syllable word, that last syllable is most often accented. *con ceal′*

   h. When there is no other clue, the accent most often falls on the first syllable of a two-syllable word. *pa′per*

Scores:

Review 23

1. a. CV/CVCC — The syllable division is between the single vowel and the single consonant.
   b. CVC/CVC — The syllable division is between the two consonants when there are single vowels on both sides of the two consonants.
   c. CVC/CV — The syllable division is between the two consonants when there are single vowels on both sides of the two consonants.
   d. CCV/CVCC — The syllable division is between the single vowel and the single consonant.
2. a. *play ful* — Suffixes and prefixes generally make separate syllables. This root word has one syllable.
   b. *ca pa ble* — The syllable division is between the single vowel and single consonant. If the last syllable of a word ends in *le* preceded by a consonant, that consonant usually begins the last syllable.
   c. *fa ther* — You usually cannot divide between letters of a digraph; treat the digraph as though it were one consonant. The division is between the single vowel and the digraph.

Scores:

Review 24

1. the smallest unit of meaning in our language.
2. we cannot divide it into smaller, meaningful units.
3. *dog, desk, hat, table*
4. a free morpheme or a free morpheme with one or more bound morphemes.
5. *collectable, untimely, enact, unneeded, childish*
6. a. morpheme
   b. cannot

Scores:

Review 25

1. prefix
2. suffix
3. affixes
4. *climbing, likeable, prehistoric, impolite, previewed, treatment, illogical, uncovered*

5. *dis-, mid-, im-, un-, non-, sub-, re-, de-*
6. *parenthood, -hood; joyous, -ous; motorists, -ist, -s; heroism, -ism; actor, -or; massive, -ive; musician, -ian; uselessly, -less, -ly*
7. *furious, D; attracting, I; wolves, I; sculptor, D; penniless, D; boyish, D.*
8. *apostrophe, yes, could've, where's, don't, they're, we'll, what'll, he'd, we'd*

Scores:

Review 26

1. When a one-syllable word ends in a single vowel followed by a single consonant, we usually double the final consonant before adding a suffix that begins with a vowel.
2. drop
3. *nicer, baker, dined, hiked, closest, finest*
4. *birds, dishes, toys, mixes, marries, bosses, quizzes*
5. **a.** consonant, *s, ch, sh, x, z*
   b. *v, es, -s*
6. *silliest, copied, denied, haziness*
7. Usually, change the final *y* to *i* when a consonant precedes the final *y.*
8. *camped, recently*
9. Do not double the final consonant when a word with a short vowel phoneme ends in two or more consonants.

Scores:

Appendix A

Phonics and Structural Analysis Generalizations

Consonant Generalizations

1. Consonant letters are fairly reliable: There is a high relationship between the letter and the sound (/ /) we expect it to represent (p. 29). However, there are irregularities:
   a. A letter may represent more than one phoneme (pp. 49, 65). Some common patterns are:

      c: /k/, /s/
      d: /d/, /t/
      g: /g/, /j/
      n: /n/, /ng/
      s: /s/, /sh/, /z/, /zh/
      z: /z/, /s/, /zh/

   b. A phoneme may be represented by more than one letter (pp. 41, 49, 65, 78). Some common patterns are:

      /f/: *f, gh, ph*
      /j/: *j, g, dg, d*
      /k/: *k, ch, q*
      /s/: *s, z*
      /w/: *w, u*
      /z/: *z, s*

   c. A letter may represent no phoneme; that is, it may be silent. When two like consonants appear together, the second usually is silent (pp. 37, 41, 49, 65). Some common silent letter patterns occurring in the same syllable are:

      b following *m*
      b followed by *t*
      c following *s*
      c followed by *k*
      g followed by *n*
      h following *k, g, r,* following a vowel and as the initial letter in certain words
      k followed by *n*
      l followed by *m, k, d*
      p followed by *s, t, n*
      t following *f;* followed by *ch*

2. When the letter *c* or *g* is followed by *e, i,* or *y,* it usually represents its soft sound as in *city* or *gem;* when *c* or *g* is followed by any other letter or appears at the end of a word, it usually represents its hard sound as in *cup* or *go* (p. 65).

3. The suffix *-ed* usually forms a separate syllable when it is preceded by *t* or *d.* When *-ed* does not form a separate syllable, the *d* may represent /t/ or /d/ (pp. 46, 49).
4. The letter *q* always represents /k/ (pp. 35, 41).
5. The letters *c, q,* and *x* have no distinctive phonemes of their own (p. 31).
6. The consonants *w* and *y* are positioned before the vowel in a syllable. The consonant *y* is never silent (pp. 58, 65).
7. We use two-letter combinations (digraphs) to represent the seven consonant phonemes not represented by single letters (*ch, sh, ŧħ, th, wh, zh, ng*) (pp. 68, 78).

Vowel Generalizations

1. A letter may represent more than one phoneme (p. 89).
2. A phoneme may be represented by more than one vowel letter (p. 89).
3. A single vowel in a closed accented syllable usually represents its short sound (pp. 95, 97).
4. A letter may represent no phoneme; that is, it may be silent (pp. 96, 100, 130).
5. When a one-syllable word or accented syllable contains two vowels, one of which is a final *e,* the first vowel usually represents its long sound and the final *e* is silent (pp. 100, 108).
6. A single vowel in an open accented syllable often represents its long sound (pp. 105, 108).
7. When *i* is followed by *gh* or when *i* or *o* is followed by *ld,* the vowel usually represents its long sound (pp. 106, 108).
8. If the only vowel letter in a word or syllable is followed by *r,* the vowel sound will be affected by that *r* (pp. 119, 120).
9. If the only vowel in a word or syllable is an *a* followed by *l* or *w,* the sound of the *a* is usually that heard in *ball* (pp. 119, 120).
10. When two vowel letters appear together in a one-syllable word or in an accented syllable, the first vowel often represents its long sound and the second is silent. This holds true most often for *ai, oa, ee, ey, ay* combinations (pp. 127, 128, 130).
11. The vowel *y* always follows the vowel or is the only vowel in a syllable and is silent or represents the phonemes we associate with *i* or *e* (pp. 97, 108).
12. Although a syllable may have more than one vowel letter, there is only one vowel phoneme in a syllable (pp. 127, 166).
13. Vowels behave differently in accented and unaccented syllables. The vowel is most clearly heard in the accented syllable (pp. 160, 166).
14. The vowel in most unaccented syllables represents the ə or ĭ (pp. 111–113).

Accent Clues

1. The vowel phoneme is the most prominent part of the syllable (p. 166).
2. When a word contains a prefix and/or a suffix, the accent usually falls on or within the root word (pp. 162, 166).
3. The accent usually falls on or within the first word of a compound word (pp. 162, 166).
4. In a two-syllable word that functions as either a noun or a verb, the accent is usually on the first syllable when the word functions as a noun and on the second syllable when the word functions as a verb (pp. 162, 166).
5. When there is a double consonant within a word, the accent usually falls on the syllable that ends with the first letter of the double consonant (pp. 163, 166).
6. In a multisyllabic word ending in the suffix *-tion, -sion,* or *ic,* the primary accent falls on the syllable preceding the suffix (pp. 163, 166).
7. When the vowel phoneme within the last syllable of a two-syllable word is composed of two vowel letters, that syllable is usually accented (pp. 163, 166).
8. When there is no other clue in a two-syllable word, the accent most often falls on the first syllable (pp. 164, 166).

Syllabic Division

1. In a compound word, the syllabic division usually comes between the "words" of which it is composed (pp. 172, 178).
2. Prefixes and suffixes usually form separate syllables from the root word (pp. 175, 178).
3. If the last syllable of a word ends in *le* preceded by a consonant, that consonant usually begins the last syllable (pp. 176, 178).
4. If the first vowel in a two-syllable word is followed by a single consonant, that consonant often begins the second syllable (pp. 168, 171, 178).
5. When two vowel letters are separated by two consonants, the syllabic division usually occurs between the consonants (pp. 170, 178).
6. In syllabication, digraphs are treated as representing single phonemes (pp. 174, 178).

Spelling Words with Prefixes and Suffixes

1. The spelling of a root word is not usually affected by adding a prefix (*unreal*) (pp. 199, 207).
2. The spelling of a root word often does not change when we add a suffix that begins with a consonant to a root word that ends in a consonant (*gladly*) (pp. 199, 207).

3. Add *-es* to words that end in a *y* preceded by a consonant and to words that end in *s, sh, ch, x,* or *z* (*berries, buses, crashes, churches, taxes, buzzes*). When a word ends in *f* or *fe* and the plural includes a /v/ phoneme, we usually change the *f* or *fe* to a *v* before adding *-s* or *-es* (*wolves*). Add *-s* to most other words (pp. 200, 207).
4. Usually, change the *y* to *i* before adding a suffix to a word that ends in a *y* preceded by a consonant (*worried*). Do not change the *y* to *i* when a word ends in a *y* preceded by a vowel (*played*). Do not change the *y* to *i* before adding *-ing* to a word that ends in a *y* preceded by a consonant (*worrying*) (pp. 201, 202, 207).
5. When a root word ends in a final *e,* drop the *e* before adding a suffix that begins with a vowel (*liked*). Keep the final *e* when a suffix begins with a consonant (*likely*) (pp. 203, 204, 207).
6. When a one-syllable word contains a short vowel phoneme and ends in a single consonant, double the final consonant before adding a suffix that begins with a vowel (*sadden*) (pp. 205, 207).
7. Double the final consonant before adding a suffix to a one-syllable word that ends in a single vowel followed by a single consonant (*hopped*). Do not double the final consonant when a one-syllable word ends in more than one consonant or has two vowels (*called, hoped*). Double the final consonant when the last syllable of a two-or-more-syllable word receives the greatest stress or accent (*be gin' ner*) Do not double the final consonant when the last syllable of a two or more syllable word is not accented (*o' pen ing*) (pp. 205, 206, 207).

Appendix B

Graphemes, Key Symbols, and Key Words

Grapheme	Key Symbol	Key Word	Grapheme	Key Symbol	Key Word
Single Consonants			**Short Vowels**		
b	b	*boat*	a	ă	*apple*
c	no key symbol	no key word	e	ĕ	*edge*
d	d	*dog*	i	ĭ	*igloo*
f	f	*fish*	o	ŏ	*ox*
g	g	*goat*	u	ŭ	*umbrella*
h	h	*hat*			
j	j	*jeep*			
k	k	*kite*	**Long vowels**		
l	l	*lion*	a	ā	*apron*
m	m	*moon*	e	ē	*eraser*
n	n	*nut*	i	ī	*ice*
p	p	*pig*	o	ō	*overalls*
q	no key symbol	no key word	u	ū	*unicorn*
r	r	*ring*			
s	s	*sun*			
t	t	*table*	**Schwa** (Vowels in Unaccented Syllables)		
v	v	*van*	a	ə	*comm<u>a</u>*
w	w	*wagon*	e	ə	*chick<u>e</u>n*
x	no key symbol	no key word	i	ə	*fam<u>i</u>ly*
y	y	*yo-yo*	o	ə	*mel<u>o</u>n*
z	z	*zipper*	u	ə	*circ<u>u</u>s*

Grapheme	Key Symbol	Key Word
Consonant Digraphs		
ch	ch	*chair*
sh	sh	*ship*
th	th	*thumb*
th	t̸h	*that*
wh	wh	*whale*
	zh	*treasure*
ng	ng	*king*
Other Single Vowels		
a	â	*care*
u	û	*fur*
a	ä	*father*
a	ô	*ball*

Grapheme	Key Symbol	Key Word
Diphthongs		
oi, oy	oi	*oil*
ou, ow	ou	*house*
Digraphs		
oo	o͞o	*food*
oo	o͝o	*hook*

Glossary

Note: The number following each entry refers to the page on which the word is introduced.

Accented syllable A syllable that receives greater stress than the other syllables in a word. 166

Affix A term used when referring to either a prefix or a suffix. (*See* Prefix; Suffix.) 190

Allophone A variant form of the same phoneme (as the /*p*/ in *pin* and the /*p*/ in *spin*). 13

Blending The ability to combine individual phonemes together so as to pronounce a meaningful word (/*m*/ + /*a*/ + /*n*/ = /*man*/). 20, 21

Bound morpheme A unit of meaning that must be added to another morpheme; a bound morpheme cannot stand on its own. *Un-* and *-ing* are examples of bound morphemes. 186

Breve A diacritical mark (˘) used to indicate the short (unglided) sound of a vowel, as the /*ĕ*/ in *red*. 90

Closed syllable A syllable that ends in a consonant phoneme (*trip*). 94

Compound word A word made up of two or more shorter "words" (*cowboy* and *rainbow*). 192

Consonant One of the two classifications of speech sounds. There are 21 consonant letters and 25 consonant sounds. 27, 31

Consonant blend A combination of two or more adjacent consonant phonemes pronounced rapidly, as the /*bl*/ in *blue*, the /*st*/ in *still*, and the /*spl*/ in *splash*. The term refers to the sounds that the consonant clusters represent. 81

Consonant cluster Two or more consonant letters appearing together in a syllable that when sounded form a consonant blend. Consonant clusters are taught as units rather than as single graphemes (e.g., *st* as representing two blended phonemes rather than an isolated /*s*/ and an isolated /*t*/. 81

Consonant digraph A two-letter consonant combination that represents phonemes not represented by the single letters, such as the *sh* in *shoe*. 68

Contraction The combination of two words into a single word in which an apostrophe denotes one or more missing letters (*isn't*). 192

Decoding Translating graphemes into the sounds of spoken language so as to pronounce a visually unfamiliar word. Teachers may refer to this process of word identification as "sounding out" words. 12

Derivational suffix A unit of meaning added to the end of a word that modifies its meaning and changes its grammatical category. The suffix *-able* changes a verb (*like*) to an adjective (*like<u>able</u>*). 191

Digraph A grapheme composed of two letters that represent one speech sound (phoneme). 28

Diphthong A single vowel phoneme resembling a glide from one sound to another; represented by the graphemes *oi* (*noise*), *oy* (*toy*), *ou* (*found*), and *ow* (*now*): key symbols *oi* and *ou*; key words *oil* and *house.* 121

Free morpheme The smallest unit of meaning that can stand alone. A free morpheme cannot be divided into smaller units (*play*). 186

Grapheme The written symbol used to represent the phoneme. It may be composed of one or more letters, and the same grapheme may represent more than one phoneme. 15

Graphophonic cues The 26 letters (graphemes), the 44 sounds (phonemes), and the system of relationships among graphemes and phonemes. These cues are used to translate the written code into the sounds of spoken language. 21

Inflectional suffix A unit of meaning added to the end of a word that changes its number, affects verb tense, indicates possession, or denotes a comparison (*cats, playing, Tom's, smaller*). 190

Key symbol Forty-four specific graphemes representing the 44 phonemes of the American-English language (as presented in this text), thus achieving a one-to-one correspondence between key symbol and phoneme: one symbol for each phoneme; one phoneme for each symbol. 29

Key word One word selected for each of the 44 phonemes that identifies the specific phoneme. 32

Long vowel The five vowels represented by *a, e, i, o,* and *u* that, in the context of the teaching of phonics, are indicated by a macron (-) and "say their names." Key words: *apron, eraser, ice, overalls,* and *unicorn.* These vowels are also referred to as *glided vowels.* 99

Macron A diacritical mark (-) used to indicate the long (glided) sound of a vowel. 99

Morpheme The smallest unit of meaning in the English language (*re-, play, -ed*). 186

Onset One or more consonant letters that precede the vowel phoneme in a syllable (the *c* in *cat,* the *ch* in *chat,* the *chr* in *chrome*). 149

Open syllable A syllable that ends in a vowel phoneme (*play, blue*). 104

Phoneme The smallest unit of sound that distinguishes one word from another. This program identifies 44 phonemes. 12, 15

Phoneme addition Attaching one or more phonemes to a word or word part (adding /*t*/ to /*able*/ to pronounce /*table*/). 19

Phoneme deletion Removing one or more phonemes from a word or word part (removing /*s*/ from /*stop*/ to pronounce /*top*/). 19

Phoneme substitution Deleting one or more phonemes from a word or word part and then replacing the deleted phoneme(s) with one or more different phonemes (deleting the /*t*/ from /*sat*/ and replacing it with a /*d*/ to pronounce /*sad*/). 19

Phonemic awareness The ability to conceptualize speech as a sequence of phonemes (sounds) combined with the ability to consciously manipulate the phonemes of the English language. Children who are phonologically aware can separate words into their individual phonemes; add, subtract, substitute, and rearrange the phonemes in words; and blend phonemes together to pronounce words. 27

Phonics The study of the relationships of the letter and letter combinations in written words (the graphemes of the English language) to the sounds they represent in spoken words. The study of phonics provides the content for developing skill in the decoding of visually unfamiliar words. 10

Phonogram Another term for the rime in a syllable. 152

Prefix A bound morpheme placed at the beginning of a word (*replay*). The prefix indicates sound and gives the reader insight into word meaning. 188

Rime The vowel and consonant letter(s) that follows it in a syllable. There is only one vowel phoneme in a rime (the /ă/ in *at*, the /ō/ in *oat*). 151

Root word The free morpheme to which a prefix or suffix may be attached. Some teachers' manuals use the term *root word* for parts borrowed from other languages, most often the Greek and Latin languages. In our study, we use root word as a synonym for *free morpheme.* 187

Schwa A vowel phoneme in an unaccented syllable that represents a soft "uh," and is indicated by the key symbol ə, which resembles an inverted *e.* Key words: comma, chicken, family, button, circus. 111

Segmentation The process of separating spoken words or syllables into their individual phonemes. 34

Semantic cues The general meaning of a passage that gives the reader useful information for word identification. 22

Short vowel The vowel letters *ă*, *ĕ*, *ĭ*, *ŏ*, and *ŭ* that, in the context of the teaching of phonics, are indicated with a breve (˘), and are heard in the key words *apple, elephant, igloo, ox,* and *umbrella.* 90

Silent letter A name given to a letter that appears in a written word but is not heard in the spoken word: *knight* has six letters, but only three are sounded; *k, g,* and *h* are silent. 37, 39

Slash marks Slanting lines / / enclosing a grapheme indicating that the reference is to its sound, not to the letters. 9

Structural analysis A word identification skill that involves the use of prefixes, suffixes, root words, the "words" in compound words, and the apostrophes in contractions. 185

Suffix A bound morpheme placed at the end a word (*played*). The suffix indicates sound and gives the reader insight into meaning. 189

Syllable The unit of pronunciation. The English syllable has only one vowel phoneme. There are as many syllables in a word as there are vowel phonemes; there is only one vowel phoneme in a syllable. 159

Syntactic cues Information from the order of words in phrases, clauses, and sentences that also gives the reader useful information for the identification of visually unfamiliar words. 22

Voiced *th* The initial phoneme heard in the key word *that* in which the vocal cords vibrate during the production of the phoneme. 73

Voiceless *th* The initial phoneme heard in the key word *thumb,* in which the vocal cords do not vibrate during the production of the phoneme. 73

Vowel digraph A two-letter vowel grapheme that represents one sound. In this text, the vowel digraphs are the o͞o in *food* and the o͝o in *hook.* 125

Vowel pair Two adjacent vowel letters that represent a phoneme associated with one of the letters, such as the /ā/ in *rain* that is represented by the *ai* grapheme. In this text, we use the term *vowel pair* to distinguish two-letter vowel graphemes that do not represent a distinct sound—that is, a sound that is not already represented by one of the vowel letters individually. 127

Vowel One of the two classifications of speech sounds. The vowels are *a, e, i, o, u* and sometimes *w* and *y*. (*See* Consonant.) 87

Word For the purposes of teaching reading, a word is a single free morpheme (*play*) or a free morpheme plus one or more bound morphemes (*replaying*). 187

Word family Words with the same rime (*at*) and rhyming sound (*cat, fat, hat*). 152